'As Irish adventures go, this must be one of the most extraordinary and difficult to date. *Unsinkable* is an astounding story, brilliantly told with a unique voice' – **Sean Conway**, author of *Hell and High Water* and *Cycling the Earth*

'*Unsinkable* is an incredible tale of glory and achievement borne from loss and pain' – **Swimming World Magazine**

'An empowering and inspirational story of the human spirit, grit, and determination' – **Jordan Wylie MBE**, Sunday Times bestselling author of *The Power of the Paddle*

'*Unsinkable* is about much more than swimming. It's about life and death, love and friendship, and grief and survival. It's about how whimsical ideas can turn into inspiring trials of endurance, courage, and resolve' – **Outdoor Swimmer Magazine**

'A roller coaster of a book with inspirational highs and lows. A voyage and an education' – **Professor Mike Tipton MBE**, Professor of Human and Applied Physiology

'Alan turns grief into greatness' – **SwimSwam Magazine**

'Compelling…Corcoran's vivid descriptions and storytelling immerse readers in his journey…filled with inspiration, humorous moments, and emotional highs and lows….this memoir goes deeper than just making a swim. He touches on the pain of losing his father and the moments of discouragement…gripping…engaging…will touch the heart of all that pick this book and encourage them to fulfil their dreams' – **Literary Titan** (awarded *Gold Award*)

'A fascinating insight of a determined novice swimmer taking on the ferocious extremes of the Irish Sea' – **Dr Heather Massey**, Senior Lecturer in Sport, Health, and Exercise Science and an English Channel swimmer

'Five out of five. A must-read…a great adventure book for everyone looking for something inspiring ' – **Reedsy**

'...captivating. *Unsinkable* describes the tragedy and teamwork behind his challenge in a sincere, comprehensive, and colourful way...*Unsinkable* will grab your attention and, like a vortex, won't let you go until the final pages. Alan's efforts are sure to inspire readers' – **World Open Water Swimming Association**

'An extraordinary account of determination and tenacity...a hugely enjoyable romp of an adventure through the treacherous waters of the Irish Sea. As *Marathon Man* was, *Unsinkable* is a beacon of inspiration' – **The World of Nonfiction Books** (book critic)

Praise for *Marathon Man*

Winner of Readers' Favorite Book Award, IPPY Book Award, BIBA Literary Award, and IR Discovery Award

'An intimate and uplifting story of grit, tenacity and healing' – **Dean Karnazes**, New York Times bestselling author and ultra-runner

'Highly entertaining...sprinkled with humour...greatly enjoyed' – **Canadian Running Magazine**

'A riveting account of resilience, courage, and the enduring bonds that tie families together' – **Irish Star**

'A must-read' – **Irish Runner Magazine**

'Bravo!' – **Eddie Jordan OBE**

'Fantastic' – **LoveReading** (awarded *Indie Books We Love*)

'...a timely reminder that life is to be seized' – **Irish Independent**

'A charming, detailed running account...sense of humour throughout...the prose is beautiful' – **Kirkus Reviews**

'Heart-warming and thoroughly entertaining' – **Damian Hall**

By the same award-winning author:

Marathon Man: My Life, My Father's Stroke, and Running 35 Marathons in 35 Days

UNSINKABLE

Cancer, Five Boats, and my ~~500~~
710-Kilometre Sea Swim

Alan Corcoran

**Tivoli Publishing
House**

**Tivoli Publishing
House**

www.marathonman.co
Copyright © Alan Corcoran 2023
All photos © Alan Corcoran unless otherwise stated

First Published in the Republic of Ireland in 2023 by Tivoli
Publishing House

A CIP catalogue record for this book is available from the
British Library

ISBN (paperback) 978-1-8383650-2-8
ISBN (hardback) 978-1-8383650-4-2
ISBN (e-book) 978-1-8383650-3-5

Typesetting by Alan Corcoran
Illustrations by Jack Spowart

You taught me that tattoos are horrible altogether, motorcycles are deadly, the sea is lethal, and running thirty-five consecutive marathons would destroy my knees. I didn't listen. This book is dedicated to you, Mam, for putting up with all my shenanigans.

CONTENTS

Author's Note

To write my memoir, I relied on my journal, social media posts, memory, interviews with participants, film footage, and video diaries from my *Unsinkable* documentary movie.

To preserve the anonymity of specific individuals, I changed the following names, listed in alphabetical order: Charlie and Jim.

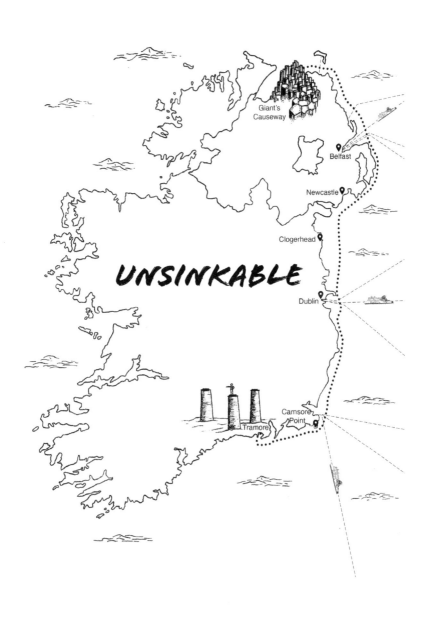

UNSINKABLE

Giant's
Causeway

Belfast

Newcastle

Clogerhead

Dublin

Carnsore
Point

Tramore

PROLOGUE

Ten RNLI volunteers assembled at Newcastle Harbour, County Down. They came prepared, wearing their yellow waterproofs, red lifejackets, and white helmets. Coastguard officials joined in equal numbers, getting dressed into their overalls and safety gear.

'Morning, Alan. You're becoming the talk of the town, a bit of a local celeb.'

'How's it going, Lisa?' I said to the RNLI (Royal National Lifeboat Institution) officer, nodding to the heavens and feeling my cheeks reddening. 'Yeah, more like a local pain in the arse. Real sorry about all this hassle.'

'That's what we're here for; not to worry. Follow me. Brace yourself,' Lisa said, leading me towards the pier wall.

'Morning, Alan!' Seamus said. I looked down from the pier. The local fisherman smiled and waved, standing in his T-shirt and trousers while up to his neck in the frigid water. A swarm of moon jellyfish bobbed around him like discarded plastic bags, but Seamus was unfazed, focused on helping me out. 'I found her like this ten minutes ago. I'm just getting her out of harm's way, is all.'

Seamus waded towards the slipway, gripping my damaged support boat with his left hand and scooping his right arm forwards like a digger.

'I think I might need a bigger milk carton to bail the water out this time. What do you think?' I said, grinning and bearing the sorry situation.

The orange and black tubing along one side of my rigid inflatable boat (RIB) held its breath, full lungs ensuring this side remained just above the water. The tubing on the opposite side of the RIB was flat as a floppy pancake and drowning.

I walked over to the concrete boat slip to assess the problem head-on. I tilted my head forty-five degrees, hoping if I matched the boat's angle, things mightn't look so dire. It was no use.

'The milk carton won't fix this one,' I said.

A volunteer patted my back. 'Ah, I'm really sorry, Alan.'

My support boat was the size of a convertible car, and I had no trailer to wheel it from the sea. The locals and I would have to lug the boat from the water for the second time this week. Five of us gripped the rubber handles on the left side, while five others took the right side. Two were on plank duty. Taking a leaf from the pyramid builders, we placed a handful of wooden posts on the incline, grunted, and heaved the boat upwards. Orange paint flaked off as the boat's fibreglass hull shrilled against the timber like nails on a chalkboard. I winced, thinking of the damage, and a chill shivered up my spine. We inched forwards in group bursts on the count of three. I stared skywards as fifty-euro notes with fluffy wings flew away.

The sight at the top of the slipway was harsher than the piercing scrapes – the battered boat laid out on the asphalt against the car park's cinder block wall.

Once we set the RIB aside, I began discussing my project's fate with the RNLI volunteers and Coastguard. With my support boat out of action, I hadn't much choice. After 210 kilometres of punishing sea swimming, Murphy's Law sank my boat and ended my charity challenge.

I saw the relief on the faces of the safety volunteers, no longer on standby for another assistance callout.

'Ah, look, it's desperate, I know,' a volunteer said. 'You put in so much effort, but it's the right call. To be fair, I would have quit long ago. It's a wonder you swam this far, so fair play to ya.'

The morning's commotion calmed, and everyone disappeared. 'Ugh, fuckin' hell,' I muttered to myself.

I could feel the warmth of the breakwater boulders through my shorts as I sat in solitude on the shoreline. Seagulls cawed overhead. The cold swell flowed towards me and pulled away, wet splashes landing on the tips of my trainers and seeping through to my toes – taunting me.

With the mighty Mourne Mountains behind me, I inhaled

the aroma of the salty seaweed and stared across Dundrum Bay, and sighed. The scenery appeared as though viewed through the bottom of a pint glass – streams flowing down my adventure-beaten face, and into my dishevelled beard.

I had hoped to become the first to swim the length of the island of Ireland – 500 kilometres of sea swimming – from the Giant's Causeway on the north coast to my home of County Waterford on the south coast.

It was June 2017. After nearly thirty days of battle, this was where I had to accept defeat.

In that moment of loneliness, I was not a twenty-six-year-old man. I was a wounded boy, mourning much more than a personal pursuit. The premature end to my adventure forced me to stop and sit still in the reality that my dad, Milo, was dead. I'd failed in my tribute to him. I'd let him down. I wanted to feel his comforting arm around my shoulder and hear his reassuring voice telling me it would be alright, that I'd honoured him in the act of giving it a proper bash, despite the wreckage. That wasn't going to happen. Wanting my dad's presence, I was alone and inconsolable. Time froze as I stewed in misery.

Those sinking feelings were a country mile from the life-affirming joy I'd experienced at the end of my previous charity adventure.

Five years earlier, by 30 June 2012, my dad had worked tirelessly for fifteen months to recover from a debilitating stroke. He stood proud, alive, and free on that glorious summer's day, embracing me with a wide grin beneath the Waterford Viking Marathon finish banner.

'You did it! Some man for one man, Al,' Dad said.

I gave him a tight hug, landing a sweaty kiss on his smiling cheek. 'Sure, didn't I tell you we would!'

Fundraising €15,000 for the Irish Heart Foundation, National Rehabilitation Hospital, and Football Village of Hope, I'd run thirty-five marathons (1,500 kilometres) in thirty-five consecutive days around Ireland's coast. Dad had returned from the brink. My family triumphed over adversity.

Five years on, though – on the rocks of Newcastle, County Down – hardship wasn't willing to let go of its suffocating stranglehold. *Where do I go from here?* I wondered.

PART ONE

HIGHEST AND LOWEST TIDE

ONE
Graduating

Running Ireland

After I became the first person to run around Ireland's coast, people often asked me, 'What's next?'

'I've no idea' didn't seem acceptable to most, but it was true. Once Dad suffered a stroke, I put my head down and blinkers on. I never strayed from thinking about what actions I needed to take to increase the probability of finishing the 1,500-kilometre charity run. As a novice long-distance runner at the time and with no substantial project management experience, the running mission required almost all the energy I had. I couldn't think of a time beyond it.

Once I had run across the finish line, I removed the blinkers, along with the Vaseline from my nipples, and the blister packs from my swollen feet. I was at ease, joyous with where my running odyssey had taken me. At the time of my dad's stroke, there had been a sense of sadness, danger, panic, and urgency. The run had served its purpose as a valuable tool in a challenging time. The daily tasks invigorated me and got me out of a hole when I most needed structure, activity, and a meaningful goal to pursue. From my family's low in 2011, we'd turned the tide. Dad had recovered to ninety-five per cent and was there to celebrate our successful fundraiser. We had reason to be content once more, basking in the warm June rays of 2012 and stopping to take in the scent of life's beautiful roses.

Rushing into another all-consuming charity endurance project for the sake of it had no appeal to me, even if that was what people expected. As a fresh-faced college graduate, my energy shifted towards gaining independence and venturing into the world on my own two feet.

MY DAD, MILO

MY MAM, MARIE

35MarathonMan.ie

THAT'S ME

EV, MY BIG BRO

Ripples

One rewarding consequence of my run was the ripples it created. Like the adventure stories that influenced my life, my actions motivated others.

Before publicly sharing my thirty-five consecutive marathon goal, I'd made a drunk bet at a house party with Darragh O'Keefe, a De La Salle secondary school friend.

'That's mental, Alo! I was actually dreaming about cycling around Ireland one day. How's about this? If you follow through with your run, I'll cycle a lap of the country?'

We shook hands, tipped our cider cans together, and I smiled through hazy eyes: 'You better get training so,' I said. 'I'm going for it.'

In September 2012, two months after I crossed my run's finish line, Darragh was true to his word. He and Conor Murphy were on their saddles, testing their physical and mental limits. They were powering around the island with purpose, choosing to raise funds for the Cardiac Risk in the Young (CRY) charity to remember our friend, Gary O'Keefe, who'd died of a hidden heart condition, aged twenty-one.

I found myself on a train from Waterford to Dublin with Mark Gunning to join them for their final stage.

Mark was a competitive cyclist and had his slick race bike, cycling cleats, and coordinated skin-tight team kit. Cycling shades completed his professional look. I was no cyclist and made do with borrowing a bicycle, cycling jersey, and *extra-padded* shorts. My running shoes gave away my disguise.

I arrived with misplaced optimism, assuming the 5,000 kilometres of running over the previous year would surely translate to the saddle – *fitness is fitness, right? It'll be graaand.*

The last leg was from Dublin City to Waterford City, roughly 160 kilometres. We cycled from Dublin to Carlow – eighty-five kilometres – before taking a break. Dehydrated, hungry, and soaked to the bone in sweat, we sought respite from the testing sun. I dismounted my bicycle for the first time since leaving the capital. My legs turned to wibbly-wobbly jelly under the weight of my body. I shuffled forwards, using my bike as a walking crutch, and flopped in a heap on the concrete, cowering in the shade cast by the support car. *Jeepers, we're only halfway,* I thought. There wasn't a bother on the multi-stage cycling men, laughing and joking as they gulped their sports drinks and gobbled their chicken fillet rolls from the petrol station.

The three lads placed their buns of steel on their seats and took off smiling after the break. I joined them, but I was grimacing. Not even halfway, the saddle squashed my untrained Play-Doh bum into a thin crêpe. Every little pebble or tarmac crack hit like a hammer.

They raced each other to physical markers to inject excitement into their cruise. While I huffed to keep the chain spinning in low gear, someone would shout, 'That signpost up there!' They'd be gone like the clappers. Once I caught them after their mini-race, they were soon off galloping to the next landmark.

As we pedalled onward, my body struggled. The lads pulled alongside me, placing a hand on my back and nudging me up the mountain sections. In reality, the slopes were barely off horizontal, but they felt like mountains to my virgin cycling legs.

They stopped to fix a puncture but encouraged me to continue ahead. Before long, the three men were back beside me. I felt like a burden in this foreign sport. Despite my friends' willing me to go the distance, I re-considered my part in the glory leg. This was their big day. After cycling 150 kilometres, I retreated to the support vehicle, not wanting to be the reason they finished late. I was never so happy to stop moving, rolling the car windows down and jeering them to the finish line.

'C'mon you lazy sods, we don't have all day. My granny could cycle faster!'

It was an epic experience to be a small part of the successful cycling odyssey. There were two main takeaways for me.

First, I learned there is only *some* general transferability of fitness between sports. Switching from one discipline to another is far from easy. The cycle zapped my legs. Although I'd trained myself to run for days without ill effect, just a few hours of cycling left me unable to sit for a week. I resembled the Leaning Tower of Pisa, alternating from one cheek to the other in a feeble attempt to relieve the pain of my broken rear end. It was a sharp reminder that if you want an activity to be enjoyable and sustainable, you must start small and build gradually.

Second, sharing aspirations, taking actions to achieve them, and talking about your experience can nudge others towards their dreams, like dominos knocking forwards. If I had kept my running dream inside my head and hadn't made the tipsy bet, Darragh and Conor mightn't have gone for their dream and raised another €4,000 for charity. In turn, their actions motivated me to write this book, hoping I could replicate this ripple on a broader scale, encouraging as many people as possible to pursue their ambitions and interests, whatever they may be.

Insufficiently Unemployed

With no graduate work in 2012's recessionary Ireland and the summer's running and cycling adventures complete, I had to look across the pond to the United Kingdom for employment. My four-year Town Planning degree from Technological University Dublin didn't satisfy the pedantic job specifications of British employers. They required a *UK-accredited* degree, which meant another year in postgraduate books at Cardiff University, Wales. With an Irish degree and a UK master's in my back pocket, but no money and no job lined up, I returned home to Waterford to continue my worldwide CV bombardment campaign – which ran into thousands of non-responses.

Countrywide, there was *one* town planning 'opportunity'. It was part of the government's infamous JobBridge scheme. I cycled to the Job Centre and waited my turn to sit like a prisoner in front of the Plexi screen that shielded the social welfare officer from the infectious unemployed.

'I'd like to apply for this internship I found,' I said, sliding a printout under the protective barrier.

'You're unemployed, you are?'

'Very unemployed, just finished college and keen to earn some dough.'

'And you're on the dole, though, yeah?'

'No. I've been offered a job in a call centre. I was going to work there while trying to get into town planning. The Job Bridge intern scheme seems to be the only thing going.'

'Oh, well, sorry. To be eligible to apply, you'll need to be on the dole for three months.'

'Huh? So, you're telling me to turn down the job offer to take social welfare instead?'

'Well, I couldn't advise that. We're the Job Centre. But, if you want the internship, yeah, you need to be on the dole for three months. They're the government's rules. What's it to be?'

'Put me on the dole, I guess … ?' I said with an amused shrug.

'Great,' he said with a delightful smile – *another satisfied customer.*

Round One, Fight

While twiddling my thumbs as I waited to be adequately

unemployed by government standards, I tried to make the most of my free time. With no money, options were limited. It so happened that the Irish Heart Foundation was organising a white-collar charity boxing fight for people with no previous boxing experience. This fundraiser offered a unique opportunity for ordinary people to test themselves in a high-stress combat situation. If fighting weren't intimidating enough, participants would put themselves on the line in front of a packed crowd of friends and family. Each participant was required to sell at least twenty tickets for the charitable cause.

I opened the rusting industrial steel doors and walked up the intimidating narrow stairs of the Raging Bull Gym in Ballybeg, Waterford City. At the top of the stairs, the sound of punches and grunts funnelled from the gym's doorway.

'I'm here to sign up for the Irish Heart Foundation fight night … I think,' I said to the woman behind the desk. 'After looking in there and hearing all that, I'm not so sure.'

'Ah, we'll look after you,' said the charity employee as she glanced up at me. 'Alan! I wasn't expecting *you* here. First the run, and now this! Holy moly, you're a glutton for punishment, so you are! Good man yourself.'

The fight camp involved training twice a week for six weeks before stepping under the ring's bright lights. Billy O'Sullivan led the coaches, with a young Dylan 'The Real Deal' Moran (now an 18–1 professional boxer) and his dad, Martin, bolstering the coaching team.

The introductory Tuesday and Thursday evenings went well, a mix of pad work, bag work, and lung-busting high-intensity circuit training – push-ups, sit-ups, burpees, and squats. The second session ended with an invitation: 'Every Saturday morning, we do sparring. It's open to anyone who wants to give it a shot.'

For those unfamiliar with the term, 'sparring' is unchoreographed fight practice between two training partners. It allows fighters to practise on a moving, unpredictable, reactive target rather than the less retaliatory pads and bags.

Of the twelve beginners, one participant and I dragged ourselves to the first Saturday morning spar. There were fifteen willing participants. Some were regulars, but most were from a local Gaelic football team. Gaultier GAA Club members were on the last week of their own six-week white-collar boot camp and were ready to rumble.

I watched as my Irish Heart Foundation companion threw himself to the wolves, getting clattered to the canvas three times within as many minutes.

'That's enough for today. Good effort,' the coach said, not waiting for the pre-set round buzzer to sound. His index finger flicked from me to the ring. 'You're up.'

My stomach was churning. My palms felt clammy inside the boxing gloves. I nodded, poker-faced, trying to hide the instinctive fear from my sparring partner.

As the coach wedged the red cushioned helmet over my head with a downward tug that could have broken my neck, I made him aware that this was my first week, my first spar, and asked what to do.

'When the buzzer goes, fight yer man there until it sounds again. You'll get a short breather, then go for the second and third rounds.'

'I know that, but—'

'You'll be grand. Enjoy.'

I didn't share his chilled optimism, my brain struggling to process why I was doing something you're programmed to avoid at all costs. After witnessing my new pal get beaten up, my eyes bulged. I thought this was what it might feel like to be that last lobster in the restaurant's fish tank, watching the simmering pot. The coaches stepped out between the ropes and hopped down to the mats. There was nowhere to look except the opposing corner. The GAA player jumped up and down, tucking his stocky legs to his chest before rolling his thick neck. My heartbeat trembled like an earthquake. Before I knew my arse from my elbow, the buzzer sounded. My opponent marched across the ring with his hands up and sixteen-ounce gloves protecting his stern face. *Shite*. The sensation of fight or flight was equal parts terrifying and exhila-rating. Having not stepped an inch forwards, I threw a reactive, defensive, jab-jab towards the attacker's head, thinking, *Feck off, leave me alone, will ya!* The next I knew, he was on the canvas, sitting there like a surprised-looking upright L. The referee sent me to a neutral corner. I was relieved to be out of danger and confused by my early success, shrugging in bewilderment as my opponent climbed back to his feet.

Punters will tell you that everyone has a puncher's chance. After my beginner's luck, I combined some flurries, but the movement robbed me of air. My gas tank wasn't what I thought it was. Fatigue forced me into a protective shell as I backed up. In defensive recovery mode, things went downhill, with me absorbing punches like no tomorrow.

The sudden drain was an insight that I could only learn through experience. Punching a bag in my own time was worlds apart. Holding my gloves up to my temples felt like lifting two sacks of spuds. I was in peak endurance running fitness but my slow and steady marathons meant diddly-squat in the ring. At least with running and cycling, you could veer to the sidelines for a breather. But here there was little rest, with a madman chasing me and punching any remaining air from my lungs.

The final beep-beep sounded and couldn't come soon enough, rescuing me from the onslaught and the verge of puking.

My sparring partner and I pumped our gloves and hugged each other. I'd lost the practice session but survived to fight another day. I was knackered, a sweaty starfish sprawled out on the foam mats, but buzzing, excited about my morning's accomplishment.

After absorbing Saturday's blows, my head pounded worse than a hangover on Sunday and Monday. If that's how it felt after being punched with balloon-like, sixteen-ounce gloves by a primary school teacher, don't ask me how humans can take the punishment from Katie Taylor and Co. I wasn't quitting, though. The fight camp and charity fundraising were the primary energising splashes of colour to my grey dole existence.

The other Heart Foundation fundraiser who'd joined me at sparring had similar but far worse problems. Puking up after the practice fight, he visited his doctor, who told him that he was concussed and must end his boxing foray. You might *play* sports, but you don't *play* fighting. By dabbling in boxing, I had a newfound respect and awe for the fighters I watched on TV, gaining a small insight into the health risks, conditioning, and skill required to have a career in combat sports.

Ginger Jabber

As beginners, we were at a heightened injury risk, going from zero to throwing full-force blows. At the end of week two, I damaged my flimsy wrist. Merely pressing my left palm against my right fist, it felt like there were smithereens of glass cutting me from the inside. The physio told me to quit and rest.

With only two weeks of training completed and four weeks to fight night, I had an easy out if I was inclined. Sedentary unemployment was an unappealing alternative.

With a decade of competing as a sprinter and having run forty-five-odd marathons, including my solo training marathons, I was well aware that things rarely go to plan. If I waited for perfection, until I was 'ready', I'd never accomplish anything. An injured wrist is a speed bump, not a stop sign. *Keep moving. I can't box. What can I do?* I asked myself. I did what I knew best and laced up my runners, hitting the road for endurance. It was good enough for Rocky Balboa; it was good enough for me. The sparring resembled high-intensity sprinting rather than long slow runs, so I returned to my old tartan track to replicate the rapid rounds.

Punching the forgiving air, shadowboxing with god-awful technique around my family's living room, I tried to engrain the movements without impacting my damaged wrist.

These sub-optimal actions were the best I could do in my circumstances. That was what mattered most and how I could look at myself in the mirror – making an honest effort with available resources. We can't do more than that.

I tested my wrist and fitness one week before the fight. I wound the strengthening cotton wraps around my knuckles, hands, and wrists, put on boxing gloves and stepped between the ropes for a third and final spar.

Landing punches still pinched my bone. This time, though, it was manageable pins in my wrist instead of shards of glass.

Forgetting 'the five Ds of dodgeball' – 'dodge, dip, duck, dive, and, dodge' – I blocked a few too many punches with my nose, and blood trickled into my 'tache, turning my foxy stubble ruby red.

The sparring went much better than the first and second attempts, excluding the wrist and nose injuries. It seemed less like a brawl and more like chess. It wasn't a blur of panicked reactive instinct. I wasn't in a shell or swinging wildly for the fences, hoping the other man would disappear. Mainly, I considered my shot selection – *one-two, hands up, jab, jab, move.* Having experienced chaos twice, I was more relaxed and in control of my actions, better equipped to handle the spike in adrenaline, nerves, and fear.

Another positive was that the weeks of shadowboxing and running meant my anaerobic and aerobic engines could complete the rounds more efficiently. Not throwing the baby out with the bathwater and choosing to work around my injured wrist had paid off. My fitness seemed as good or better than those who kept up the prescribed training regime, and I was still in a position to show up and compete.

I sold twenty-five tickets to friends and family, raising €500 for the Irish Heart Foundation. After I'd chosen the compulsory fighter's name and walkout song, the announcer beckoned me to the ring as the Dropkick Murphys' 'I'm Shipping Up to Boston' blared. The hairs on my arms rose like the cheering crowd from their seats.

'Alan "The Ginger Jabberrrrr" Corcoran!' said the MC on the mic, unable to hide his grin.

My chosen fighter's name was a bit of craic, but I wasn't smiling. I was focused. The competition was a real boxing fight, not a restricted practice spar. My black hood was up, and I was stony-faced. I inhaled as deeply as my damaged nose would allow, exhaling through my mouth while jiggling my arms out to the side, trying to remove the jitters.

The metal bell ding-dinged, and my opponent and I marched towards each other with intent. The first round was even, replicating the recent sparring. Decisions felt measured as the local shoe salesman and jobless graduate struck each other tit-for-tat. Things took a turn towards the middle of the second round. Mike Tyson famously said, 'Everybody has a plan until they get punched in the mouth.' For me, it was my softened nose. I couldn't feel pain – adrenaline numbing all receptors – but I could see the crimson puddle burst onto the ring's white canvas. I tasted the copper flowing into my mouth. I tried to inhale, only to swallow blood.

My corner team pressed a tatty, faded green towel on my face at the end of the round to stem the bleeding. The old rag was sandpaper on my skin. When they removed it, the towel was violent red.

They looked me in the eyes and asked, 'Do you want to continue?'

'Yeah, all good.'

The referee walked over to assess the damage. 'Are you okay? Want to carry on?'

I knew things mustn't have looked great for me if they all suggested I quit.

'Yeah, yeah, I'm grand. Let's rumble.'

The bell for the third and final round sounded. Self-control leapt from the ring, and a monkey took over the joystick. No more crisp hooks to the body and tight straight jabs. *That fucker broke my nose!* I began swinging automatic right-handed haymakers with wild abandon, one after another, trying to knock him out. One swing was so reckless that my fist flew wide of the intended target and momentum twirled me off-balance to the floor.

My opponent capitalised. I lost. I had a deviated septum to show for it, the bone in the middle of my nose resembling an S, but I'd enjoyed the experience and learned a lot about combat and myself.

Tyson was right. Fighting is an extreme example, but things don't go as planned in the ring or in life. Sometimes, you'd take a punch in the mouth rather than absorb some of life's curveballs. How we respond is what it's all about and sets the trajectory of one life apart from the next.

Reflecting on my fight, I decided I needed to be an objective sniper homed in on the target, not an AK-47 blasting in all directions with collateral damage.

I was annoyed at not remaining calm. I lost blood but gained experience, feeling better equipped for an improved response during my subsequent trials and tribulations.

Climbing

There wasn't anything I could do about the recession and lack of jobs, so I just had to serve the government's three-month unemployment sentence and wait things out. Sadly enough, that meant leaping for the only two town planning opportunities in Ireland – nine-month unpaid internships. I at least retained some semblance of dignity by getting invited to interview for both.

First up was a private-sector Dublin city-centre firm. The business targeted its internship at graduates, requiring no prior experience. After five years of full-time study, I had a degree and a master's. I trimmed my stubble, spent my dole money on a half-price suit and a haircut, and was office-ready.

In addition to the €144 the Irish state and taxpayers would be paying you anyway in unemployment benefit for doing nothing, the lucky winner would get an extra €50 to cover the thirty-five-hour workweek: €1.43 per hour of work, despite minimum wage laws. *How high could the firm's expectations possibly be?*

As I floundered in a sea of questions fit for a ministerial post, I realised they expected a lot. After all, businesses had the pick of five years' worth of unemployed recession babies, plus the previously employed town planners who'd been wiped out by mass lay-offs.

I didn't know what was more demoralising, the thousands of ignored applications or getting rejected for an unpaid job after spending years studying the subject. It raised doubts about myself. I felt like giving up on my career aspirations. *Maybe I should see if the hotel will have me back to scrub their pots, or the sports factory might have me back to pack their boxes.*

With yet another rejection absorbed, I had to do better. I clambered back on the horsie and, although this one was an unpaid position too, prepared for my interview with Monaghan County

Council as though they would pay me the big bucks. With my sword sharpened by battle, I secured the internship.

Nine months later, with still no paid career prospects on the horizon, I was resigned to moving back home to my parents to regroup and figure out my next step. A UK recruiter contacted me out of the blue. They invited me to a job interview with an employer offering *actual* money for work. I couldn't believe it.

Within weeks, I landed in London after securing an admin role in the London Borough of Ealing Council's Planning Department.

Some may see that as an underachievement after college, a bajillion job applications, the dole, and interning for months. There's always room for improvement, but it's about the small wins. The new job was a personal best and a step forward from yesterday. If you trudge through life, waiting only to appreciate the peak, you'll miss the fun in the climb. It's worth highlighting that many don't reach their envisaged pinnacle. What then, if you've belittled each modest progression?

I moved into a six-person houseshare in West London, spending £360 per month to share a former living room that the owner had turned into an extra bedroom. It came equipped with a bunk bed, biting bed bugs, one desk, and a large man who spoke no English. He snored like a banshee with a head cold just four feet to my right and fumbled around most mornings at 5 a.m. to get to his construction job.

My friends thought I was cracked. They weren't willing to slum it, and spent a much bigger chunk of their similar graduate salaries on more comfortable housing. My roommate was in his early thirties and sent his earnings abroad to his wife and infant child. At the age of twenty-three, I wasn't going to complain about my circumstances.

We were six adults crammed in a typical two-storey, three-bedroom, one-toilet terraced house. I didn't want to spend time there. On my first weekend, I explored on my own, boarding the underground with no destination in mind. Flushing red, pressed between the belly and the bum of two strangers and gripping the blue pole for dear life, I could feel London's glamour was fading fast. Desperate to restore my personal space and avoid a heat stroke, I squeezed my way out of the sardine can, finding myself in Fulham.

I wandered for half an hour before pulling my second-hand iPhone out and opening Google Maps to get my bearings. Born and raised in Waterford, Ireland, I couldn't believe the street I found myself on – Waterford Road. Feeling heart-warmed by coincidence, I floated around the next corner, and a building caught my eye. The red-brick structure curved around the bend, emblazoned with the distinct orange, black, and white of the Harley Davidson emblem. Rows of shiny toys lined Warr's show-room. It was love at first sight – destiny. *How do I get my hands on one of those?*

Daydreaming of motorcycles, I returned to the Tube and resurfaced at Ealing Broadway station. Moseying around to kill time and get my bearings, I stumbled on a Waterstones bookstore. As usual, I went in search of the sports and adventure section. A black-and-white cover with bold orange text beckoned me – *Hell and High Water: One Man's Attempt to Swim the Length of Britain* by Sean Conway. I was intrigued by the idea of a multi-stage swimming adventure and bought Sean's book to escape the reality of my grim accommodation.

I knuckled down at work and management rewarded me, pulling me from the admin team and welcoming me to the major projects team as a town planning officer. The turning tide was building behind me. My ambitions could rise from survival. I kept my cost of living lower than my peers – instant coffee, packed lunches, jogging to work, and cheaper housing. I used the difference to invest in my new muse – the Harley. I took motorcycle lessons and was licensed to drive bikes of any engine size within months. Learning the skill and saving to beat the band, I walked back to Warr's showroom a year after stumbling upon it. With the help of a bank loan, I became the proud owner of my dream motorcycle

– a 2015 matt black Iron 883cc Harley Davidson Sportster.

There are few chances to surprise unsuspecting parents as adults, and I wasn't letting this whopper pass me. My mam, Marie, and dad, Milo, had no clue that I'd spent the year learning to drive bikes, never mind that I'd bought one. They knew I planned to visit home.

'What time does your flight land at Waterford Airport?' Dad asked over the phone. 'We can pick you up and we'll go out for some breakfast in Tramore. How does that grab you?'

'Great stuff. The flight's landing at 10 a.m. Thanks for picking me up. Looking forward to seeing you.'

Two days after collecting my bike from the London show-room, I roared down the M4 away from London, my motorcycle's backfire popping like a playful firecracker. I drove onto the ferry at Fishguard in Wales and didn't look back until I reached Waterford, Ireland.

Like a giddy schoolchild wanting to show his parents his crayon drawing, I danced while sitting on my bike in front of the airport. When I saw Dad's car pull up, I smiled and waved like a madman on day release, forgetting the tinted solid chrome visor that hid my face. They had no idea who this flapping weirdo in the astronaut helmet was. I started the engine and rolled up next to Dad's window.

'Are you alright?' he said.

'I'm doin' great, and you?' I said, brimming ear to ear.

Dad looked at me confused, seeing his reflection in my visor, head tilted back, and eyebrows scrunched together. He looked at my more puzzled mother in the passenger seat and returned to me.

'Eh, can I help you?'

'Do you not recognise me voice?' I said as I roared with laughter and shoved the helmet overhead.

The look of gleeful bemusement on Dad's face and the sound of his laughter was something money could never buy. He jumped out of the car to hug me and rev the engine for himself.

Mam looked less pleased, glaring at the death trap and letting her mild motherly disapproval be known.

'Ah, Alan. You're not serious?'

'Come on; I'll take you for a spin.'

'You will not,' she said as she hugged me.

I was a working man on a mountain's peak, enjoying the fruits of my labour. The year's work, the scrimping, and the days of lessons were worth it to experience the joy of the road trip and the sight of my parents' jaws hitting the ground.

TWO
Olé, Olé Olé Olé!

Tour de France

After spending 2015 working towards proving myself in the office and pursuing my motorcycle dream, 2016 was about accumulating annual leave, saving, and progressing my next brainwave – creating enjoyable memories to cherish.

I loaded my motorbike steed with my sleeping bag, tent, backpack, and a red steel canister of emergency fuel. It balanced on my passenger seat, held together by a hotchpotch of bungee cords. The Buckaroo! looked like it was ready to bolt under the load.

I'd booked two weeks off from the London desk job and was away to France for a once-in-a-lifetime trip.

In the summer of 2016, the Irish soccer team qualified for the UEFA European Football Championship. My dad was flying to France with the Irish squad as part of the Football Association of Ireland's (FAI) delegation.

Dad loved football and would watch it morning, noon, and night if he could. He'd climbed from being a fan in the local team's supporters' club in the '80s to becoming the FAI's vice president in the '90s and president in the 2000s. Dad chaired the FAI's International Committee and helped establish and chair the cross-border Setanta Cup competition. He'd enjoyed attending all the major championships Ireland had qualified for – Euro '88 in West Germany, Italia '90, USA '94, Korea and Japan 2002, and Poland 2012. He wouldn't miss this footballing extravaganza for love nor money. I couldn't wait to share the experience with him.

The overpriced campsite on England's south coast had a two-night-stay policy. Only needing a few hours, I decided to wing it and find a free patch of ground to pitch up.

My exhaust pipes growled beneath the dim glow of streetlights and interrupted the stillness. Two-storey houses formed a wall to my right, some in darkness, some downstairs windows aglow with TV screens. To my left was an ink-black canvas where I knew the waves of the English Channel crashed against the White Cliffs of Dover.

As I killed the engine, eyes peeped through the curtains of a dark upstairs room opposite. Although I was the intruder, I felt uneasy about being watched. *I should have booked the feckin' campsite.* I unclipped the steel hooks that secured my belongings – the tapestry of bungee cords slingshotting every which way. Bundling everything into my arms in one lazy man's load, I scurried into the shadows of the neighbourhood green and hoped the residents wouldn't call the police.

With Neighbourhood Watch on high alert, only a few hours to rest, and no experience erecting a tent, I decided to start the micro-adventure with a bang. *I'll keep a low profile and sleep beneath the stars.* That reads as romantic as it sounded in my head. It's a stark contrast to the reality.

I hid on a narrow, paved path behind a red-brick building that smelled like public toilets. Laying my backpack and jacket down as a pillow, I layered up, clambered into my sleeping bag, and fell like a twit off-balance onto my camping mat.

Pebbles prodded. The toilets hummed with an occasional clank that flashed my eyes open. Although six-foot-two and around eighty-five kilograms, I was half asleep, half on guard, waiting for the shadow of an attacker to loom over me.

My first fractional glimpse into 'sleeping' rough rattled me. Remove the barriers, and stress kicks in. My unease forced me to appreciate the basic comforts that many, including myself, often take for granted – a roof, walls, warmth, security, and a fridge with food. It made me consider London's 11,000 rough sleepers in a more compassionate light. Watching a documentary on homelessness beneath a warm duvet is one thing; sleeping on the pavement has a visceral impact. I can't recall one experience in the office or at home in the months preceding this, but this memory stands out from the pages like a bookmark.

My instincts woke me with a fright. I shot upright and couldn't breathe. I tried to open my eyes, but somebody had glued them shut. My heart pounded like I'd downed a quadruple espresso. My hands raised, one open and one closed, partly in defence, part in surrender.

The hysterics were short-lived. My jacket pillow had my phone in the pocket beneath my head for safekeeping. I'd set my alarm to the siren to ensure I didn't miss my train. That accounted for the heart attack. As for the attacker that had glued my eyes shut with a yucky yellow crust, that was the fresh-cut grass I hadn't seen when I'd arrived under nightfall. My bleary eyes were hanging out of my head. I was hay fever personified. My nose allowed no air in, but allowed a river out. My tongue scrubbed the back of my throat to relieve an itch that no amount of scratching could soothe. I hadn't packed antihistamines or eye drops, nor did I have time to find a pharmacy. Feeling sorry for myself, I grumbled while struggling to load all my gear back onto the motorcycle before dawn.

Adventures are never straightforward, and comfort is rarely an ingredient. Nonetheless, there are always lessons from leaving the comforting armchair and a story to be told.

Green Army

Driving my bike off the train, I continued from Calais to the centre of Paris and pulled up to our Airbnb to meet my childhood friends. Some had just flown from Dublin, while the rest had got the direct train from London.

'Jeez, state of you. You alright?' Tommy said, referring to my devil-red eyes and pilot's tone.

'Let's just say it was a rough night and I should have got the train with you lot. What about your eyes then?'

'That'd be the cider and mimosas. It was a great aul' train ride, in fairness.'

'Glad you lot enjoyed the feckin' trip at least.'

After dumping our bags, we did what any self-respecting Irish football tourists did when arriving in a cultural capital – we Googled 'Irish Pub Paris' and set out searching for some craic (via the pharmacy).

We Irish don't know how good we have it when globetrotting. We're never too far from a taste of home. As expected, a ready-made community of merry compatriots were enjoying the French wine and exotic Stella Artois Cidre on the Boulevard de Clichy. The crowd stretched from The Harp Bar, past Corcoran's Irish Pub (no relation), and in front of the Moulin Rouge – a 200-metre shamrock-green river containing approximately one zillion boisterous Irish fans.

It wasn't long until the singing and playfulness engulfed the street, everyone's hair flowing wild by dinnertime. At first, the French police approached us like we were football hooligans – heavy-handed, attempting to impose law and order. The Irish retaliated, plonking their arses on the road with straight faces and singing spontaneously in chorus:

Sit down for the French police,
Sit down for the French police,
Sit down for the French police,
Sit dowwwwn for the French police!

Right on cue, without a conductor, the masses erupted skywards in smiles as beer filled the air:

Stand up for the French police,
Stand up for the French police,
Stand up for the French police,
Stand uuuup for the French police!

The jovial choir of strangers flung their arms around their neighbours' shoulders – an Irishman, a passing shopper, or even a police officer – and jumped in song. The confused locals couldn't help but smile. The Irish giddiness was infectious, radiating the essence of bonhomie. Realising they'd mixed us up, that we were not the furniture-throwing fans from other countries shown on the news, the police adjusted their strong-arm attitude to crowd control. The guards took their new position at either end of the block and left us to frolic around our meadow of cans in peace.

One Irish fan did get aggressive and instigated hassle with another reveller. A wobbly bystander holding a plastic bag of cans sang acapella:

Are you English,
Are you English,
Are you English in disguise?

A chorus of twenty strangers harmonised to repeat the verse, and forty joined in for the third verse. Travelling English football fans don't have the best reputation, and the Irish usually don't like people mistaking them for English. The green-shirted aggressor bowed his head, denied the accusation, and apologised profusely.

'No, no, you're right. I was bang out of order. Sorry. I'm Irish, lads. I'm Irish.'

The chant stopped, and the merry mayhem continued in high spirits.

Quality Time

There was a late start to my second day in Paris. I drove to the western edge of the city, to Versailles. Dad was due to arrive with the team and officials, and I would stay with him for two nights.

Pulling in across the road from the walled hotel grounds, I admired the elegant stone columns on either side of the opulent wrought-iron gates. My neck tilted backwards to appreciate the golden spikes piercing the sky.

A gang of security guards protected the entrance, looking like

Men in Black. I didn't think my biker aesthetic and denim jacket decorated with bludgeoned flies conformed to the grandiose surroundings of the five-star Trianon Palace Hotel. I knew security would tell me where to go if I tried to breach their defensive line, so I phoned Dad to come out and let me in. He didn't answer, despite me being bang on time.

The heavens opened, and the rain poured – an omen for the calamitous events. I unloaded my gear and sought shelter. Standing alone beneath the pleached lime trees, I admired their perfection, forcibly woven together by skilled arborists, forming an ordered marching column of leaves up and down both sides of the broad, straight boulevard. After two hours of waiting in the torrential rain and more unanswered calls and texts, I grew more concerned. I approached the guarded gates.

'Bonjour, sorry, fellas, might you know when the team arrives?'

'They're already here, but fans can't enter.'

Walking back to the tree, I was confused about my dad's whereabouts. I hadn't known him to be late. If he was ever running behind or there was a change of plan, I'd get a text or call. He was dependable. He wouldn't leave my calls unanswered unless he was in a meeting. *He must still be in a meeting.*

To my relief, a text from Dad vibrated on my phone:

'Hi Al, sorry to leave you waiting. I've had to get a later flight. If you go to the gates, I've arranged for someone to let you into the room. See you tonight.'

Five hours after we'd planned to meet, there was a knock at my hotel door. It was Dad and a colleague helping him with his suitcase. My dad's full head of curly snow-white hair and characteristic moustache was as perfect as ever, but he looked battle-worn, paler, skinnier, and had bags under his eyes.

'What happened?' I said. 'You had me worried. All okay?'

'I'll be fine after a good night's kip. I just felt a little light-headed at the airport, was all. The team doc didn't want me flying unless I got checked out. Straight to the hospital, got the green light, and took the next flight out. Better late than never. I'm only fit for bed.'

'Are you sure? That sounds serious enough?'

'Yeah, I'll be grand. It's great to see ya,' Dad said with a hug. He skipped unpacking and went straight into bed.

The following morning, Dad seemed himself again. A smile had returned to his face along with colour to his cheeks. He was an inch or two taller, with his shoulders broadened.

Dad had been to Paris before for football and was eager to show me the neighbouring Palace of Versailles after some tea and grub.

At first, the extravagant grounds appeared fake, a synthetic form of perfection, with diamond-shaped trees sliced with laser precision. One man stood on a ladder, chiselling away with a cordless hedge trimmer, while another filled the air with the clawing of his rake. Green Lego blocks of knee-height hedges formed flawless squares along the sandy gravel paths, their centres brimming with a rainbow of flowers.

I noticed Dad falling behind on our sauntering stroll. He was short of breath.

'Are you *sure* you're okay? Want to take a rest?'

Unusually, he accepted the offer to pause. We sat on a marble bench while he took deep breaths in through his nose and out through his mouth to recharge his batteries.

He'd made a phenomenal return to life in the five years since his stroke, thanks mainly to the National Rehabilitation Hospital in Dun Laoghaire. His health was never one hundred per cent after the stroke, but Dad wasn't far off in the grand scheme. He'd regained and enjoyed his independence; he could do everything he relished – walking lengths of the local Woodstown Beach, meals out with the family, attending hurling and football matches, and going on the odd sun holiday to Portugal. He didn't sleep as well as before the stroke, tiring faster, and often experienced pins and needles down his right-hand side, but it didn't hold him back from living to the full.

At the Euros, he was sixty-five, on the verge of retiring with Mam. I chalked this excessive fatigue up to his age, the stroke, travel stress, and his immune system having a catnap.

Slowing the pace, we ambled around the grounds and enjoyed some quality time with each other.

'You're good company,' he said. 'Thanks for coming out to visit me. I know your friends are probably having a mad one in the city.'

'Not at all. This is perfect here. And you're not bad company yourself,' I said with a wink, putting my arm over his shoulder as we continued to the palace.

The palace's grandeur matched the 2,000-acre grounds.

'I can see why it's a UNESCO World Heritage Site, the size of that place!' I said. The seventeenth-century limestone château extended for days. A succession of royals had decorated it with more and more ornate sculptures and pillars. 'Unreal, isn't it?'

'Fuckin' lovely,' Dad said, with a cheeky grin and a squeeze of my shoulder.

I was twenty-five and standing on my own two feet. We'd grown beyond a pure father-and-son relationship and had bonded as equals, adults, friends.

Dad walked to the viewing platform. Standing between two bronze statues, he looked out on the vast symmetrical orangery, ponds, fountains, and intricately patterned lawns. He tilted his face towards the sun's heat, his hands on his hips, and closed his eyes. Watching him soak in the serenity, I didn't want to be anywhere else or with anyone else.

I'm a Little Teapot

On Monday, I was back in the city to find my friends for the first match against Sweden, while Dad put on his navy suit and tie to join the FAI delegation at the Stade de France.

The city was a rowdy carnival and a world apart from the tranquil palace grounds.

It was just a few hours before the 5 p.m. kick-off. A white work van made the schoolboy error of trying to navigate through the middle of the buoyant Irish contingent, now encamped on the Boulevard de Clichy. The inevitable happened. A middle-aged man clambered atop the snail-paced van with the help of encouraging friends and strangers. The thousands drinking on the street celebrated his successful ascent as if we'd just scored a World Cup-winning goal. The adulation of the cheering crowd raced to the man's head. The van-man celebrated by removing his green jersey and whipping it overhead in circles, proudly displaying the slate-grey forest of chest hair attached to a mighty dad-bod. It looked like this might have been his first holiday away from his wife and kids in twenty years, and he loved it. A faint *ooh* became two, then five, gathering pace as hundreds joined to create a deafening cheer. In the excitement, he dropped his fawn trousers to the van's roof with a poise worthy of a role in *The Full Monty*. Jigging from one foot to the other in his black boxer shorts and white shin-high socks, he put his hands to his hips, like a little teapot, short and stout. The crowd was enthralled, glued to the show. A happy *ooh* began rumbling again, louder and louder in anticipation, until the public reached a climactic roar – an emperor's thumb of approval. The crowd burst into laughter and cheered in divilment as the man merrily jiggled around with his boxer shorts now hanging around his knees, the teapot's spout on full display.

Our national team probably wouldn't get out of the tournament group stages. We weren't there for a long time, but everyone came there smiling and was ready for a good time. We drew the opening game 1–1 against Sweden. The result did little to dampen spirits, the craic in front of the Moulin Rouge's electric red glow pulling the Irish to it like a moth to a flame.

Go Home, for the French Police

With Paris behind me, I faced a two-day, 800-kilometre ride south to Mam, who was flying into Biarritz.

I indicated onto the dual carriageway and roared towards the southwest tip of France.

After a few hours, a brooding cloud appeared on the horizon. Dark and ominous, it might as well have been the apocalypse. Exposed and vulnerable, my concern grew at the same speed as the inky blackness swallowed the sky.

The clouds shot a million pellets at me, flooding through my denim and soaking my body to the bone. The deluge smashed into my visor with ear-splitting clinks and placed a veil over my eyes. Forks of lightning cut the horizon in two as thunder rumbled, making my pipes sound like squeaking mice by comparison.

I didn't want to be a biker anymore. I wanted out, but there were no lay-bys or escapes. A wall of articulated lorries filled the slow lane, perilous gaps with an impenetrable mist sprayed by monstrous tyres. There was no choice but to remain in the overtaking lane. I shouted, 'Fuck off!' at the glaring blur of car headlamps on my back wheel, forcing me to maintain speed. My eyes wide with energy-drink focus, I turned on my hazard lights. Gusts caught my backpack and shoved me towards the steel crash barrier. My body stiffened as I clenched the handlebars, wishing the nightmare to end.

A lay-by appeared. Blindfolded, I swerved between lorries to escape to safety. I paced back and forth until the storm passed, trying to avoid catching my death while giving my body an outlet to release the heightened adrenaline.

Continuing to Biarritz felt like being blasted by the world's largest hairdryer, flicked to its coldest setting, wind shooting up my sodden jeans and denim jacket.

'Where on earth have you been? You're drenched,' my mam said when I shivered into Biarritz. 'I've been hiding from the sun all day, reading my book at the beach. Come on, and we'll get you warm.'

We strolled to the seaside with puddles squelching in my boots and footprints stalking us. I set my clothes to dry on the sunbed, changed into my boardie shorts, and waded into the azure waters. I turned to see if Mam was following.

'What is *that* yoke?' she said, staring and pointing at my ribs.

Whoops-a-daisy, I'm nabbed. I plunged my torso into the water. 'Nothing.'

'Ah, Alan.'

My mam disapproved of the stag I'd got tattooed on my ribs.

With not so much as a participation certificate for running a lap of Ireland, I wanted a souvenir. With all the stags on the training trails, it felt fitting. The stag was out of the bag now and in permanent ink. We laughed at our mother-son differences, bobbing for an hour as the hug of the warm water and time with Mam re-warmed my core.

After two days on Biarritz's beaches with my mother, our family regrouped in Bordeaux. My big brother, Evan, and his wife, Deirdre, landed from Ireland, and Dad made it down from Paris with the Irish team for Ireland's match against Belgium.

Ireland lost 3–0, but fans celebrated as though we'd won. We flocked to the streets around the Irish pub. Wine bottles popped open with the heels of shoes. Hours flew.

After the last orders in the pub, the police shooed the fans out the door. It was lashing raining. The crowd didn't pay a blind bit of notice. The police encouraged revellers to go home, but the craic was ninety, so they may as well have been trying to herd cats.

One reveller wandered off course. 'Over here, lads, c'mon.'

The hijinks moved out of the rain and into a tunnel. Red and blue police flashes followed and illuminated the shelter. They unintentionally turned it into a nightclub as the crowd danced and sang their version of Gala's 'Freed from Desire':

Shane Long's on fire. UH! Na-na-na-na-na, na-na, na-na-na, na-na.

A tired police officer became desperate, wanting nothing more than to go home to bed. He directed his speaker into the echo chamber and pleaded in song:

> Go home for the French police,
> Go home for the French police.

Fuck Yeah!

Returning to Biarritz, I was relieved to find my motorcycle where I had hidden and shackled it.

I skirted the Pyrenees mountains for 300 kilometres, the saw-tooth wave following me to Toulouse for lunch. After another day in the saddle, I arrived at my night's campsite in Saintes-Maries-de-la-Mer, a quaint Mediterranean fishing village east of Montpellier.

When I awoke and unzipped my tent, my map lured me three hours east to the deepest and most spectacular European canyon – Gorges du Verdon.

I was as giddy as a puppy in a ball pit as I queued up to rent a pedalo on the shoreline. The natural wonder was breathtaking, the surreal turquoise water illuminated by the sun's glare. As I pedalled the pristine Verdon River, I stared in awe, mesmerised by the sheer cliffs of glistening limestone decorated with lush greenery. *It doesn't get much better than this.*

With my wanderlust quenched for the day, I went hunting for an Irish pub to watch the next match – Ireland vs Italy. The game was in Lille in the north of France, a good 1,000 kilometres from my postcard surroundings in the southeast. We were unlikely to beat Italy to advance from the group. Still, I wanted to watch and cheer on my nation.

I climbed up to Moustiers-Sainte-Marie, a charming village of 700 residents perched high in the mountains. It lived up to its reputation as one of France's 'most beautiful villages'. I found myself content in being lost, meandering the narrow pedestrian maze lined by pastel yellow terraces, clay tiles, and wooden window shutters. I followed a hiss to a cobblestone bridge and watched the stream flow far beneath, bisecting the town with a deep forested valley.

They say you must first get lost to find yourself. I found myself back looking for the pub. There were only two in town, and they were screening Sweden vs Belgium. A phone stream in a quaint square beneath an olive tree would have to do.

'Sorry, bai, are you watching the Ireland game there?' said a man with a thick Cork accent. 'Mind if we pull up two seats?'

I laughed. 'That's gas. No matter how off the beaten track you think you are, there's always a roaming Paddy nearby, huh? Yeah, pull up two seats, and we'll grab some pints.'

To our surprise, Robbie Brady scored a leaping header to snatch a now-famous late Irish victory, sending President Michael D. Higgins jumping to his feet on my phone. The win secured a qualifying spot to advance Martin O'Neill's Irish team from the group stages and into the last sixteen to face the French.

The next game was four days away, in Lyon. I checked the map. *Four hundred kilometres north. I'm here now, may as well.* I called Dad to tell him I was coming to meet him, and texted my boss to tell him I needed an extra week off work.

'Unfortunately, all of your work cases were overturned by the planning committee. The councillors and committee members recommended sacking the planning officer, but don't worry about that, Al, you just enjoy your time off ;),' his response read.

In the morning, I zipped open my tent to the sights and sounds of Verdon Natural Regional Park and stepped out into the woodland dirt. Twigs crunched, pine aroma wafted, and birds twittered as the sun hit me through the thick canopy. With a grateful smile and a yawn, I stretched my arms wide before dismantling my home and loading it up in record time. *I'm getting the hang of this craic,* I thought.

Helmet fastened. It was time to rock 'n' roll.

'I'm so fucking lucky!' I cheered, my voice muffled by my exhaust pipes and the Red Hot Chili Peppers in my headphones.

Ripples miraged between the dark molten asphalt and sweltering sky. In my brown leather glove, my sweaty hand ripped the throttle back. Leaning to the left and zooming to the right,

I swooped around the winding track, the footpegs sparking and rattling off the road when I leaned too far.

I waved to passing motorcyclists with an outstretched leg. Their extended legs returned the gesture, and I became part of the community.

The beaming sun highlighted forty shades of green along the French countryside. I was in a watercolour painting, soaring through farmlands lined by trees, patchworks of small woodlands, and alpine peak after peak spanning to Austria. People pay thousands for artwork, but nothing matches the spectacle and feel of being in it at 160 kilometres an hour. Goosebumps of delight tingled my arms.

'This is the life! Fuck yeah! Wooh!' I sang from the top of my lungs as my cheeks began aching from smiling since dawn.

Don't Take Me Home

Matchday was upon us, 60,000 filling the Parc Olympique Lyonnais. 'La Marseillaise' – *incredible!* The national pride was palpable as the French nation sang with gusto on home turf. The elated Irish joined their singsong, forgetting there were sides to this duel: 'Dada-da-da-da-da-DAAA-DADA!' It served as a vocal warm-up.

Ireland's 'Amhrán na bhFiann' vibrated through the air. The national anthem penetrated the souls of the Irish, teleporting their psyche to an ancient hilltop overlooking the battlefield alongside Cú Chulainn and his warrior clan. The moment overpowered me. There was a visceral gut response standing shoulder to shoulder with Dad and compatriots, singing our anthem, invoking strange, prideful tears of Irishness and unity.

France's Paul Pogba fouled Ireland's Shane Long within a minute of kick-off. The referee awarded Ireland a penalty. Two minutes in, we found ourselves 1–0 up against a tournament favourite, Robert Brady converting the high-stakes opportunity. The green corner went berserk, unbelieving Irish fans jumping to their feet as liquids filled the air. Dad and I hopped up with our arms around each other in bliss. We were grateful the doctors had cleared him to make that late flight and experience this priceless ecstasy.

At half-time, we couldn't believe our luck. It was the most exciting game of the entire tournament. We were playing out of our skin and deserved the lead.

'Where's the next match for the winner?'

'Paris, next weekend, against the winner of Iceland and England. Don't count your chickens just yet, Al.'

'If we win, I'm staying another week.'

'What will work say?'

'Yes or no, but I'm staying. It's only a job. I'm twenty-five and will have forty-odd years of typing reports in an office. How many chances are there to experience all this with you, eh? I've got qualifications and three years' experience now. I won't starve. Someone will have me.'

'I suppose you only need enough money to do the things you want to do. Yeah, you can always find another gig, I suppose.' Dad smiled. 'I don't think your mother will agree, though.'

'No point having a great job at the expense of an enjoyable life.'

We snapped a photo together to mark the occasion and returned to our seats for the second half, unaware of the sentimental value that image would hold.

The Irish fans shared our feelings. Thousands sang:

Don't take me home,
Please don't take me home,
I just don't wanna go to work,
I want to stay here and drink all your beer,
Please don't, please don't take me home!

In the fifty-seventh and sixty-first minute, Antoine Griezmann put paid to our plans, scoring two goals in quick succession for the French. Our remaining hope disintegrated as the referee raised a red card to Shane Duffy in the sixty-sixth minute, reducing us to ten men. Ireland lost 2–1.

The Irish fans remained in the stadium, singing as eagerly as ever, appreciating their team's effort as the French supporters disappeared. I stood with Dad, absorbing the moment, watching our players walk over and applaud the thousands remaining in the green corner. We mightn't have had the footballing prowess, but nobody could question our spirit. I had jumped around with Dad in the hopping O2 Arena in 2014 when Ireland's most decorated mixed martial artist, Conor McGregor, beat Diego Brandão in the first round of UFC Fight Night 46. McGregor famously told interviewer Dan Hardy and the Dublin crowd that the Irish were not there just to take part in the UFC but to take over. The Irish football fans had different values. They were delighted to be on the journey, celebrating it, and painting the town green in any outcome.

I put my arm around Dad's shoulder, and he threw an arm around mine. Emotions took me by surprise again. We were choked for words. It didn't matter. Being there with each other, high on life, was more than enough.

Though we got knocked out of the tournament, we made international news with our afterparty on the streets of Lyon. I slept in the back of a hand-painted green, white, and gold van with five hometown strangers I'd met in the hostel the night before, and couch-surfed through Reims en route back to London.

I'd done what I was supposed to. I had gone to school, got my degrees, clambered from the welfare queues, and moved up the career ladder. I was young and free, loving the gift of standing on firm ground, saddling my motorcycle, and soaring to a crescendo.

THREE
Cancer.

Crash

The pressed office trousers, ironed long-sleeve shirt, and polished black shoes were back on in Acton, West London. I pushed my shamrock socks to the bottom of my drawer and pulled up my navy ones.

An avalanche of e-mails, meetings, and reports replaced the excitement of the road. Little did I know then that the post-holiday drizzle would brew into a life-altering tsunami.

Dad was home in Waterford, feeling his health decline. He went to the doctors, who referred him to specialists for further testing. I spoke to Mam and Dad throughout July, calling as soon as my staff card swiped the office exit chicane. I'd listen to their updates while sitting on my motorcycle in the emptied staff car park. Our chats got more concerning over time.

'There's the possibility this might be cancer, Al. The doctors haven't ruled it out yet, but we just don't know until we get the results,' Mam told me.

I was up to high doh with how my life was going. The contentedness had left me flatfooted. *Cancer.* The word knocked me for six.

While awaiting his results, Dad didn't waste his freedom. He'd be damned if he would sit at home and wallow in dread. My dad wanted to live and do the things he loved doing. That vigour for life had got him through his stroke. On Wednesday, 27 July 2016, he mustered the energy to attend Waterford's Walsh Park and encouraged the Waterford Minor (under-eighteen) hurling team in their Munster Semi-Final clash with Limerick. He drove two hours to Turner's Cross Stadium in Cork the following day, taking in the atmosphere of Cork City FC vs KRC Genk, competing in the Europa League.

'I'm shattered, Al,' Dad said to me on Friday's phone call.

'You might look at some flights home,' my mam suggested. 'We're due in for the test results on Monday.'

I booked a last-minute flight from London and boarded the plane on Sunday morning.

It was one thing to hear how exhausted Dad was. I wasn't prepared to see how much his health had diminished in the four weeks since the French escapade. He couldn't stand for our usual embrace. It was as though he had aged twenty years, resembling an eighty-five-year-old – gaunt, fragile, and depleted. I lowered myself to him as he lay on our living room couch. There were no words, just a long hold.

I bottled my feelings and focused on the practicalities of the dire situation. When it was bedtime, I hoisted Dad from the settee like a wounded soldier from the battlefield. We retreated down the short hall to his bedroom with his arm around me.

With Dad tucked in, I went to bed in a daze with a ringing from the bomb blast. The soft, warm blanket in my silent room was little comfort as all I could whisper in the darkness was, 'Jesus Christ'. The bolts burst open with the rising pressure. Tears flowed.

The following day, my brother, Evan, called over so we could face this appointment together as a family.

After helping Dad wash his hair, the four of us waited in the sitting room, counting down the hour-like minutes.

'Ten-forty-five. Everyone right to go?' Mam said.

It was time to head to Waterford University Hospital. Ev and

I went to help Dad from his seat. He was having none of it.

'If I'm walking out of my home, I'm doing it under my own steam.'

Dad was psyched up with a fire in his belly. His sentiment increased the moment's gravity, suggesting this could be it. The notion that he mightn't return home wasn't on my mind until those words stabbed my lungs, robbing me of oxygen. Life had started to spiral too fast to catch up with it.

Though the car was metres away, Dad's fight to walk solo had him running on empty when we reached the hospital five minutes later.

He sat in a wheelchair. We pushed him through corridor after corridor. The wheels' black rubber squeaked with every turn on the bandaid-beige lino. A gallery of paintings lined the walls on either side, trying to soothe the tension within the maze. The odour of antiseptic overwhelmed my senses – surgery, sickness, death – rendering the artwork's efforts worthless.

Crumpled magazines covered a table surrounded by empty steel benches with foam bursting from their worn seams. My family approached the receptionist, despair and worry etched on our sleepless faces.

'We're here for Milo Corcoran's appointment.'

'We're running behind. Sorry. Eh, you'll have to wait. If you can come back in, say, two hours, the consultant should be able to see you then.'

It was a brutal blow to the gut of a family already beaten to the floor. We looked around at the empty seats with anger bubbling to a boil.

'But this is our appointment time. It's urgent,' Mam said.

'Sorry, the consultant's swamped. There's nothing I can do.'

The information was delivered casually, as if we were just there to get a routine haircut, but it was my dad's life on the line. *Look at how shattered my dad is! He needs help. NOW!* We were despairing and powerless.

Despair

Back at home for two hours, I could only think of how much time the doctors were wasting when they should have given my dad the medical attention he needed and deserved. It was torture, being forced to watch his strength wither before my eyes. A storm of anger, fear, and sorrow engulfed me as I looked across at Dad, resting his head in his hand, almost paralysed with fatigue.

We left home once more. The delay had extinguished Dad's morning fire. This time, he had to accept our assistance.

The door closed with a slam. Mam, Dad, Ev, and I sat down to the clinks of the chrome leg chairs colliding. The consultant's desk bisected the office, pinning our backs to the wall. Grey filing cabinets lined one side of the room, exacerbating the crushing feeling of being trapped.

Nothing needed to be said. Nothing could be said, deep-seated emotions strangling my vocal cords. Ashen faces looked at me when I peered left or right. We were deer caught in the headlights of an oncoming car.

The doctor knocked and entered with a brown A4 folder gripped to the chest of his lab coat. We all shimmied our seats in the available inches to allow him to his chair.

'Let me open these blinds and let some light in first.'

His effort to brighten the sombre room did little. Instead of staring at dated vinyl blinds, we faced an oppressive pebbledash wall of a tiny courtyard.

We did all we could to brace ourselves for his words, intuitively forming a defensive chain by placing our hands on each other.

'Okay, I'll not make you wait any longer. I've got the results from the biopsy and X-rays. I'm afraid, Milo, it's not good news. You do have cancer.'

Nothing could prepare us for those words as they entered our ears and shot our hearts. The room filled with audible breaths as optimism sank like a cement block to the seabed. My lower lip quivered as I locked my jaw to fight the heartbreak. The little pulsing squeezes of my dad's hand on my leg were enough to break me. Nobody's head moved in my teary peripheral vision, everyone remaining fixed on the doctor, willing him to provide us with an olive branch.

'The cancer's advanced. It's stage four, which means it's grown and spread to other organs.'

The doctor removed an X-ray film from his folder with a violent wrist flick. His gold watch rattled as the plastic sheet whipped like a face slap. Daylight illuminated the black-and-white image that the doctor held overhead for us to see. He ran the black cap of his plastic biro from stain to stain.

'Here's where cancer originated in the bowel. Here you can see that it's spread to the liver. Have you any questions?'

Time was warping. Dejected silence lingered for a second or an eternity.

'How bad is it?'

'What can we do?'

'What does this mean in plain English?'

'Can it be treated?'

'It's serious but by no means fatal. I've seen many bouncing back from this and worse. All's certainly not lost by any means. We need you ready for a fight, though. We'll admit you and get your energy up with a drip and a feed. Once we've got you feeling a bit stronger, the next step is chemotherapy. I'll give you a moment. There'll be someone outside to take you to the ward when you're ready.'

The horrors of life clobbered us like a wrecking ball, smashing the rapture of France into the stratosphere. It had only been four weeks ago, but a lifetime amid today's sickening reality.

First the stroke, now this? He was in the wars. *It's cruel,* I thought as I stood up, on the verge of crumbling back down.

Once Dad settled into his ward and visitation hours finished, my mam, Ev, and I walked towards the hospital's exit. The weight of the world forced our heads and shoulders downwards as we walked in silence.

The automatic doors swooshed open. I blinked hard as the cool breeze stroked my arms and cheeks. The evening air entered my lungs but hit differently. The waterboarding torture paused, and the suffocating wet cloth fell from my face. I felt grateful to breathe the fresh air. I thought of Dad as we left him behind, deprived of the breeze he cherished. I thought of him stuck there, surrounded by patients but alone behind his flimsy curtains, worried, and forced to share the stagnant, disinfected air of the floodlit room.

I had spent the day in the ward watching my dad cling to life, a young father recovering from a fall that had impaled him on a branch, and a nurse helping a frail older man to the communal toilet.

Time froze while we were in the hospital. I forgot the world continued to spin outside, where layers of amber merged as the full sun dropped towards the horizon. A butterfly flapped its tiger-striped wings above a group of young nurses on their break. They laughed about something they'd seen on *Love Island* as they puffed their cigarettes and sipped from their mugs of steaming tea. It felt surreal to go from such a harsh extreme to beauty and frivolity in a matter of steps.

I smiled at Mo, our Jack Russell terrier, who rolled onto his back for belly rubs once we opened the front door. Our innocent doggy was oblivious to the sadness and trepidation. I clipped his tiny red harness around his chest, and we traipsed laps of the housing estate, while I tried to make sense of it all.

Each sentence of grim medical news had seared a fresh cattle brand onto my exposed skin. In the ward, I had absorbed it without flinching. The pain was so much that my mind shut it off. I had to stay focused, solid, and optimistic while in Dad's company.

The shell shock and numbness wore off as darkness fell, tears dropping as I passed beneath the buzzing streetlights.

Spending each day in the hospital ward, surviving with my family, and cranking the pressure cooker shut, only for it to explode in the night as I walked Mo, became my routine. These solitary moments of decompression created the space needed to endure the next day's devastation.

Hope

The superhero doctors and nurses kept my dad alive with healthy doses of humour, an IV drip injected into the top of his hand, and a feeding tube up his nostril. After two days, Dad could eat for himself. His energy improved, and he could lift himself to sit in bed and toss and turn without assistance.

'You're sounding a little nasally today, Milo, talking through your nose a bit,' the nurse said.

'Talking through my arse, more like it.'

We all laughed. Despite the distressing situation, Dad held onto his playfulness, an essential tool for survival. His humour and chuckle fixed and broke my heart simultaneously.

As the days passed, we monitored the results of regular blood tests, hoping that the numbers would improve to the point where chemotherapy was possible. Chemo was our only hope, but poor bloodwork tormented us, keeping treatment out of reach. I had no idea what the names and numbers on the medical spreadsheet meant. The oncologist set the target figures. Anything below the target, and the chemo would likely kill Dad, but he had a fighting chance if the bloods could improve just a bit more. Internally, I was a crazed gambler who'd pinned his every possession on one horse. *Come on! Leukocyte, move, for fuck's sake!*, I thought with my fists clenched and teeth gritted.

The blood counts improved for several days, aligning with Dad's energy and mood. I'd think he was getting better and was ready for chemo, only for the numbers to decline or stall, ripping the rug from under us.

'I'm proud of you, Al, and Ev. Ye've done brilliant,' Dad said to me one day. 'And your mother, she's as strong as an ox. I was with her when Tom, your grandad, had cancer. There's nobody better to have in your corner. Look after her when I'm not around.'

'I'm proud of you, too, but you're mending,' I said to him. 'I'm sure you'll be starting chemo any day now, so don't be thinking like that, okay?'

The lack of control was unbearable. My dad's life swung in the balance, and we could only sit with him and hope, trying to comfort him with our presence.

I'd been living abroad and unable to return home when he suffered a severe stroke in 2011. I'd struggled with my absence during his recovery in my early twenties. It meant everything to be there with him in this time of need, but it still didn't feel like enough. I hated waiting, unable to influence the outcome.

'I bet you never imagined you'd be brushing my false teeth in your twenties. Ugh, Al, I wouldn't wish this miserable disease on my worst enemy.'

A week after the doctor admitted my father to the hospital, the oncologist gathered my family at Dad's ICU bedside.

'Right. Some good news today for a change.' Our eyes opened and watered as we leaned in. 'The bloodwork's improved. We feel it's the right time to start chemo. Does that sound okay? Think you're ready, Milo?' she said with a comforting hand on Dad's forearm.

'I'll give it my best bash,' Dad said as we fought back the tears.

I sneaked Dad a Turkish Delight to mark the occasion, his favourite chocolate, drawing the curtains just in case we got in trouble as he savoured the sweetness and spiked blood sugar levels.

'That's hitting the spot, Al,' Dad said with a wink. 'It's great to eat and taste again instead of having that shaggin' tube wedged up my nose.'

The bloods continued in a favourable trajectory for the following week as Dad began his course of chemo. The conversation turned from knocking on death's door to a drawn-out marathon war, bouts of chemo over six months or more.

With imminent disaster averted and the urgent timeline extended, we had to recalibrate our pace and raise our gaze towards the longer term.

At the same time, my rent was due, and I'd already taken off two unpaid weeks from work. I had to return to my town planning caseload in London.

'You're doing unreal, Dad. That first week was scary as fuck, but you look ten times better now, and the bloodwork's looking up, too,' I told him before I left. 'Great to see your colour and smile back. I'll be home again in two weeks. Love you.'

'Looking forward to it already,' he said. 'Love you too, my man.'

Care

Hopeful of the vast improvements and start of chemo, I returned to London on the last flight out on Sunday night. I did what I could at work on Monday morning, but it wasn't much. On Thursday, Mam phoned.

'You might look at flight options for this weekend.'

On Friday morning, it was urgent.

'What's the earliest flight you can get? Best you come home as quick as you can.'

Arriving home to Waterford on Friday evening, my mam and brother relayed what the doctors had told them.

'He's off medication. They've stopped chemo. They said he's not going to make it. They're not sure when it will happen, sometime in the next couple of days, maybe a week or two.'

'*Weeks?*'

'They don't know, Al.'

There had been hope with the IV drip hydrating Dad, the nasal tube feeding him, and blood transfusions assisting blood counts. When Dad had returned to eating and drinking for himself and had begun chemo, that hope had grown significantly. My dad had overcome a stroke five years previous. *If anyone can beat cancer, Dad can*, we told ourselves. Although mostly bedbound with limited energy, Dad was still Dad during his first two weeks on the ward. We could talk for hours, reminisce, discuss the future, share our fears, cry, laugh, and comfort each other.

The medical team removed Dad's lifelines and cast him adrift with an offshore gale on that life-shattering Friday. They reduced his chance of recovery and survival to zero with their decision to begin palliative care – strong painkillers to provide 'care and comfort'. He was neither dead nor alive, forced to lie in a laboured sleep. It was horrifying to learn he could be in this sedated purgatory for days or weeks. We wouldn't impose that on a dog or cat but insist on inflicting it on people. It made me sick. It made me angry. I wanted to grip the doctor by the scruff and ask for mercy. *Stop this! Help him!*

The following days were the cruellest of my life.

'Why does he have to go through this? Why do we have to watch? If Dad were an animal, we'd do him a favour, show compassion, and put him out of his misery.'

The doctors and nurses said he wouldn't feel pain with palliative care. *How do they know what he's feeling, lying there dying?* It was unnecessary and cruel. It was torture seeing my dad drugged up as death slowly strangled him. He was no longer responsive, taking laboured breaths fifteen, twenty, or thirty seconds apart. The visible deterioration was impossible to bear, but I couldn't leave him.

I thought about putting a pillow over Dad's face and stopping his needless suffering. It's the most harrowing thought I've ever had. I couldn't speak. My stomach churned, and I sobbed. The legal alternative of protracted sedation and days of suffocation didn't make me feel any better. *Just make it stop!,* my tormented mind pleaded.

When there's a chance of survival, we fight. When some quality of life can be maintained – coffee with a friend, a sit-down outside, a nice meal with your family, sharing yarns – we squeeze every last drop out of life. But I don't know why laws and society force us to endure sedated non-existence when doctors guarantee death within a week.

Irish doctors and nurses ask families if they want medical staff to resuscitate their loved ones if they go into cardiac arrest. Saying no is a common and acceptable answer. They will respect that wish because the person is terminally ill. Cardiopulmonary resuscitation (CPR) will only cause more distress to the person and their family, ripping the patient from the brink only so they can continue suffering. Though immeasurably tough, it can be a humane and merciful decision.

Yet we in Ireland can't choose assisted dying, whether active, passive, indirect, or physician-assisted. To reduce people's misery and pain, Irish lawmakers must examine examples in Canada, New Zealand, Belgium, Luxembourg, Spain, Portugal, Switzerland, and the Netherlands, and reconsider their stance. I certainly wouldn't choose to go through what my dad had to. Nor would I want my family to endure what we did.

With no choice, my mother Marie, Aunt Cora, Ev, Deirdre, and I took shifts 24/7 as we sat and waited in hopeless despair by Dad's bedside.

Dad was lifeless on Friday and Saturday except for laboured and sporadic gasps. I was left to realise this was it as the seconds, minutes, and hours ticked.

On Sunday, I felt pressure around my fingers that held Dad's hand. He was squeezing in pulses. The subtle touch, a sword to my gut. The most intense feelings known to man. His eyelids flickered as he fought to open them with all his strength. They opened and focused on mine. *He's alive!*

'I'm here, Dad. Mam's here.' I squeezed his hand.

'Alan,' he whispered, squeezing back.

His energy faded, and cancer dragged his eyelids shut after two seconds. I kept squeezing his hand. I was desperate to feel his presence, hear his voice, and be with him, not his body. I stared at his hand in mine, willing him to respond. I would have done anything to feel one more squeeze, hear one more word. I never wanted anything so much.

We hit the nurse's button with urgency. She strolled in and fiddled with some tubes and valves.

'I gave him some more medicine. He should be fine now.'

The nurse's lifetime of care had desensitised her to the trauma we were experiencing. Dad hadn't been awake or responsive for two days, but he could speak to me today, look me in the eyes, and squeeze my hand. Thoughts of his pain and state of mind tormented me. I wondered if he could hear our voices or feel my touch. *He hasn't eaten or drunk in days. How is this the right way, the only way?*

Twenty-four hours later, on Monday, 22 August 2016, three weeks after his diagnosis, my dad, Milo Corcoran, died aged sixty-five with his family around him.

I'd emptied my tear ducts and had no tears left to cry as I retreated to the corner of the room. I felt a sense of relief that Dad no longer had to lie in that hellish state. We no longer had to be observers of the cruel process.

I think we *can* and *must* do better for our dying.

Drown Your Sorrows or Raise Your Joy

The adage goes, 'If we don't learn from our mistakes, we're bound to repeat them.' I don't think there are many arguments there. It's important to reflect on what *has worked* and try to repeat those things, too.

I'd never experienced pain and loss like the death of my dad. I wanted to suffer less. Drowning my sorrows seemed akin to my erroneous boxing reaction, swinging destructively out of control and burning in a blaze of flames. Things were bad enough. Why make them worse? Dad wouldn't have wanted that for me. I wanted to control my response and choose to raise myself to a higher standard.

The last time my life had tested me to this extreme was when my dad had had a stroke, when I was twenty, alone, and living on foreign soil for the first time.

Absorbing the punishment without retaliating had seemed a stupid response to that adversity. I couldn't be passive. I'd needed to do *something* back then. Learning ultra-distance running, shuffling my fitness forwards, and pursuing my outdoor sporting interest had regulated my emotions and made my life more satisfying. Being able to help charities and inspire others had been two more layers of satisfaction.

After Dad's death, my mind drifted to this process of recapturing a semblance of control over life, in the hope that I might be able to ignite a flicker of light in the darkness of catastrophe.

My mind drifted towards Sean Conway's swimming book. His story inspired me, like the Eddie Izzard TV documentary that had planted the seed for my lap-of-Ireland run. Sean's book and Eddie's documentary forced me to recalibrate what I might be capable of accomplishing in my life. They impressed me. I wanted to impress myself and extend Dad's legacy.

Why not swim around Ireland?

After being so helpless, I needed to do something. I needed to move and express myself. The millions of practicalities didn't enter the equation. I clung to the idea; the rest, I could figure out once I got going.

Carrying your parent's coffin and lowering their body into the earth is the heaviest load a child of any age can bear. After doing my duties as a son and burying my dad, I felt dazed, lost in a fog. I walked two minutes from my family home to the Solas Cancer Support Centre to meet a bereavement specialist.

This incredible local charity supports people affected by cancer, their families, and their carers. They provide counselling and group support sessions, including meditation, yoga, mindfulness, walking, art, and crochet.

At first, I was apprehensive about speaking to a stranger, albeit a professional, but I thought no harm could come from trying. Maybe they would say something that would unlock a flood of feelings, and my heart would be 'fixed'.

There was no breakthrough moment for me on the therapist's chair. I was exhausted, drained of all tears during the previous weeks.

'Dad's no longer suffering. That's something, at least.'

I felt uncomfortably pragmatic once I said it. I was blunt in accepting Dad was gone. The stress and shock of the diagnosis and the torture of witnessing his final weeks and last gasp removed grief's first stage of denial.

The therapist reassured me that, although grief is universal, everyone's experience is different. Still, I felt uneasy and guilty about shedding buckets of tears every day while Dad struggled in the hospital but little to no tears after his death.

'Grief is overwhelming and started before he died,' she said. 'The timing of your tears bears no correlation to your love for your father. Try not to overthink it or judge yourself harshly.'

She advised that my body was coping with the pain in its own way. My mind tried to rationalise the devastation.

'Dad suffered a stroke five years ago. The way I look at it is that it's unlikely that he would've survived if it were any other point in time or a poorer part of the world. Even if he had, he more than likely would have been disabled or speechless without his freedom. I thought the stroke was it for him, but he got a second life. Dad borrowed the last five years, really. After that, our hugs were different. Each hello and goodbye meant more to us, you know, like they could be our last. Those borrowed moments were priceless. I have to be thankful for that extra time. I know he was.'

I could focus on the resentment, anger, and pain at Dad's life ending seventeen years prematurely, according to the average lifespan of an Irishman. I had these feelings but didn't want to overfeed them. Bitterness would only make life more challenging. Whether right or wrong, I framed Dad's death in a different light to try to dampen the suffering in my mourning. I'd do my best to focus on his life lived and the fact that I had the privilege of a loving father for twenty-five years. Many don't have that fortune. I'd continue his heritage through my thoughts, words, and actions.

Dad was the first person I had spoken to about my 2012 charity-run ambition. Without him there to share my dreams, I expressed my aspirations to the therapist.

'I want to take this nightmare and try to create *something* good. I'm thinking about doing a charity tribute swim.'

Dad had loved sports. Because of that, sports participation became an integral and joyous part of my upbringing. There was no better way to honour his memory than to get active, follow a sporting interest, and generate funds for cancer and stroke charities.

'A charity swim sounds like a lovely idea, a nice positive aim.'

I welcomed her supportive words and stopped there with the details. I didn't want her to retract her support and refer me to a padded room.

Although there was no watershed moment in my counselling, the information and the words of support dispersed the storm clouds on my walk home to Mam and Mo, the doggy.

PART TWO

MAYDAY

FOUR
Splashing in the Shallows

Upturned Tortoise

In early September, I reached out to Chris Bryan. Chris was a friend of a friend and an Irish open-water marathon swimmer.

The marathon distance is 42.2 kilometres (26.2 miles) when running. A *marathon swim* is defined as ten kilometres (6.2 miles). Although one is four times the distance of the other, the events do share similarities. The marathon run and swim world records are both around the mind-boggling two-hour mark. Average recreational participants who train for the marathon challenges can expect to complete the run or swim in about four hours, give or take.

In 2016, Chris Bryan was Ireland's top open-water marathon swimmer, narrowly missing out on Olympic qualifications. There seemed to be nobody better placed to help get me from novice to a ten-kilometre-per-day open-water swimmer.

Before meeting Chris for an introductory swim lesson, he wanted to know more about me. Below are the ratings I gave myself for some attributes he asked about:

Swim fitness – 1/10   Swim speed – 1/10
Open water skills – 0/10   Knowledge of swim – 1/10
Ability to handle cold – 2/10 Swim technique – 3/10

With an ambition to start my 1,500-kilometre lap-of-Ireland sea swim in eight months, these weren't promising figures.

Chris sent me an assignment to better understand if the dismal ratings I gave myself were accurate or pessimistic. He instructed me to swim one hundred metres three times, with thirty seconds rest between each swim sprint. I was supposed to record my heart rate before starting, after each sprint, and again sixty seconds after the final sprint. The swim times and heart rate would reveal the truth.

Darragh O'Keefe, from the cycling bet, was an experienced swimmer, and he came along to support me on the test. Although a lifelong runner, I was way out of my depth swimming any distance. I felt reassured to have Darragh on standby for a rescue.

As we entered the hotel leisure centre reception, I felt sweat dripping down my sides. The mission became real as the smell of the pool's chlorine overwhelmed my senses, triggering a stampede of elephants in my belly and flashbacks in my mind.

While I was attending Ballygunner primary school, they'd started entering teams into local swim galas. The swim club kids who'd trained to compete were winning the races but I hadn't been too far off the pace. Aged ten, my weekly swim lifesaving class and athletics and soccer training had given me enough gas in the tank to mix it at local and provincial finals.

With encouragement from Mam and Dad and confidence from the handful of school races in the pool, I'd found myself at Newtown Cove, Tramore, for an open-water race.

A steep grass verge flowed from the hilltop car park to the small cove where the sea gently swashed in and racked out over the pebble shore. Parents supervised from the hillside, one picnic blanket after another, as their screaming kids smothered the soothing noise of the backwash. A concrete slab jutted from the bottom of the cliff, and a queue of children waited to leap off the diving board. Older swimmers had climbed the ladders or tip-toed over the algae carpet that hugged the narrow slipway to the sea.

I wolfed down my enormous ice-cream cone in the sunshine

and joined the twenty kids around the start zone. *Hmm, they're all getting into wetsuits*, I noted. I didn't own a wetsuit. I stood in my baggy football shorts in the cliff's shade, gripping my hands across my torso to cup my shoulders and fend off the sea breeze.

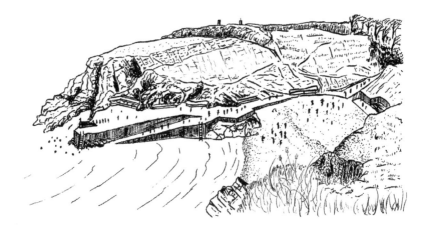

How are they going to start us? I pondered, seeing no starting blocks in sight.

'Right so, down ye go, lads,' the enthusiastic race starter said, pointing at the slimy green slope into the sea.

The tide was nearly in, lapping against the walls with a clap. Water submerged half of the slipway. I thought fast to get a competitive edge and let the neoprene competitors lead the way – *suckers!* With a smug grin, I planted my feet on a nice dry spot at the top of the slope, envisaging a launch that would propel me halfway across the twenty-metre cove before making a single stroke.

'Here, tall fella, you swap with one of the shorter guys down there,' the starter said, clamping his hand around my scrawny bicep and pushing me towards the deep. 'Keeeep going,' he said with a flick of his finger as I inched down the ramp, holding the rusty handrail and looking back every half-second to see if I was allowed to stop yet.

'Jesus! It's feckin' freezing, lads! Oof!' I said as I squeezed behind the giggling, warm, and unfazed wetsuit boys.

'That'll do ya grand!' the starter said with a nod as the water bobbed just below my heart.

Easy for him to say with his big happy, dry head on him.

My childish spite was fleeting as the Baltic water demanded my full attention. My pasty twig legs vibrated, and my teeth chattered.

'Come on, blow the whistle, will ya, before I freeze to death.'

The starting whistle shrilled around the cove, launching families to their feet. Applause and cheers thundered down the hillside, filling the amphitheatre with excitement. The raucous crowd and bitter water injected adrenaline into my veins. I unfolded my arms from my lanky frame with Hulk energy. I bent my knees to generate force. Race efficiency, speed, and medals were on my mind. My arms shot overhead, my biceps glued to my ears, one hand atop the other.

As I launched myself, I slipped on the seaweed underfoot, and my face slapped through the water's surface. Despite the summer's sun splitting the stones, the seas were 15°C (59°F). Race efficiency, who? Survival took over – cold shock! I jolted to an abrupt stop, my startled eyes filling my goggles as I sucked for air as if someone had zapped me back to life with a defibrillator. My chest tightened, the pressure of the cold water crushing my lungs.

The neoprene field ploughed onwards without pause. I fought not to sink like a lump of lifeless lead. Catching my breath and resubmerging my face, I gave chase. It was no use. I couldn't keep the air in my compressed lungs long enough to swim as I knew how – fast, face down, with no breath for twenty-five metres. My traumatised gaze remained fixed straight ahead for an uninterrupted oxygen supply. When I elevated my head, the movement lowered my kicking feet, pumping the brakes like an anchor dredging the sandbed.

I was traumatised when I returned to the slip's safety. I rattled from the sea and shot up the hill at a world-record pace in a desperate search for a towel and my parents' warmth.

'Good try, my man,' Dad said.

Mam placed the towel around my shoulders. 'Hard luck.'

They looked sympathetic, fighting the urge to giggle at their little defeated boy.

I hugged the towel around myself.

'So, how was it?'

'Bloody freezing! Did you see the state of me? I couldn't breathe! I'd beaten most of them before, but I couldn't breathe. Last place, feckin' hell.'

'*Watch* your language.'

After primary school, I had an eight-year hiatus from swimming, focusing instead on football and track sprinting.

Aged twenty, I made a brief return to the water. I signed up for a sprint distance triathlon on a whim after seeing a race poster while queuing at the chipper. I had one week to 'prepare'.

With six years of swimming in the bank, I thought the swim leg would be a doddle provided I wore a wetsuit for warmth. I hadn't factored in the passage of ten years and learned my lesson the hard way as I failed in two attempts to swim the 700-metre race distance in my two days of pool preparation. Unlike in my childhood, I was stopping to beat the band, struggling for air after each length.

Despite the concerning practice sessions, I toed the start line on Tramore Beach, County Waterford. Haunted by my childhood open-water experience, I was determined not to repeat the errors of my ways. I'd built a sauna sweat, wearing my friend's undersized winter surf wetsuit. Overshooting the mark this time, I thought, *Start the race before I melt to death!*

I questioned my life choices while clawing the sand with my toes, seeing the inflatable course markers floating above the waves in the distance. There were no refuge points every twenty metres as in the training pool. The bite-sized leisure centre didn't compare to the intimidation of the sea.

I stared at the crashing waves. Something I hadn't considered until it was too late was how I would navigate the surf and crowd once we all hit the water together. That problem didn't arise in the pool's slow lane. Jumping first and asking questions later can sometimes land you in a spot of bother. At this late stage, I could only chuckle at my predicament. *Eh, this should be ... interesting.*

The buzzer sounded in the raised hand of the race official. One hundred triathletes sprinted at the foaming surf. The mob of swimmers answered my question. Everyone who could swim just bulldozed through me, striking me with limbs from all angles.

I had gasped for air during my week of flat-calm leisure centre practice. Now, when I turned for air in the sea, I found competitors chucking buckets of saltwater down my gullet. Not only was I deprived of oxygen, but my vision was also stolen by a combination of fogged-up goggles and swinging baseball bats of neoprene. My line of travel was impossible to gauge amidst the pandemonium. It was lethal stuff altogether!

It was a relief when the competitive swimmers glided ahead, and I survived the initial shemozzle to tell the tale. I found some space towards the back of the pack, reverting to breaststroke, which allowed me to catch my breath. To say I nearly drowned isn't much of an overstatement. My lack of swim fitness forced me to backstroke, breaststroke, and do something that might have resembled a front crawl. I was moving forwards, but my peculiar racing style drew concern from a safety kayaker.

'Are you okay? Do you want to hold onto my kayak for a minute?'

'I'm. Grand. Don't. Worry. About. Me.'

What a joy to step onto the beach. The *firma* the surface, the less the *terra*!

My second sea-swimming event was as rough as my first one over a decade earlier. That's a large part of why my around-Ireland swimming dream was so appealing – swimming's hard as hell. It was a tall order. I'd have to grow taller to meet the challenge.

I was sitting on the timber bench in the men's changing room, delaying the inevitable discomfort of Chris's baseline fitness test, when Darragh snapped me out of my daydreams.

'Come on, Alo, we better get moving.'

'Do we have to?'

'Sure look, aren't we here now?'

'I suppose. C'mon so.'

'Three, two, one, GO!' Darragh said from the poolside as he clicked the stopwatch.

My hand let go of the wall, and my feet pushed off the slippery tiles as I pursued childhood race times. I felt powerful. I rotated for air after every fourth stroke – smooth with all-out effort.

That changed after one length. I was spent after twenty metres, my body screaming for oxygen after every two strokes. My mind requested swim precision, but my haggard body couldn't accommodate it. After thirty metres, any technique was out the window, my arms and legs demanding more fuel than my poor lungs could process. The more I suffocated my muscles, the more they burned, the heavier they became, and the slower I moved.

Forty metres in, I cranked my neck forwards and upright to prevent asphyxiation.

'Come on, that's it, lad, keep it going.'

I touched the wall with a desperate outstretched arm to survive round one. Darragh stopped the watch and jotted my time down in his notepad. I keeled over, looking like a beached seal, my chest and cheek glued to the tiles at Darragh's feet as my dead legs floated behind me.

'How are you feeling? One down, just two left. You got this, bud.'

'Fucked.'

I pressed two fingers to my neck, doing my best to count the rapid beats in vain. The river of blood pulsing through my jugular was too fast to count, two or three beats per second. My lungs were pistons on their max setting, pumping my body up and down from the poolside tiles. Except for my one-word response, I focused on deep breaths, desperate to calm my heart and catch my breath during the fleeting recovery seconds.

'Five seconds. Get ready.'

I turned my reddening head to the deep end, catching glances of bemused regulars. They were accustomed to older breaststrokers and children playing with floats, not beginners panting like asthmatics and ruining the leisure centre's serenity.

'GO!'

I inhaled deeply, kicking harder off the wall this time and trying to cheat my banjaxed body to the deep end. When I resurfaced, I was no longer under any delusions. The lactic acid flooding my muscles erased notions of trying to reproduce my schoolboy performances. I just wanted to make the finish, preferably afloat.

'Two down. Yes, that's it, great stuff!'

I was slowing. My lungs, heart, and head felt ready to explode at any second, blood boiling up to the surface and sweat steaming from my pores.

'Agh!'

'Three, two, one, GO!'

The pool's floor was a magnet dragging my limbs downwards. I was battling to maintain enough momentum to remain on the water's surface.

It wasn't pretty, but I survived, just. I clambered from the alien environment, feeling ten stone heavier than when I'd entered. I rolled onto my back, stuck there like an upturned tortoise.

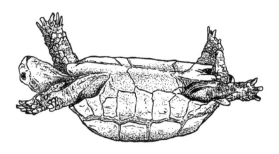

My mouth moistened with saliva, and my face flushed lava red. Instinct kicked in. I sprinted to the men's and dropped to my knees, gripping the toilet seat as breakfast erupted from my mouth.

What a way to spend a Saturday morning. The experience made me ponder, *What if my parents had encouraged me to play the guitar instead of sports?*

Leaving the vomitorium, I returned to Darragh, who was waiting poolside. With years invested in competitive swimming, he knew full well what my post-session dash meant and patted me on the back with a chuckle before he jumped in for his turn.

Darragh put me to shame, demonstrating what swimming was supposed to look like. His effort remained smooth and consistent yet fast, his hands slicing the water like a hot knife through butter.

His times thrashed mine while also maintaining a lower heart rate throughout. Luckily, I wasn't competing against Darragh. He had no interest in trying to swim a lap of Ireland. I was in the pool to test my baseline and improve it over the following months.

The opening test reinforced what I already knew – I was not a swimmer, and I sucked at swimming. Many people give up here before getting going. The realisation that they're incompetent at something scares them from showing up the next time. They give too much weight to the negative voice in their head that says, *You're crap, you've no right being here or pursuing this.* But competence and confidence only come from action and repetition. The dire results didn't faze me. It's okay to be a beginner, and you must commit to your goal long before achieving it. I'd have been foolish to expect anything else during my opening gambit. If anything, it excited me because there was so much room for improvement. The potential motivated me to keep chipping away to see how far I could advance.

Inflatable Armbands

I'd been a beginner long-distance runner, just twenty years old, when I gave myself eight months to prepare to run around Ireland's coast. I'd exceeded the five-kilometre distance just once – a school fun run in my early teens. Having created my project of thirty-five marathons in thirty-five consecutive days in March 2011, I committed to my chosen charities in September 2011. At the end of October 2011, with just four weeks of marathon 'training' – two weeks of 'volume building' and two weeks of 'tapering' – I lined up for the Dublin City Marathon to foolishly try my first 42.2-kilometre run.

I'd been a competitive sprinter throughout my teenage years, and my football team was in Ireland's top sixteen. I reasoned that the accumulated high-intensity bursts, time on the feet, and hours in the weights room would count for something. They did, to a degree. I completed the distance in a quicker-than-average time – four hours and thirteen minutes. On the surface, I'd run it with no endurance-specific training, which was somewhat reassuring.

The reality was starker under a more critical light. Twists and turns on the pitch and short track sprints had little to do with pounding the pavement for hours. I couldn't walk the following two days, lying bedridden, stiff as a poker, nursing joint and tendon pain. Running another marathon the next day was out of the question. No way, José. Beginners should not try to take marathon bites. It's a recipe for failure. I needed to give the distance and my body much greater respect.

Once I could walk the stairs again without the handrails, I began rebuilding brick by brick, training session by training session. The idiom says, 'There is only one way to eat an elephant: a bite at a time.' I couldn't safely run 42.2 kilometres, but I could manage consistent, slow, bite-sized pieces that wouldn't injure me or crash my immune system. So, that's what I did. I ran eight kilometres on Monday, sixteen kilometres on Tuesday, nine kilometres on Wednesday, took Thursday off, ran sixteen kilometres on Friday, lifted weights on Saturday, and ran twenty-four kilometres on Sunday. Week in and week out with gradual increases in training load.

I invested four months in this style of structured preparation before running the marathon distance for a second time: a solo training marathon around the trails of Phoenix Park, Dublin City.

Running a marathon untrained versus trained, unsurprisingly, was chalk and cheese. My body's development through consistent small steps was eye-opening. I finished the training marathon in a similar time to the Dublin City disaster. But I wasn't bedridden like before; I was off out the door for a twelve-kilometre recovery jog the next day, energised from experiencing the fruits of my labour.

The months of ultra-distance running taught me the method of success, not just for endurance running but for any goal. After the Dublin Marathon, running thirty-five consecutive marathons had been impossible but I didn't allow it to intimidate me. I made a start, broke the overwhelming goal into daily and weekly tasks, and adapted to the challenge's demands over time.

If you complete the method once, you have the knack and confidence. The process is transferable. You need to start with what you have and accept and be willing to grit past the initial failings and poor performances – fall, flounder, and mosey on. That I could do.

This swim would require much more beginner thrashing than the lap-of-Ireland run. Whilst capable of completing a slow marathon run without specific training, I didn't have a hope in hell of *swimming* a marathon.

I hadn't gone anywhere near preposterous endurance extremes in the five years since running a lap of Ireland. Endurance training is time-consuming and often interferes with other health factors. I wanted bang for my buck – the best overall health outcomes for the least time and effort. I went to the gym, lifting weights and doing some mobility and stretching three times a week. I did the odd walk around the park at lunchtime, yoga class, and a twenty- or thirty-minute jog or row with a dollop of all-out sprints here and there to counterbalance the decaying effect of the sedentary desk job. Though my endurance capabilities diminished, this routine gave me free time and a healthy mind and body.

In light of that, throwing me ten kilometres offshore would guarantee my death at this point in my story. Put me five kilometres offshore with inflatable armbands, and I'd die of drowning, hypothermia, or exhaustion before making the beach.

Unlike running, you can't rest to re-energise. The stakes at sea are much more significant. Stop moving, and you will sink and drown. Tread water, and the cold will immobilise and kill you. As daunting as running 1,500 kilometres was, this swim could have seemed insurmountable. As we know, there's only one way to surmount the impossible: taking action, one simple step at a time.

My next baby step was to drive from Waterford to the University of Limerick to meet Chris and show him the true scale of the mountain we had before us.

It's impossible to calculate how much larger Limerick's Olympic-size pool is than my local twenty-metre pool, but it looked at least a hundred times bigger. The pool's dimensions churned the nerves around my stomach.

'Swim up to the top there and back down for me,' Chris said. 'Any stroke will do. I just want to see what we're working with here.'

I peered over the edge into the water. There was no shallow safety net here. I got that dizzying rush like looking off a roof's ledge.

As nervous as a kid performing the nativity play in front of the parents, I dived in and began front-crawling. Air soon became scarce, like breathing in and out of a brown paper sweet bag. I hoped it wouldn't explode. I sighted forwards to get my bearings – *Shite, halfway to one length, twenty-five metres.* I fought the urge to grab the floating lane divider at my side. *Keep going!*

Touching the end wall, I flipped on my back to give Chris a look at my backstroke abilities. The reality was that I needed to go on my back to keep my mouth out of the water. After one lousy fifty-metre length, I couldn't hold my breath to maintain the front crawl for the return leg.

'You were telling the truth on your Q&A form,' Chris said with a nervous smile when I eventually made it back to him. 'Right, well, the good news is you didn't stop.'

'I was allowed to stop? Why didn't you tell me? I nearly drowned out there,' I said, making light of the challenge on our hands.

'You can do one hundred metres anyway. We can make a start.'

Grief

My mother had just retired from working after forty years in the haematology lab of Waterford University Hospital. Dad, Ev, and I had planned a surprise meal out to celebrate her career success and mark the beginning of my parents' post-work life together. Cancer killed that plan. When my compassionate leave ended, it broke my heart to leave my bereft mam at home alone in Waterford and return to earn my living in London.

Returning to town planning work and 'normal life' was jarring. I ironed my work shirt and wore the window dressing that concealed my inner sorrow. I accepted condolences as I typed letters onto the screen.

My work felt trivial in the context of what had happened to Dad, but it did help to distract me. During office hours, I engaged in the job, assessed planning applications, and looked for solutions to steer them from refusal. Concentration was a temporary anaesthetic. The therapeutic drug would fade throughout the day, and I'd become conscious. In wakefulness, I retreated to the sanctuary of the toilets, hiding in solitary silence. *What the fuck happened!* I'd text Mam and Ev:

'Hope your day is going okay.'

The text without contact felt utterly inadequate.

The security man nodded goodbye each evening, and the exit doors yawned open on my approach. Without work to occupy me, the cold shock of reality waited, the summer breeze splashing over me like a cauldron of frosty water. I walked to my motorcycle in a trance. Tears dropped as I straddled my bike.

Is this real? What am I doing here? How can things get better?

Flashes appeared like a slide show. Dad's smiling face in our last photo together at half-time in Lyon. The dark contrast with the next slide at Dad's wake, his body dressed in his navy FAI suit as we mourned.

Leaning forwards on my bike's petrol tank, resting my forehead on the cold metal, I closed my eyes and wished it weren't true. My thumb flicked the ignition switch. The rumbling engines drowned the despairing voices in my head as I weaved in and out of London's evening traffic.

Method to the Madness

I met my friends at the Alexandra Pub in Clapham, South
London, to discuss what I should do next. Alex, Billy, Tommy,
Ciarán, Sinéad, and Tara, childhood friends from Waterford, were
there for me.

We placed our pints on the wooden table and wet our whistles.
I shared my idea of swimming the 1,500-kilometre lap of Ireland.

'It was attempted once, by a pair, last year,' I said. 'The lads got
from Dublin around to the west coast but couldn't make it up to
the north. One stopped after four months and the other after six
months.'

The idea of circumnavigating the country was exhilarating, but
I didn't carve it in stone by any means. I knew I wasn't thinking
straight, so I was keen to hear my friends' opinions to see if they
had any better ideas.

'The next project just needs to be exciting, interesting, and
tougher than my marathons. It can't be too bonkers. I need some
hope of finishing the thing, though, to raise a few bob for charity.'

Putting my skills to use and generating charity funds meant a lot to me when Dad had had a stroke and even more to me now after cancer. Learning from my lap-of-Ireland run, I knew that finishing was integral to the success of the fundraising component. On my run journey, I'd completed more consecutive marathons than most in history. Still, as I neared the final day, I'd only fundraised about €7,000 for stroke and sports charities. Crossing the finish line forced the media and their subscribers to take notice. Charitable contributions exploded, doubling to €15,000 within two weeks of cartwheeling over the line.

'Love it, Al,' Sinéad said. 'Over the moon you're trying to create something positive. I was wondering what you might do next. How long do you think the swim could take?'

'With five weeks to run around, you're probably talking maybe six months to swim it?' I said. 'The weather, boat, and crew seemed to slow the last guys a lot. They still had a ways to go after half a year.'

'Yeah, I dunno,' Tommy said. 'Would people follow that long and donate, or just lose interest and not bother their arse?'

Alex chimed in, 'You couldn't get sponsors for the run, so you couldn't? If it's the same craic swimming around Ireland, that'll cost you a small fortune. You won't earn an income either when you're off work.'

'I'd say it'll be a struggle to get sailors for that length of time,' Tara said. 'Even getting some for a week might be hard. It's not like asking someone to sit in a support car with their driver's licence.'

The discussion was pulling me back to earth. The chances of success seemed to hover around ten per cent at best.

'What about the *length* of Ireland?' Billy said. 'If the lap could take six months, the length might take, what, a month? Two? That's reducing your variables and upping your chances by a fair whack.'

'It'd be more sheltered down that east coast, too,' Ciarán said. 'So, you could probably swim more and spend less time faffin' about and waiting for weather windows.'

'You might get away with a small motorboat instead of a

sailboat if you avoid the west,'Tommy said. 'That's big wave surfing territory over there.'

Three pints in, I was glad to have consulted the lads. The risk-to-reward ratio wasn't stacking up without any significant sponsor managing logistics and covering costs.

We concluded that swimming the 500-kilometre *length* of Ireland would be much more demanding and complex than running thirty-five consecutive marathons. I didn't doubt it after two dire opening sessions in the pool and two dismal sea races on my record.

The same physical, psychological, and logistical challenges were present, although moving the goalposts closer shifted more control to me and risked less in the hands of mother nature and strangers. It was more a swimming challenge than a spending and project management one.

Swimming the length of Ireland met the brief. If completed, I'd accomplish something nobody had done before, far beyond my comfort zone and current ability. It would be a fitting tribute to Dad, and had the potential to inspire and raise some money for charity.

Charity

I was passionate about fundraising for causes related to diseases that devasted my family. With stroke and cancer attacking Dad, these conditions were as real as possible for us. Fundraising added a considerable layer of meaning to my efforts. It wasn't merely swimming but doing my utmost to help others and soften disaster's blow.

The Irish Cancer Society and National Rehabilitation Hospital (NRH) were standout picks, the latter playing a fundamental role in my dad's remarkable stroke recovery in 2011.

After Dad's stroke, he couldn't speak, walk, or control his emotions, never mind dream of driving or returning to work. The local hospital wasn't equipped to rehabilitate him. Their care was limited to sporadic physiotherapy sessions and a bed to vegetate. Once Dad got into the NRH, the new demanding schedule energised him. Monday to Friday, he worked in a structured recovery pro-gramme with an interdisciplinary team of dieticians, occupational therapists, speech and language therapists, and physiotherapists. They worked wonders on him.

When I'd raised €15,000 for the Irish Heart Foundation, Football Village of Hope, and NRH by running around Ireland, I had done it without telling the NRH. I surprised them with €2,600. It meant a great deal to my dad and family to offer a small token of our appreciation.

The NRH were thrilled with our unexpected donation. After my dad and I handed them the cheque, they told us to give them a heads-up for the next challenge. They wanted to be a part of the project, supporting me, and capitalising on the fundraising opportunity.

With those words reverberating, I contacted the Irish Cancer Society and NRH as soon as possible. In September 2016, I shared my intent with their fundraisers.

'Next May, I'm going to swim the length of Ireland in memory of my dad, Milo, and in aid of your charities.'

One topic of our conversation was my previous experience fundraising for a charity.

The man I'd worked with in the Heart Foundation had vol-unteered to organise several bits and bobs for my run, but left me hanging. One sore point was his asking me to get permission so the charity could do a big bucket collection at the Aviva Stadium. My dad got him the permission, but the guy fumbled the opportu-nity, only finding one volunteer after nearly half a year to organise it.

Flagging this at the outset, I floated the stadium collection to the Irish Cancer Society and NRH.

'The FAI are doing a minute's applause during an international match on 24 March to remember Dad,' I said. 'That's six months away. Would you be interested in organising volunteers to collect money at it if I can get access permission, or would it be too much hassle for you? If you're out, that's grand. I'd rather you say it than commit and bail. If you're in, perfect, but I can't have a repeat of 2012's collection. Have a think and let me know.'

The emails came back positive.

'*The opportunity to bucket collect at an Irish football international early next year is extremely exciting for us and one we are really excited about working with you on. I have already commenced discussions with our volunteer coordinator, putting a strategy in place to secure these volunteers to take advantage of this amazing opportunity you have offered us,*' the NRH's Fundraising Manager wrote.

'*Getting a collection day at The Aviva is amazing. I would certainly work on finding a group that would be available on the day. I'll contact the volunteer bureau and start working on that. I'm hopeful we will source sufficient volunteers for the evening,*' the Irish Cancer Society's Ulster Community Fundraiser echoed.

Sorted, I thought. *We know where we stand. It won't just be applause for Dad but money going to causes that can help people.*

FIVE
Shocking

Training Camp

Action's the best teacher. With the challenge defined and charities needing no convincing in September, it was time to jump into the deep end.

I hit Ealing's public pool with my new bag of torture toys. Sorry, training tools:

Finger paddles   Hand paddles
Short flippers (fins)   Long fins
Snorkel   Pull buoy
Kickboard

The two introductory sessions only covered 400 metres. It was time to knuckle down and let the real work begin. I slid into the slow lane with 1,500 metres to cover (see Appendix One for session one of week one).

I was no longer a track athlete sprinting in an Irish Team singlet. I wasn't an ultramarathon runner stringing together a heap of consecutive marathons. I was a beginner swimmer thrashing about, trying to keep in a straight line and fight the urge to stop and rest before reaching the end of my lane.

My two calves kept cramping, squeezed by invisible vice grips. The clenched muscles shot pain signals to my brain, pleading for me to stop fighting the water's resistance with each flutter kick. My land legs couldn't hack my feet's new flexed position.

Claustrophobia and panic overwhelmed me from the discomfort of forcing my face underwater, time after time, while desperate for air. I often took an exhausted breath to the front instead of efficiently to the side. Sometimes that wasn't enough, and I had to tread water to relax and regain my composure. Chlorine seeped into my goggles and seared my eyeballs. My beard was a brillo pad scrubbing the skin on my shoulder rawer with each twist and turn.

I was asking a lot of questions of myself. I'd have to answer them in deeds, not words or thoughts. My shoulders, calves, and lungs were in tatters, but I struggled to the end of training session number one of 200.

Allowing time for my cramps to subside, my lungs to refill, and my frantic mind to calm all added minutes to the clock. The first week's training took nearly twice as long as it should have. Nonetheless, I completed the distance I needed to swim in week one – 4,450 metres.

My training volume increased each week from there. I had an easier recovery week every fourth week before tackling the next four-week training block.

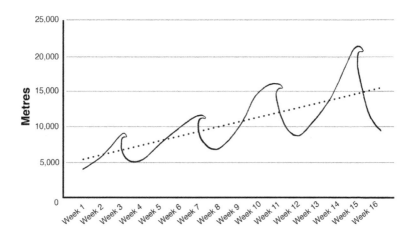

I had no coached lessons besides my first session in Limerick with Chris. After that, I was on my own to figure out the puzzle. I knew if I floundered a little each day, those uncoordinated splashes would eventually turn into powerful strokes. I was aware of the arguably impossible 500-kilometre end goal, but I paid nearly all of my attention to the present, to that day's workload. I kept showing up and repeated the often-frustrating stop-start process. Although nothing seemed to change from day to day, when I looked back on my completed training volume, I had gone from three swim sessions and 4,450 metres in week one to eight swim sessions and 22,000 metres in week fifteen. My steady work accumulated by taking it a metre at a time. I covered 171,750 metres over the first four months of camp. Inevitably, somewhere along those training blocks, my heart rate lowered, my lung capacity increased, and I relaxed in the water. I was progressing along the right trajectory.

The hours of solitary pool time provided space and an outlet to process the trauma of losing Dad. I wasn't numbed, lingering on the couch, distracted by TV, or endlessly scrolling through social media while soothing myself with cigarettes, alcohol, and excess comfort snacks. The project wasn't about running away from problems in a world of distractions but about facing them.

The training got me out of the front door and into the real world to express and soothe my pain in a meaningful way. I built rather than destroyed. Sometimes I cried while swimming, thinking of old times, and sometimes I smiled to myself. I always felt better for showing up, getting off my ass, and onto my toes, propelling my body forwards and ticking each little training session off my calendar.

As well as the alone time to process, it created an outlet to open up and talk about Dad. After the initial, 'Sorry for your loss,' people generally don't want to discuss death and grief. We don't quite know what to say to people in mourning. The topic can be intimidating, and we don't want to risk burdening others by bringing up their pain. The thing is, I was already thinking about Dad every day. Having the chance to speak about him, and hearing people say, 'Milo,' while sad, still made me feel better. It kept him alive in a way. People were excited to talk about my charity swim, which often acted as a safe segway for them to say something about my dad in a more uplifting way that felt natural rather than awkward or insensitive.

Fool Me Twice

It was February 2017, four weeks from the Aviva Stadium sell-out. The charities had no volunteers confirmed for the bucket collection.

I was surprised, yet not, at the same time. Been there, done that, and wore the big charity T-shirt. It felt like a middle finger to my dad, the FAI, and my efforts.

This stadium collection was more significant than the botched one in 2012. Of course, both games were 52,000-seater sell-outs, but this one was deeply personal. The stadium announcer would pay tribute to my dad's life, and there would be a minute's applause in his memory.

The FAI facilitated our bucket collection request. Their match-day programmes had gone to print, including an article about Dad and the meaning behind the Irish Cancer Society and NRH collectors around the grounds. It was too late to back out. Whatever the charity's values, *I* would be ashamed to have nobody collecting, least of all because it would steal the fundraising opportunity from other clubs or charities.

With history repeating itself, I had to step in and take matters into my own hands, again asking friends for help. Twelve volunteered within forty-eight hours. *That was pretty easy.* I couldn't for the life of me understand how the national charities organised no volunteers with a lead-in of almost half a year. I passed the details of my volunteering friends to the charities and reminded them of their enthusiastic words about the opportunity they'd assured me they would not waste.

Chlorine

The swimming goal was consuming my life. I spent most mornings and some evenings in the pool. I swam up and down the twenty-five-metre treadmill, doing my best to overcome its monotony, reminiscing on dreamy trails surrounded by oak trees, squirrels, and stags.

When preparing to lap Ireland, most run sessions focused

on long, slow (zone one and two heart rate) time-on-feet miles. Slow repetition works when moving through an ever-changing landscape of sensory tickles. Apply that approach to the dull pool setting, and you'd be sure to do your nut. We mixed things up to make the training more engaging and playful, injecting medium- and high-intensity bouts into the slow endurance volume. The toolbox of training aids helped here, too. I might swim one set with flippers to another with hand paddles and a pull buoy, one set water-polo-style with my noggin up, and another with a snorkel on and my face fixed down. The variety taxed and stimulated my body and mind with a slight twist (see Appendix Two for session 119 of week twenty-three).

Using training equipment wasn't always possible, though. My local 'Everyone Active' pool cited the health and safety document – HSG 179 – to me.

'Sorry, mate, you'll have to lose the fins,' the lifeguard said, interrupting me an hour into my training.

'Why?'

'It's after nine.'

'Ah shur, what difference does that make? I have the lane to myself, and you've seen me swim just fine for the last hour. It's only adding two inches of plastic to my feet.'

'Sorry, health and safety, mate. The 'Swim 4 fitness' slot is over. No training equipment's allowed.'

'There's only three people in the pool and two lifeguards watching us. What if I had size thirteen feet? Can we not be pragmatic here and let me plough on with my training, no?'

'We'll have to ask you to leave otherwise,' the computer said.

To get my training done, I had to fork out the cash to join a second pool further away to overcome the braindead application of HSG 179. The second pool applied the rational approach: if you're interfering with others, stop, and if you're not interfering with others, regardless of using training equipment, keep doing your thing. It ate into my limited time, getting in and out of my motorbike gear and driving to the more distant pool instead of walking to my local pool. But it had to be done.

Despite the hurdles, my physical conditioning was coming

together – each session adding a wafer-thin layer of progress to the previous one. By February, I no longer needed to pause, and could swim nonstop for over three hours.

Regulated swimming pools had several downsides, especially compared to the freedom of running, but pools were my best option in London. The nearest beach was some hundred kilometres from me, so that wasn't a runner. The River Thames was tidal, and I would risk getting struck by boats or catching God knows what from the water. Though training in a lake was possible, it wasn't nearly as convenient as the pools, especially since leisure centres were open for an extra twelve hours per day compared to the nearest lido.

That lido was one hundred metres long, but most training sessions needed me to do twenty-five and fifty-metre reps before pausing and going again. The local twenty-five-metre pool worked best.

Plus, I was a wimp at getting into and staying in cold water. I didn't want to suffer needlessly through the UK winter. Re-learning how to swim and building volume on volume was challenging enough.

Training swim efficiency and endurance were my primary goals. Like any pursuit, consistency would be critical to accomplishing them. To give myself the best shot at success, I removed as many potential barriers and excuses as possible, choosing the closest and least uncomfortable venues to get the work done – heated public pools.

I drove an hour across the city to the Olympic pool for my first ten-kilometre marathon swim. At fifty metres long, London's Aquatic Centre was twice the length of my local pool. I thought it would be easier, mentally, to swim 200 fifty-metre lengths than 400 twenty-five-metre lengths.

I entered the architectural specimen that resembled a spaceship. I recognised the massive pool from watching the 2012 Olympic Games on TV, only there was a slight difference. There were no swimming lanes. A gigantic children's obstacle course of floating inflatables occupied the waters.

Staff diverted me to the twenty-five-metre warm-up pool of slow, medium, fast, and family lanes. *Four hundred lengths it is so.* It was chaotic, with fifteen swimmers-plus in some lanes, and screaming and crying kids echoing around the hall. I hated it. I remembered there was something so relaxing about the simplicity and peace of putting runners on, starting training at your doorstep, and having the privilege to roam where you wanted, when you wanted, and at any speed you wanted.

I did my best to control my 'lane rage' when, regardless of a traffic jam of swimmers behind them, the daydreamer wouldn't stop to allow the queue to pass them on the turns, or would manspread across the end wall for a breather instead of shrinking to the side. Slow swimmers would plod in the fast or medium lanes, breaststrokers swam in the middle, and backstrokers went anti-clockwise despite the clockwise sign. Don't get me started on the rare and unwieldy butterfly-stroker who showed up to wipe out every man, woman, or child in their path.

The odours of the cleaning chemicals I inhaled with each breath compounded the discomfort of the overcrowded and noisy setting. *Ugh, set me free and get me into the open sea,* I vented, trying to flush the frustrations from my head.

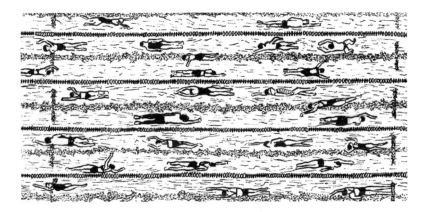

Two hours into my stressful marathon swim, I noticed everyone scattering across lanes to escape like a scene from *Jaws*. Lifeguards waved their arms and shrieked their whistles. I removed my silicone earplugs.

'Out! Everyone out!'

Swimmers watched poolside as the pool's floor raised like a lift and the water emptied into the gutters. The lifeguard stepped with his blue plastic shoe covers onto the white canvas. He mopped baby Jaws' brown mark from the floor before lowering it and refilling the fish tank so I could continue for another two hours.

I survived what Chris titled 'Hell Week' – with a total of 35,150 metres of swimming over seven days. With the accumulating training hours, I gained confidence in my ability to be ready for the 500-kilometre swim come May.

After morning sessions, stinking of chlorine, I was straight to the office for porridge and a homemade smoothie laced with more oats for breakfast at the desk – calories in, while town planning reports and emails went out.

On my lunch break, I'd eat my homemade cold potatoes, salmon, and peppers from my lunchbox at my desk, while project-managing the swim's logistics – boat, crew, safety, navigation, sponsorship pleas, and publicity requests.

After work, I was either en route to the pool, or home to boot up the laptop. There was rarely downtime in this dash to address the never-ending list of management tasks.

Behind training, securing a support boat was my next priority. Unlike my road-running adventure, the risk of going unsupported would be reckless at sea. A solo effort would lead to death, hospitalisation, or at least one mayday call for rescue. Safe entry and exit points along the island's coast would be too dispersed to swim between, interrupted by long stretches of sheer cliff faces. As well as the unrealistic point-to-point swim distances, there were variables and dangers, including commercial shipping lanes, recreational boats, changing tides, wind, and waves. My body and mind's inability to handle extreme conditions or distances could also cause significant problems if I went solo and came up short. Without question, I needed a support boat and team.

Sean Conway used a twenty-seven-foot sailboat for swimming up Britain's west coast. Maghnus Collins and David Burns, the two men who tried to swim around Ireland, had a rigid inflatable boat (RIB) supporting them along the east and south coast and a thirty-eight-foot yacht on the west coast.

I couldn't afford a yacht and didn't know anyone who could sail. I couldn't much afford a RIB either, and I didn't know anyone who could drive one, but it seemed the more straightforward choice.

I contacted an old athletics club friend in Dunmore East, a small County Waterford fishing village. After a week or two, he relayed some great news.

'I have a local chap who says you can borrow his RIB for two months, provided the drivers have a powerboat licence.'

'Serious? For free?'

'Yeah, he's happy to help and be part of it.'

'Unreal! That's perfect. Thanks a million for sorting that. Here, I'm pushing my luck, but might you see if you can find a plan B, too, just in case? I don't want all my eggs in one basket.'

Another week or so later, a second person agreed to be a backup sponsor, offering a loan of their RIB for the swim's duration.

Securing a boat sponsor and backup were massive pieces of the puzzle that allowed me to focus on the other significant part – finding a qualified crew.

Cold Shock!

Finding friends to drive a support car on the run had been a doddle compared to locating competent and willing volunteers to crew a small open-top RIB.

I emailed every sailing and boat club I could find to no avail. I turned my attention to the media, sending email after email, hoping a spotlight on the project might attract somebody to volunteer to operate the craft.

Peter Grogan offered a helping hand. He's a family friend and co-owner of Emagine, a creative agency. He suggested creating a short promotional video to help launch the campaign and try to attract crew members and sponsors.

It was early March. I drove down a country lane only wide enough for my mother's Renault Clio. All was black as a bat except the half-moon in the sky and my headlights illuminating the empty car park. Emagine's three-person film crew pulled up.

'Grand aul' morning for it,' I said, fog streaming out of my mouth.

Ted rubbed his hands together. 'Awh, shtap, gorgeous, so it is.'

I shivered into my brand-new Sailfish wetsuit as Peter, Ted, and Róisín captured dawn breaking on the empty Kilfarrasy Beach in County Waterford.

'For the next shot, just wade in up to your thighs, do a cool headfirst dive, and swim straight out about fifty metres towards the island there. We'll have the drone flying overhead. It'll look class.'

'Deadly. No bother.'

By March, I could swim over 10,000 metres in the pool without pause. Fifty metres would be a piece of cake. I strutted towards the flat sea, trusting my high-end triathlon wetsuit to protect me. I couldn't feel the water's bite as I waded in with purposeful strides.

I dived in with a cinematic flair when the sea reached my thighs.

The sea felt as cold as an arctic night on my unprotected head and punched me in the gut with the full force of a heavyweight boxer. It was a cheap shot when I wasn't looking, naive in the false security of my wetsuit.

For context, the sea I had experienced in my childhood race was a comparatively balmy 15°C (59°F). Those summer waters were still cool enough to cause a traumatic cold shock response. Your local swimming pool is a boiling 28°C (82°F). Even that can give you a shiver and make you very cold over extended periods. As it turns out, March has the lowest sea temperatures in Ireland – a life-threatening 7–8°C (45–46°F).

While my wetsuit covered me from my ankles to my neck, nothing protected my feet, hands, or head. I hadn't realised you could get cold shock while wrapped in an insulating wetsuit. I became acutely aware as the freezing water flushed between my body and the neoprene. Nor did I know cold shock accounts for most immersion deaths and that these occur within the first minute of entering the water. I was beginning to see why. I gasped like someone with a punctured lung on a ventilator. We inhale roughly 600 millilitres in a standard breath. In response to being submerged in cold water, our deep gasp reflex can inhale two to three litres. Getting into cold water also multiplies our breathing rate from twelve breaths per minute to sixty-six. Gasping is an obvious hazard in water when aspirating just one and a half litres of seawater is all it takes to kill an adult.

Those startling facts demonstrate the importance of not diving into cold water and ensuring we don't submerge our mouths during the cold shock phase.

All my pool mileage and accumulated fitness were worthless. One stroke in, the ice-cold water's dangerous stranglehold mimicked the effects of sprinting 400 metres.

Cold water reduces your ability to hold your breath from around sixty seconds to less than ten. My lungs could barely hold enough air to manage two face-down front crawl strokes before the pressure crushed my lungs as effortlessly as a sumo wrestler stepping on an empty can. Reflexes forced my mouth open just in time as I rotated to gasp.

If we find ourselves unexpectedly submerged in frigid water, experiencing a cold shock response, we must fight the urge to flail and scream for help. Listening to your natural reflex to splash and shout will increase the chance of drowning.

Experts advise us to roll onto our backs, try to float, and relax our breathing for a minute or two. If you manage this, your body will regulate your breathing and heart rate spike. Panic's hazy fog will lift. You'll be able to think again, cry for help, or swim to safety.

Cameras were rolling, and the crew had sacrificed sleep to help me create awareness for my charity project. *Suck it up! Come on! Agh!* The water burned my exposed skin like liquid nitrogen and exacerbated the raw panic as I ploughed ahead. Every fibre screamed, *Lift your head out of the feckin' water! You plonker! Get back to the beach!*

As well as stressing my lungs, the extreme cold caused my adrenaline, heart rate, and blood pressure to soar from zero to one hundred in a half-second. This physiological response to cold water immersion causes some to suffer heart attacks and bleeds in the brain.

I unknowingly put myself at further risk by forcing my face into the water to continue my front crawl. Breath holding and face immersion trigger another physiological response called the diving response, which *slows* your heart rate and increases blood pressure. The mixed signals of simultaneous cold shock response and diving responses can cause cardiac confusion (dysrhythmias and arrhythmias), which can be fatal, even for young and healthy people.

These points highlight why it's essential to consult your doctor before taking up cold-water swimming and not submerge your face until you've got your breath back. Swimming within your depth and with people who know CPR are other sensible practices, especially for beginners.

Survive the cold shock response and diving response, and you've bought yourself some time to escape before the water attacks your nerves and muscles after about ten minutes. If you haven't been moving to generate heat, your ability to use your hands, arms, and legs declines over time.

Clinical hypothermia strikes after about twenty to thirty minutes of cold water immersion. Though it depends on the individual and circumstance, it usually takes this long for an adult's core temperature to drop close to and below 35°C (95°F), even in the coldest waters.

I'd been in my cosy house an hour earlier on a clear, brisk Irish morning. The sea transported me from safety to the most extreme environment in a second. Though all was calm mere metres away on shore, I was on Mount Everest. Five people die per year climbing into the death zone of the world's tallest mountain. Two hundred and seventy-seven people drowned in the UK in 2021. Over the last decade, roughly one hundred drownings have occurred annually in Ireland, while the World Health Organisation estimated 236,000 people drowned in 2019. That's twenty-seven drownings per hour. I'd only swum five metres. It was far enough to realise how unprepared I was for the life-or-death actuality of the homicidal Irish Sea.

I pushed beyond my limits, persevering until I could no longer submerge my alarmed, glacial-blue face. I ripped my head from the sea, rescuing myself from the immediate dangers. *Air! Much better*, I thought. Stopping to tread water, I turned to face the lads on the beach, giving them a thumbs-up while on the verge of passing out from hyperventilation. *Jesus, I only made it twenty metres! I'm gassed.*

My heart still thumped like a jackhammer as my feet sank into the safety of the wet sand.

'Do you think you can go again?'

Christ. I'm swimming the length of Ireland in two months; I can't say no!

'Yeah, no worries, lads. Do you want me to go the same distance?' I said, trying to hide my fear and lack of breath.

'A little further, if you can manage? Fifty metres.'

'Okey-doke.'

My confidence had plummeted with my skin temperature. Now terrified of the sea's murderous power, I wanted to go straight home. My brow furrowed as I turned and stared seaward. *Christ almighty, what am I doing?* Now, I was more anxious than when Dad had taken me to a farmyard in Tipperary to jump solo from a plane at 4,000 feet.

'And ... ACTION!'

The second exposure was no less traumatising than the first. *Please tell me you got the feckin' shot, lads!*

'All good to call it a wrap?' I said.

'Could we do it one more time?'

Deflated as last year's birthday balloon, I chose to tell them, 'I think I have just one more in me.' The sea stripped me bare for all to see. I reached my limit, exhausted by the stress of three swims that couldn't have totalled more than sixty lousy metres.

I scuttled to the car and whacked the heating to full. There was no natural high for me as I thawed. My acute response to the elements sowed severe seeds of doubt and concern during this significant step on my journey to become an open-water swimmer. *How am I going to fix that, in the name of Jaysus?*, was all I thought during the startled drive home.

I couldn't influence the torturous environment, but I could be better equipped. Being fat, fit, and cold-adapted are three pillars of open-water distance swimming. I didn't have the time or desire to pile on an insulating fat layer. With my body fat composition on the lean end, extra layers of *synthetic* blubber seemed a sensible place to start. I jumped online and searched 'thickest swim cap'. I found a ten-millimetre-thick neoprene hood and added it straight to the basket. *Sod the cost.* I ordered some silicone swim caps for protection, a large snorkelling mask to cover more skin than my tiny pool goggles, neoprene boots and gloves to protect my hands and feet, and an extra thermal vest to go beneath my wetsuit.

Abandon Ship

The charities emailed me to declare, *'We must withdraw with immediate effect from this fundraising project.'*

You're taking the piss, I thought. There was no phone call, meeting, discussion, or warning, just an abrupt robotic U-turn. I re-read it five times in case I was mistaken. *Yeah, they're jumping ship twenty-four weeks in, two weeks before the stadium collection, and ten weeks before the swim start.*

'*What's the problem?*' I replied. '*Can't we figure out a solution? It's in memory of my dad, who died last summer. You know all this. I've been busting my balls the last few months to make this a success for us.*'

'*As previously outlined ...' yada, yada '... no choice but to withdraw.*'

'*There's always a choice,*' I wrote. '*What's the problem? You're still doing the stadium collection like you said you would, aren't you?*'

'*As per our previous communication ...' blah, blah, blah '... support structures required for your safety and the safety of your support crew have not fallen into place. In withdrawing from your swim, we are also withdrawing from the Aviva event.*'

Safety concerns seemed a bizarre excuse because neither charity had mentioned the word 'safety' or set any safety criteria for me to meet during the preceding six months. Besides, I still had ten weeks until showtime. They could have raised their concerns, and I could have addressed them before the launch. They didn't care. They'd taken their ball and fled.

Ev, my brother, couldn't believe the emails I forwarded to him. Although I gave up after the poxy 'as per our previous email' responses, he thought it was worth another try. Angered, Ev ventured up the food chain and emailed the Irish Cancer Society's Head of Fundraising, with whom I'd had no dealings.

'*Given the personal risk involved in such a fundraiser and the fact that the necessary supports (support boat and crew, Irish Water Safety approval etc.) are not in place, we could not sanction this fundraiser on behalf of the Society.*'

'That's bull,' I said to Ev. 'They were all systems go September to December, then jumped ship in March. That email, there, is the first I'm hearing of them requiring Irish Water Safety approval. I'm sure they risk-assess every unhealthy marathon runner that raises funds for them, they do? That's their bed made, fuck 'em. I'll give the money to charities that want it.'

It's their organisation, and they can do what they like. Safety concerns are legitimate for endurance events, especially when open water is involved. My problem was the initial words of support, followed by no meaningful action to the team effort, and sudden withdrawal by email, without any conversation, citing unmet safety criteria that hadn't been discussed. Hey-ho, that can be people and life. If someone wants to slam a door in my face, it's okay; I'll walk to the next door and the next door until I find a way. Dust it off and keep going where you're going.

The Irish Heart Foundation and Waterford's Solas Cancer Support Centre did want donations. I'd fundraised for the Heart Foundation when I did my run and boxing, as they're Ireland's national stroke charity. Having used the services of the Solas Cancer Support Centre, it was an honour to help fund them.

The Irish Heart Foundation required me to get a safety checklist from a water safety body and give them confirmation I'd address each item.

With this hoop jumped through, demonstrating my readiness, they stepped up at the last minute to manage the stadium collection, grateful for the fourteen friends I'd secured to volunteer for them in the meantime.

'In memory of Milo Corcoran,' said the announcer over the Tannoy.

The 52,000 people in attendance rose to their feet. The words shook me, sending a shiver up my spine and tears from my eyes as I held Ev and Mam at my sides.

The Welsh and Irish players stood around the centre circle, and the football fans began thunderous applause. I was bursting with pride to be Milo's son and see €2,600 fundraised in his name on game night. With the night's tally, and online donations, we'd put over €5,000 in the Heart Foundation and Solas Centre's coffers by the end of March.

Boat Four

I secured two teams for the first two weeks of the swim. I was thrilled to get this locked in. It gave me the certainty that I could launch.

I had Tim Haines, Paul McCarroll, and Darren Doheny sign

up for week one. Tim was a friend I'd met in London who had grown up on boats and crewed in yacht races. Paul was a friend's fiancé who played semi-professional rugby and had just completed his studies as a physio *and* a doctor. Growing up in the same housing estate, I'd known Darren for donkey's years. He was on land operations – transporting us to and from marinas, and finding food and accommodation sponsors.

I had Gavin Downey from my old athletics club for week two. He'd supported me on my marathon runs and had gone to the effort of earning his powerboat licence to help again. Derrick 'Skinner' O'Neill, who volunteers with Waterford River Rescue, would join him on the boat. DJ Magee would work remotely, hitting up bars, B&Bs, and hotels to help us with food and accommodation.

By April, I'd accumulated a handful of five- to six-hour pool swims and around 400,000 metres of training since September. I was feeling fit as a fiddle. Fitness doesn't mean anything to mother nature. It was time to test my new neoprene layers in the open water.

As though getting ready for a deep-sea Antarctic dive, I donned my ten-millimetre-thick hood at the edge of East London's Royal Docks. I felt overdressed with a clunky snorkelling mask and thick gloves and boots to accompany my wetsuit and hood. I was overdressed for sunny, dry land but not the rat-black waters of the capital's dock.

Trepidation still screamed after my last open-water submersion as I cannonballed in with 10/10 for the splash. To great relief, the investment paid off – little to no cold shock. I cruised for two hours and felt almost as comfortable as I had in the pool, except for feeling queasy when I passed a floating dead pigeon. After the swim, I discovered the city's water was close to 15°C (59°F). I couldn't get too carried away with the success of the neoprene and my relatively mild response to the cold. The Irish Sea was due to be much cooler.

Did I say 'certainty' and 'launch' before? Few things in life are guaranteed. Four weeks from blast-off, I received a phone call.

'No easy way to say this, man. The two guys with RIBs have both changed their minds. There's no support boat.'

'Shit. Did they say why?'

'No. Maybe they just want to use the boats themselves or are worried about them getting damaged. Look, I know one more person who might come good with their boat. I'm waiting to hear back from them, so I'll do my best and keep you posted.'

'That'd be great. I'm desperate at this stage. I've got a crew for the first two weeks and did all the big training mileage. I can't start without a boat, though.'

The next day, a new Mr Plan C agreed to lend me his RIB to act as a safety boat for the swim … until … he, too, changed his mind another week later, three weeks from the swim's start.

At the end of April, I left London and the planning office behind and returned home to Waterford in the sunny southeast of Ireland. I didn't think it sensible to go straight from the desk and pool to the sea swim challenge. I gave myself two weeks to get used to the ocean before the official start. I knew London was much warmer than Ireland, and the dockland waters were flat and toasty compared to the untamed Celtic Sea.

Again, I squeezed my body into the neoprene rigout and took the gear for a test swim at Woodstown Beach, Waterford. It was nothing like the sea swim at the start of March. Swimming in the shallows parallel to the shore in the bearable May seas, my cold sensors felt protected, with no heart rate and breathing spikes.

When I waded ashore, satisfied with my trial, I saw my mother striding over in a tizzy.

'What were you doing all the way out there? I nearly called the Coastguard!'

'What are you on about? I couldn't have been more than twenty, thirty metres out.'

'I saw your orange tow float miles off in the channel! You'll have me driven bananas with this swim.'

I turned around. 'Mam, that's a feckin' channel marker to help ships navigate up to the city.'

'I'm not watching you swim again, giving me grey hairs.'

'Jakers, I hope the lads have better sight than you when they're keeping an eye on me.'

'So do I!'

I issued a pleading statement on social media. I had learned how to swim and devoted hundreds of hours to the project over the preceding months. Failing to even start would leave scars to last a lifetime.

Thomas Barr phoned me. He's an old athletics training partner, competitor, and friend. By 2017, Thomas was the fastest Irish person in history over 400-metre hurdles and had finished fourth in the Rio 2016 Olympic final.

'Here, I saw you're struggling for a support boat? I'll sponsor you a boat.'

'Seriously?'

'Yeah, serious. We can't see you failing because of a boat after all that, Alo.'

'You're a legend. I can't afford a boat, but I can go halves on something small?'

'Great stuff. I'll check online and see what I can find.'

I'd gone wakeboarding with Thomas a few times and seen him fine-tuning the boat's engine while on the fly. I left the boat-savvy engineering graduate to it.

Two RIBs fitted the budget, one in nearby Wexford and the other a few hours away. A former Coastguard showed us around his RIB. He seemed reliable, and the boat seemed to be in decent nick. We took it for a test spin on the sea, and all seemed in working order. We shook hands, signed the paperwork, and exchanged €5,500. The swim was back on with less than one week to spare.

I wanted a chilled cider and a deckchair to relax and celebrate finding a RIB, but more problems needed fixing. We couldn't sleep on the open-top contraption or leave our gear there overnight. I had been trying hard to secure a car sponsor for the challenge, to get us from marinas and ports to wherever our beds and meals would be. Ideally, the car would have a trailer hitch so that I could transport the damn RIB from the south coast, 500 kilometres to the north coast.

No garage or rental company wanted to support the endeavour, most citing insurance as their reason since I'd have a different support team each week. I'd exhausted the sponsorship possibilities without success, so I checked the rental prices. They hovered around €5,000. *I can't afford that! The start is Sunday and today is … Monday! Who signed me up for this craic, eh?* The project was a bucking bronco trying to shake me loose. I was clinging on by my nails.

Monsters and Rubber Duckies

The Carrick-on-Suir River Rescue volunteers saved the day by responding to my social media plea forty-eight hours before the advertised start. The generous crew drove me and the RIB for five hours to Portrush, a small seaside town on the Northern Irish coast. Though the scrambling and uncertainty had me dazed on my feet, there was no wiping the smile off my face when I saw my boat primed in the Portrush harbour the day before the swim. A strange man approached.

'Saw you with the Carrick-on-Suir River Rescue guys launching that wee boat there. What is she, five metres?'

'Yep, five metres,' I said, answering with the only fact I knew about the boat.

'What are you doing so far from the River Suir?'

'I'm swimming the length of Ireland for charity, starting tomorrow.'

'Watch out for those orcas.'

'Will do,' I said and laughed, not giving weight to his words.

'No word of a lie. There's a pod of them out there. A few fishermen saw them this week. Huge six-foot fins, so they were.' His face was as serious as a heart attack. 'Well, cya now.' He walked away, just like that.

Standing alone on the pier wall, I looked around to figure out if that had really just happened. *Why did he come over, tell me about the four-tonne apex predator that can kill great whites and stroll off without a bother on him?* I took out my phone to distract myself. *Oh, a text from Elizabeth at work.*

'Monster six-gill shark caught off the Irish coast,' read the day's

tabloid news article she sent me.

Ah, for feck's sake! There went the unerasable smile from my face.

Darren, Paul, and Tim arrived three hours later. I led them along the pontoon past some sailing boats to my mooring.

'Here she ... Ah, shite.'

'The state of that,' Darren said.

'Mate, what's with all the water?' sailor Tim said, looking down at the waterlogged RIB.

'Not a clue. It was perfect on our test spin, and the seller never mentioned any leak. Balls on it anyway.'

Over the three hours since launching the boat, it had taken on a foot of water and resembled a bathtub. The fuel tank, fenders, and flare box bobbed like rubber duckies.

'Right boys, we'll need to go to the chandlery straight away,' Tim said.

Paul, Darren, and I nodded, unsure what that word meant. Moments later, we filled a basket in a marine supply store – duct tape, sponges, and tools. Tim chucked on his sailing boots, boarded the tub, and got tinkering.

'What's the good, the bad, and the ugly?' Paul asked.

'Well, the good is, it's still floating. The bad is that it lets on a lot of water. And the ugly is, it's sort of sinking,' Tim said.

SIX
Attempt One
May 2017 - 500 Kilometres Remaining

Battling Giants

Nobody had swum the length of Ireland from the north or south coast to the opposing shore. I could make the story more epic with just a bit of extra effort.

Around the corner from Ireland's northeast tip is the Giant's Causeway, a UNESCO World Heritage Site. An ancient Irish warrior giant, Fionn mac Cumhaill, forged the outcrop of 40,000 hexagonal basalt columns to help him walk across the Irish Sea and battle the Scottish giant, Benandonner. I'm not sure about you, but jumping into the deep from giant 60-million-year-old volcanic pillars sounds damn more exciting than waddling in from Ballycastle Beach.

Around the corner from the southeast tip of the country is my hometown of Waterford. Since I'd already decided on the length of Ireland, what was another little bit between friends?

I wish I could say there were more considerations in the equation and that I had researched hazards before extending the route, but I hadn't. I always wanted to see the Giant's Causeway, and swimming home felt right.

Though the waypoints were *around the corner* on a map, the ill-considered decision had its pitfalls. It added a thirty-kilometre section of the north coast, the most hazardous area of the route. I'd just learned about the orcas lurking in the waters. It also had the coldest and deepest waters, fastest tides, overfalls, eddies, and whirlpools! The additional south coast section from Carnsore

Point to my home passed through 'The Cemetery of a Thousand Ships' and added roughly one hundred kilometres of swimming to the task. The things we do for love.

The National Trust opened its doors early for us before the crowds of tourists arrived. Mam, Ev, and I followed our tour guide through the visitor centre and out the back of the modern structure submerged in the protected landscape like a villain's lair. There was a wall of green dotted with rock and gorse bushes to our right, the paved descending path straight ahead, and the never-ending Atlantic Ocean below to our left, lapping against the magical shore.

The giant's black steps loomed four storeys over me at the base of the towering basalt cliffs. I got into my tried-and-tested wetsuit that ranged in thickness from 1.5–4.5 millimetres – thicker around the core for warmth and thinner around the joints for ease of movement. I also donned my ten-millimetre-thick neoprene hood and five-millimetre-thick neoprene gloves and socks.

I wish Dad could see this. I'd meant to visit the legendary natural wonder with Dad when we'd recced the around-Ireland run route over a long-weekend drive, but we'd run out of time and had to keep moving. It was an experience we never got to share.

I hugged Mam and Ev and climbed to the top of the hardened magma steps to get a photograph with the Waterford flag raised overhead. To reach this point, I had endured early mornings of crying in grief en route to the pool in sub-zero temperatures, thousands of lengths, pain, exploding lungs, freeze-thaw, vanishing boats, and grey hairs. It was a victory for me to reach the start line. *I did it. I can do this.*

The orange RIB motored into sight and bobbed 400 metres offshore.

'Looks like they're floating,' I said. 'That's promising.'

'Best of luck, Al. Some achievement already, in all fairness. Mind yourself, okay,' Ev said.

'Please be careful, *please*, Al,' Mam said.

I slipped on my small green fins, clipped my tow float around my waist, and dived with a splash. I waved goodbye to my family alone on the rocks and turned to swim towards Tim and Paul.

Oh, Christ! I was out of breath. *What's going on? Maybe you're going too fast with the adrenaline. Slow it down, nice and flowy, relax, calm yourself.*

I'd put in months of consistent training, swimming for hours at a time. I'd splurged on all the right gear and had had no severe reactions to the cold during the recent open-water test swims. When I reached the support boat, I felt like I'd finished a race and was more than a bit concerned.

The wild coast of Northern Ireland wasn't the London Docklands in the blistering southeast of England, nor was it shallow water above the underfloor-heated, sandy, south-coast beaches of Ireland. One hundred metres of icy blackness flowed beneath me. The sea temperature hovered around 8°C (46°F), about half the temperature of the open training waters and just three degrees shy of meeting the International Ice Swimming Association's regulation 'ice swim' temperature. The cold shock chopped me down with the crash of falling timber, humbling me back to the dirt from which I thought I'd risen.

I looked to land, the sea splashing my bearded chin. Removing my head from the sea provided relief and a moment to catch my breath. The giant's rocks looked like organ pipes chiselled by a master sculptor. From the sea, it was a modest mound at the feet of the sheer lush cliffs. I was half a kilometre from the rugged Area of Outstanding Natural Beauty and felt awed by nature's allure and power.

I looked up to greet the crew. I didn't know whether to laugh or cry. Paul, a six-foot-seven, twenty-stone bearded mountain of a man, was sitting in the back of the oddly balanced boat, scooping water from around his feet with a sliced plastic milk carton and plopping it back into the sea.

'How're you feeling? Alright?' he said.

'Probably better than yee, by the looks of things,' I said, deflecting attention from my panic and hoping they didn't notice my shortness of breath. I didn't need them worrying about me from the word go: *He's gasping at the start; has he done any training whatsoever?* 'How're things looking up there? Much water on board?'

'Leave us to worry about that,' Tim said. They looked concerned, but I wasn't sure if it was because of the state of me or their slowly sinking ship. 'It's alright when we're moving. The second we sit for a minute, water's creeping in, but we can manage it.'

An hour in, I was scared about the impact of the cold. Although I had experienced and coped with cold shock on a few occasions, prolonged cold exposure was something new. My hands and feet were blocks of ice. I'd never felt an intense deep freeze like this before.

I'd bitten off more than I could chew. It was all too much. I wanted to get out and felt pathetic for feeling this beaten so soon. I told that nagging voice, *shut it for another hour and see how you feel then. You're not quitting.*

Every fifteen minutes or so, I paused to pee in a futile attempt to feel warmth's hug. I was determined to put in a good showing on day one and maximise the tide. I kept telling myself that it would be okay if I relaxed a little and kept moving. *Keep kicking, keep stroking – that's it; stay warm.*

Moving was difficult. I was accustomed to training in flat waters and tiny chop – the pool, docklands, and my local beach. There was no rhythm to the exposed deep sea. The waves kept frustrating me, slapping me to the left and right. Waves submerged my hands mid-stroke and rushed over my head and into my mouth when I was twisting to breathe. I strained my neck above the drowning chop, almost turning onto my back to reach for air.

'Here, Paul, can you take a look at my neck, please? 'Tis stinging like a mad yoke.'

'Ouch, that's nasty, Al. Where's the Vaseline?'

I'd made a rookie mistake and forgotten to lubricate my neck before swimming. This hadn't been a problem in my wetsuit trials, so it hadn't crossed my mind. In the rough swell of the open water, my movement was more exaggerated, which caused more friction. The wetsuit lacerated my neck and set it ablaze.

Coldness and pain intensified. I was stressed and tense. Fighting. *Shit! What was that?* I slammed the brakes and lifted my head as if not looking beneath me meant that the aquatic world didn't exist. *I can't see them. They can't see me.* The boat was some 200 metres ahead of me. *Probably nothing; you're grand.* I took a few deep breaths and resumed. Another white plume whizzed beneath. It kept appearing, and I kept stopping.

'Are you okay? We noticed you pausing a fair bit?'

'I keep seeing things moving. I think they're jellyfish. It's freaking me out. The idea of something touching me in the water. I'm telling myself there's nothing there, and I'm swimming alone.'

Paul and Tim had seen seals take an interest in me, but had decided it best to withhold the information. I continued, the white clouds shooting past my face every so often, which triggered a natural response to panic. Then it clicked. *Feckin' gobshite! It's just bloody bubbles from your stroke! Ugh, the stress of this!*

'That's not Rathlin Island, is it, lads?' I yelled from the water, earplugs tampering with my volume gauge.

'Yeah, you're flying it, mate, and Ballycastle's just there.'

After three hours and nineteen minutes of swimming, my watch read 16.54 kilometres. We called it a day before the racing tide turned on us. I clambered aboard, the rugby player hoisting the hefty dummy over the lip of the RIB's inflatable tube.

I pulled the hood off overhead as Paul zipped down the back of my wetsuit. The soft towel grated my perished skin. The wicked wind caused a violent shake to erupt throughout my body, which started vibrating like an auld fella's knee after ten pints of stout at a trad session. I raced to stick the woolly tea cosy on my head to slow the dying heat's escape. Leaving my legs in the wetsuit, I hurried into a T-shirt, a hoody, emergency foil, and a Dryrobe. Even with the layers, hugging myself, cuddling up to Paul, and breathing down my blouse, I couldn't get the heat into my bones. The engine revved and then quietened as we hit the ramps and crashed down on the other side with water spraying up. As Tim navigated the waves to Ballycastle Marina, I grabbed the seat and stared at the floor in silence, exhausted from the day's stress.

Children of Lir

The swim had three phases. Phase One of the swim was to survive the dangers of Rathlin Sound, Fair Head, and Torr Head, before crossing Larne and Belfast shipping lanes. We'd have to sprint across the mouth of Strangford Lough and, depending on the tide, hopefully not get sucked into the lough or spat miles out to sea. St John's Point Lighthouse, Downpatrick, County Down, was the finish line for Phase One.

Phase Two was a tidal hole from St John's Point Lighthouse to Clogherhead, County Louth. The sea rushes around the northeast corner and down the Irish Sea at the same time as it surges around the southeast corner and up the Irish Sea. The converging tides nullify each other in the middle, neither flowing north nor south, creating a large expanse of slack water. This section would be pure elbow grease with no tidal assistance.

If I were to survive the dangers of the north, the dead waters of the mid-section, then Phase Three would be the long homeward swim, a few hundred kilometres of tides, from Dublin to Waterford. Though the surging waters would increasingly propel me from Dublin to Wexford, we wouldn't be in the clear. There were still busy shipping lanes and navigation risks at Carnsore Point and the Saltee Islands.

Many sailors warned us of the boating risks within the opening stretch of Phase One. They had *huge* sailboats. I was a support swimmer for a sinking RIB and felt uneasy about the dangers.

We spent the night in a cottage that Darren had booked while Tim, Paul, and I were at sea.

Darren made us breakfast while Paul brewed us coffee with his cherished Chemex carafe. I stood next to Tim, examining nautical charts splayed across half of the kitchen table.

Tim ran his finger over a blue section of the map. 'Ideally, we want to look at a chart and see blue seas and no features or names.'

I pointed to the next section of the swim and chuckled. 'So, not this?'

It seemed a toddler had been let loose with a black biro – spirals, squiggles, names, and lines with arrows swooshing down, up, and across in no apparent pattern.

'We could certainly do without all of this.'

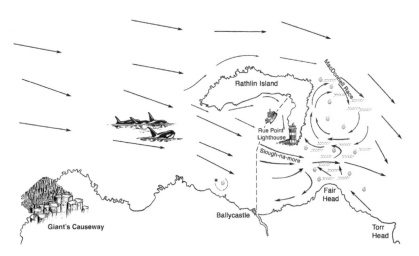

'What's that squiggle?'

'That's Slough-Na-More, the whirlpool I was telling you about. I looked it up. It means Swallowing of the Sea or Hollow of the Sea.'

'Jesus. What's this one about?'

'That's MacDonnell Race that whips around the north of Rathlin and down here to where you'll be swimming.'

'And this wall of squiggles?'

'We'll try to keep you away from the whirlpool and race, but there won't be any avoiding the overfalls.'

'Well, this should be … *interesting*.'

Paul brought the coffee over. 'What are overfalls?'

'The sea gets churned up where rapid tides collide or rush over something like a deep gully. It's like turbulence in a plane but with one difference.'

'And what's the one difference, then?'

'Oh, eh, turbulence can't crash a plane. Overfalls *can* sink us. We're starting early to be safer. We're in a good position after yesterday. I hope to be out of harm's way and around the corner before the tide picks up and this area gets scary.'

Darren set breakfast on the table. 'When does the tide pick up?'

'It changes every day by about an hour, flooding for six hours in one direction until high tide, then ebbing six hours the opposite way until low tide. The flow is the weakest at the start and end of each tide. That's *slack* water. The tide's force steadily builds to a peak over three hours and weakens back down for three hours.'

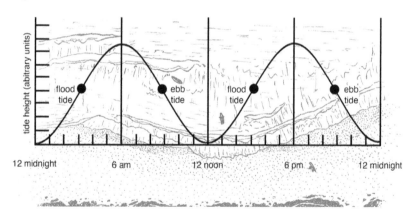

'Shouldn't we be getting Al in during peak flow for the biggest push?'

'Generally, yeah, we would, but not here. There's too much water volume converging around rocks and into funnels. The faster the tidal push here, the bigger the overfalls and the more dangerous it will be. We want to get out of danger when it's slack.'

I was ill with nerves once we reached the marina's car park. I'd lost the previous day's naive excitement and assuredness. I knew the neoprene wouldn't protect me as much as I'd hoped. The water's cold intensity petrified me. The narrow channel's sea creatures, dark depths, whirlpools, racing tides, and ship-sinking overfalls added layers of apprehension. I had competed in stadiums for Ireland as a track athlete, skydived solo, been interviewed before crowds on TV, presented planning cases to the public, slept rough, driven motorcycles through storms, and fought a man in a ring; but nothing compared to my dread of this morning.

After going to the public toilet twice, I tugged my wetsuit over my shoulders and stepped onto the RIB. I barely spoke to the lads for the thirty-minute rollercoaster to the previous day's finish coordinates. I fidgeted my legs to release some tension and turned inwards, singing 'Zombie' by The Cranberries in my head as a mind-focusing battle cry.

When I coaxed myself off the boat, it was like the previous day – feckin' freezing. The only change was that my raw, chafed neck stung like hell as the saltwater seeped into the open wound. My heart thumped. I entered a heightened, stressful state of fight, flight, or freeze, struggling to calm myself as I stroked after the boat with a quarter lung of air. *You wanted a challenge; this is it. There's no courage without fear.*

There wasn't an ounce of quit in me when running thirty-five consecutive marathons. Bar getting hospitalised, I was confident I could soldier through the 42.2 kilometres distance on foot within each twenty-four-hour slot. I never once felt like I wanted to go home or couldn't finish the job. It made me feel somewhat invincible to complete all those marathons without having doubts. The swim was the polar opposite. From jumping in off the Giant's Causeway, I had to goad myself to do another minute, another stroke. I didn't think I could keep withstanding the murderous environment for another day, never mind weeks and months. *Don't quit on Dad! Don't quit on yourself! You survived yesterday; you can do it again today. Suck it up, come on, ta fuck!*

The initial panic and frazzled mind induced by the cold seemed to last thirty minutes. Once I survived the state of shock, I got my bearings and calmed down momentarily.

The sea state was relatively peaceful. Because it was the slack part of the tide, there was little friction between the wind and the resting waters. More space for wandering thoughts became available without the desperation of trying to clear the barrage of waves.

What was that? Did something move? Why did he tell me about killer whales? Where's the boat? Jesus, they're ages away? Relax; it's just your mind. Breathe. Stroke.

I'd never had much fear of the sea. Fear didn't enter the equation when training in the pool or fifty to one hundred metres from the docks, rocks, and beach. Now three kilometres from soil and a few hundred metres from the RIB, my mind raced at a hundred miles per hour. I hated these discoveries about myself. The primal heebie-jeebies of a sea critter becoming visible, touching, or attacking me stressed me out and exhausted my taxed energy system. I tried to rationalise that it was Ireland. *There are no great whites, but didn't that website say there are thirty-five shark species in Irish waters? Calm your tits! They're not here! It's grand.*

All of a sudden, I was in a washing machine. The ancestral fear of sharks, whales, and stinging jellyfish tentacles left my mind as I grappled with the more imminent danger. Waves shoved. I froze. The boat pulled alongside me for my second feed of the morning. I checked my GPS watch, but it had fallen off and joined Rose's necklace on the seabed.

'I thought the wind wasn't picking up this morning?' I said to Tim. 'This feels sketchy. Are we okay, or do we need to get ashore?'

'This is the area of overfalls. We don't want to hang around here. It'll get worse before it gets better. We just need to push through, and things should calm down in a kilometre or so. We have you if you're okay to swim.'

The lads were elevated and could see far beyond my limited range of vision in the water. All I could see were menacing white horses sloshing all around.

I trusted Tim's instructions, put my head down, and didn't

look back until my stomach was cramped. *Aw, shite.*

'Lads! I need to go toilet again. Eh, think I can go in the wetsuit?'

'I wouldn't, mate,' Tim said.

'No! You're not allowed back on this if you do, and I'm not helping you out of a shitty, manky wetsuit either. Don't forget that open neck wound, too,' the doctor added.

I struggled aboard the tiny boat. Paul unzipped me, and I rushed to a squat next to the engine. This day was my eighth time in Tim's company and my third day in Paul's, who was face to face with me, holding toilet paper at arm's length.

'What a way to spend a Sunday,' Paul said.

It was the least dignified moment of my life to date and why I wanted to go in the wetsuit. Things were as grim as could be, so shitty that we could only but laugh at diarrhoea's concerto as we drifted offshore without a sinner in sight.

The pitstop sent me into a shiver; the half-removed wetsuit allowed my core temperature to plummet as the cold air attacked my freezing skin. I wanted to call it a day and wrap myself in a blanket. Paul zipped me back up.

'Can you get me back to where I climbed aboard?'

The roaring tide pushed us south, so we drove north, and I plopped back into the soiled sea.

Within an hour, my stomach was rumbling again. It was near impossible to get aboard and drag myself back to the freezing waters. I didn't know if I had the fortitude to do it again, and I was determined to hack the conditions for five hours. I didn't want to get out if I could hold and continue.

'Ah! Lads! Sorry! I can't bear the stomach cramps any longer – code brown. I repeat: code brown.'

The dire circumstance tested my resolve to the limit. I wanted a private, warm toilet, a roasting shower, and a cosy bed. I felt sick as a dog and was rattling with the cold. We were making phenomenal ground, and I needed to get as far south as possible to attract boat crew for week three onwards. I cajoled myself back into the sopping wetsuit to swim some more.

'Five hours!'

'I'm done! Can you get me outta here?'

In Irish mythology, Lir was a god of the sea. The Children of Lir's mother, Aobh, died, and Lir remarried her sister, Aoife. His new wife grew resentful of her beautiful step-children, Aodh, Conn, Fiachra, and Fionnula, and the attention Lir gave them. She lured the children to the local lake and inflicted a curse to be rid of them, turning them into swans for 900 years. The swans lived a peaceful 300 years on the calm Lake Derravaragh in the midlands before enduring a *miserable* 300 years on the fearsome and cruel Sea of Moyle on the northeast coast.

Swimming from Rathlin Sound, around Fair Head, and into the Sea of Moyle, I concur that it's no place for magical swans or chilly-willy swimmers to linger.

With the GPS watch lost within the first hour, we looked at the boat tracker for an indication – 38 kilometres. Tim and Paul were spinning back and forth on the RIB, so we knew it wasn't an accurate read of my swim progress, but it wasn't too far wrong, the tide slingshotting me from Rathlin Sound to the headland at Glenariff.

After motoring to shore, I sat in Glenarm's marina shower for the guts of an hour, decompressing, letting the warm water wash over and soothe my depleted soul.

Breaking Point

We checked the wind apps and saw what we felt. The gusts were red, blowing from twenty-five to thirty knots. The air rushed north while we wanted to swim when the water raced south. Wind against tide makes for the worst sea conditions.

The bay looked tranquil, with hardly a ripple, so we thought things mightn't be as bad as the forecast and flying flags suggested. I got kitted out, and we took the RIB towards the previous day's finish with a cautious but open mind. We ventured all of ten seconds beyond the protection of the headland's skyscraper cliff and grassy hillside farms. The swell sloshed above us in the exposed open waters as we shouted in unison over the brutish winds.

'Nope. Nope.'

'Jesus.'

'Not today.'

There were no doubts that we would be asking for trouble in these foolhardy conditions. We retreated twenty metres.

'Ah, that's better. Well, at least now we know.'

We returned to Darren onshore to live to fight another day.

The weather dictated the schedule, and forced us to take two days off. Paul and I drove to buy another GPS watch, a cheaper model. I'd learned an expensive lesson and bought some cable ties, too.

While we were away, a local committee of men left their tea and biscuits in the marina office and helped Tim and Darren yank the boat out of the water. The kind sea lovers opened their toolboxes and did their best to make the RIB watertight.

The gusts eased, and I had the all-clear to swim on day five. I asked the crew to try to stay close, thinking it might ease my fears. It did, but it also brought its problems – the loud thudding engine, the overpowering pong of a petrol station, and the choking, grey diesel fumes. When the wind and waves blew the idling RIB towards me, they'd try to correct their course, and I'd waste energy following them in the wrong direction. We decided it best for them to remain a few hundred metres ahead, prioritising progress over my fraught nerves. We struggled to get the balance right. Sometimes they pulled too far away, and I couldn't see them in the trough of the waves. I only got glimpses every fourth breath when they rose to a wave's crest.

Fears grew. Clocking my hysteria, I did something about it. I redirected my unhelpful thoughts towards useful ones. *How's your swimming form, Al? Make yourself more streamlined, c'mon. Head downwards and body horizontal. High elbow. Glue that arm to your ear. Better. Where's the boat? Crap. You've gone in a circle. That way.*

I swam for five hours, then stopped before Larne's shipping lane with a further 16.7 kilometres on the scoreboard.

Day six saw the fundraising tally reach €7,000. With this great news came matching weather. The donations and sunshine helped counterbalance my unease at seeing the massive P&O Ferries ship steaming from Larne Port across my swim route as I dunked from the boat into the sea.

I trusted Tim and Paul and scuttled through the shipping lane. I swam for four hours and thirty minutes and covered another eighteen kilometres.

The drying and warming procedure became more fine-tuned, and the post-swim shakes were less violent.

I wrapped the fleece-lined changing robe around myself, and Tim started the engine. False start. Tim tried again. No dice, only splutters. We were drifting close to the jagged water-torn cliff without any power.

'I'll give it another few tries, but it's not sounding too promising.'

Tim gave up and turned his attention to the much smaller backup engine. It worked for five minutes, shifting us away from the rocks, before also dying a death.

'We might have to radio for a tow sooner rather than later, boys,' Tim said, taking his tools to the motor.

We were in luck. A boat was driving south en route to Belfast. Tim, Paul, and I stood up and flagged them down. The two generous men threw us a rope, welcomed us aboard, and tugged my flailing RIB behind them. Their machine was a RIB on steroids. It had a rigid hull and an inflated belt around the base, like my boat, but that was where the comparisons stopped. It had two engines bigger than fridges hanging off the back, and a toasty indoor cabin with no wind, a kettle, and seats with armrests – heaven.

'Would you like a cup of tea, Alan?' the skipper said.

'Oh, I'd love one, thanks a mil.'

I took a comfy seat and cradled the mug in my hands. It was relaxing not having to grip on for dear life as we progressed.

I awoke in Bangor, Belfast, without my cup of tea.

'We wrestled the tea from you. You were out for the count within thirty seconds of your backside touching the cushion. We didn't want you scalding yourself.'

Tim got the engine working again. Day seven's swim started north of Belfast Lough. I felt secure with Tim and Paul minding me, and I was keen to cross the hectic shipping lane before the next crew tagged in.

The conditions were the best we'd had so far. The crew wore their shades, floating on the sea that was smooth as glass. The first thirty minutes passed with relative ease compared to the opening days. There was less shock and panic to fight through. My body had adapted somewhat to the stress of the cold over the eighteen hours and eighty kilometres of sea swimming completed over the first six days.

Still, my mind spiralled like an alpine slalom skier down the blackest slope. *This is miserable. Just go home.* My strokes became lethargic. *You're fine; you got this.* Saltwater splashed in my mouth. I stopped to dry heave several times before continuing to swim. My internal thermometer lowered, the icy waters seeping into my capillaries. *Get yourself together. This is the best weather we've had. You need to capitalise and bolt across the shipping lane. Let's relax the cacks and just get to Blackhead Lighthouse at the start of the lough.*

I knew I could survive for five hours in the sea, but I had only been going for an hour and thirty minutes and couldn't explain the darkness engulfing me. Better to be honest than brave.

'Here, guys! Just a heads up, I'm not doin' well. No pain, but I feel shit and cold, real cold. I might take extra food. Can you chuck me a banana and some of that carb drink? Sound.'

If I could compare it to something, it was like the one time I had 'hit the wall' during marathon training. My legs had turned to jelly while running on the trails, and extreme fatigue bulldozed me as I flopped from my left foot to my right foot. I slowed to a walk and ate all my rations to overcome it and make it back home. I thought the extra swim feed would plug the holes in my perforated bucket. It didn't. Though my goggles were the same as always, they clamped around my head like a tourniquet and felt like vacuums sucking my eyeballs out. The veins in my head bulged. I wanted to quit like never before. I stopped and retched. I reasoned it was just in my head, and I could dig myself out of the hole if I persisted. I didn't want to continue. I didn't want the shame of quitting. I thought of Dad and doing his memory proud. *I can't quit.* Tears filled the fish bowls around my eyes.

'I've counted your stroke rate, Al, and it's way down,' Paul said as Tim pulled the boat alongside me.

I felt empty and wanted to go home. *This is too hard.*

'I'll see what I can muster for the next thirty minutes but keep an eye on me, please. I feel like a flat battery.'

Each stroke was a struggle, like lifting dumbells in my dead claw hands with each flop of my arms. It was a vicious cycle. Exhaustion made me swim slower than usual, and the slower pace allowed the sea to sear my nerves and muscles with dry ice, working its way to my core. The temperature drop zapped my speed, strength, and coordination, making me colder, slower, and more negative in my thoughts. I reached quitting point and squeezed out another thirty minutes of slow progress.

'I can't do any more. That's all I got. Sorry, lads,' I slurred, no longer in complete control of my mouth.

'Right, let's get you up, big guy,' Paul said.

I was shaking uncontrollably in the water for the first time, my body desperate to generate warmth. It worried me. I was too stubborn for my own good, aborting the mission later than I should have. Staying in cold water to the point of shaking is playing with ice, toying with drowning and hypothermia. Dr Paul grabbed my arm, then a leg, and yanked my depleted body from the water to land the day's biggest catch.

I wasn't in the clear once Paul ripped me from the blue. Far from. Once on board, my core temperature continued to drop. Post-swim cooling can last thirty to forty minutes even if the air temperature is significantly warmer than the sea. After this, core temperatures stabilise and start returning to normal levels. Even if you don't feel cold when leaving the water, continued cooling can still trigger hypothermia, and re-warming can take several hours. That's why it's essential to get dried, dressed, and warmed without delay. Already showing signs of hypothermia, with some of 'the umbles' present – grumbles, fumbles, mumbles, and stumbles – I didn't give myself a sensible safety margin. We had to move fast, although I couldn't. I was grateful for my new friends. Tim and Paul rushed to get me dry and warm, my shaking more alarming than ever. Paul lent me an extra layer, his knitted pullover made by his granny, and handed me a flask of hot chocolate to sip. Tim sped us over the lumps and bumps towards the safety of Bangor Marina. The tremors persisted as Paul wrapped around me to shelter me from the biting wind.

Despite my swimming abilities and cold experience, I was edging towards swim failure. If it weren't for my wetsuit's buoyancy helping me stay horizontal, I'm not sure I would have stayed afloat. Like an insect in a spider's web, the sea had spun its freezing net around me, trying to immobilise and devour me. I only pushed the envelope because I had a fail-safe. I wouldn't have been able to return to shore without the support boat and safety team to get me out of danger.

'I think we underestimated the toll all these hours of cold swimming has on you,' Paul said in the evening.

I was gutted to crumble and waste an excellent opportunity to take advantage of the favourable conditions and cross Belfast Lough. 'I'm fried after that ten-K, lads. I'm hitting the hay early tonight.'

Saline Sausage Fingers

We loaded the RIB the following afternoon, day eight, for Darren, Paul, and Tim's last day in support. I was desperate to cross the busy shipping lanes.

'I didn't think you'd continue after yesterday,' Paul said. 'I thought that might have been it. I talked to Jess last night about ways to convince you to keep going.' His partner, Jessie Barr, is a childhood friend and an Olympic athlete with a PhD in Sports Psychology. 'But you seem a different man today, ready to hit the ground running.'

'Live and learn. It's a new day, a fresh slate. I'm ready to rock.'

'That's what I like to hear.'

I thought I'd crashed and frozen because I'd misjudged my

calories, and things had spiralled out of control from there. I hadn't eaten enough that day, or close enough to the swim. It was already too late when I scoffed the banana and carbohydrate supplement.

It was impossible to settle into a routine because the start time changed by roughly an hour each day due to the ever-changing tide. I had to account for nerves and seasickness with boat commutes to the swim start that could take an hour or two and factor in the discomfort of having no toilet aboard. I wouldn't swim with an empty stomach again, that was for sure.

Tim manoeuvred the RIB out of Bangor Marina, past row after row of moored sailing boats. Once into Belfast Lough and out of the marina's slow zone, he pressed the handle to accelerate north. The engine sputtered and then died. He got it working before it gave up the ghost again. We trundled back to our mooring in the marina with our tails between our legs, concluding that a high-traffic shipping lane of monster tankers was the last place we wanted to cut out. I booked a service from a mechanic, and we went to the pub to drown the day's frustrations and celebrate the week's ninety-eight-kilometre triumph.

Gavin Downey and Derrick 'Skinner' O'Neill swapped in on boat support, and DJ Magee worked from home, phoning restaurants, pubs, hotels, and B&Bs to ask for help with my costs.

Sailfish sent me a new wetsuit with an extra half a millimetre of thickness to help my struggles with the cold – up to five millimetres now around my chest. I gladly accepted the offer of additional insulation.

With forced rest on days eight, nine, and ten, we were back in action with a fully serviced boat engine on day eleven. The swim began on the north side of Belfast Lough. The plan was to swim in a higher gear for a shorter duration – a sprint across the shipping lanes to get out of the collision zone.

As well as the pressure to zip across the shipping lanes, I needed to maximise headway in week two to attract people to help over the following weeks. No boat operators had answered my online pleas to volunteer in weeks three and four. It seemed there was little chance of enticing volunteers all the way up to Belfast from the sunny southeast or Dublin region. I felt I needed to make the Republic of Ireland border by the end of week two. With speed and momentum in mind, I swapped the small fins for the longer fins to gain more propulsion. I didn't like switching to long fins as it compromised my vision for the challenge, but it seemed like a necessary evil to give myself the best chance of reaching the finish line.

An hour into the swim, I stopped to pee and looked around. I couldn't help but laugh. *What are you up to? This is mental.* The penny dropped as I saw the tankers and ferries zoom in and out of Belfast. I was swimming across a damn shipping lane.

'We need you out of the water, Al,' Skinner said.

'Now or in a tick?'

'Fairly lively, I'd say; otherwise, that thing's going to flatten you, kid.'

A cargo ship was heading our way at a rate of knots. I jumped aboard and paused my GPS watch. Skinner shoved the throttle down as I huddled with the robe gripped around me. We watched the ship steamroll over the coordinates we had just fled.

'Some first day at the office,' Skinner said. 'Right craic altogether.'

They dropped me back in the middle of the lough, and I swam until I reached the south side of the inlet. We'd passed the considerable milestone of Belfast, swimming another fourteen kilometres in three hours and twenty minutes.

After only five hours of kip, we left the B&B before dawn for the morning's tide. We were the only boat out on the seas as we chugged out of the marina. It was the first time the sea had resembled a pool. *Finally, I can swim in my training conditions,* I thought. The icing on the cake was starting clear of the shipping thoroughfare – one less variable to fear. I felt calm, my body flowing as effortlessly as the tide through Donaghadee Sound. Copeland Island rose to my left, and a row of coastal homes and cars followed on the mainland to my right. No ferocious boxing today, just graceful ballerina dancing. The two hours of zen-state swimming flew as we progressed to the next port of Donaghadee.

Donaghadee is a small harbour town known as the start line of the North Channel swim. While mountaineers have the Seven Summits – a hit list comprising the tallest peaks on each continent – sea swimmers have the Oceans Seven, consisting of seven of the world's most brutal channel swims. This intimidating list includes the Cook Strait (New Zealand), Molokai Channel (Hawaii), English Channel, Catalina Channel (California), Tsugaru Channel (Japan), and Strait of Gibraltar. The most challenging channel, however, is the thirty-five-kilometre North Channel swim from Donaghadee, Northern Ireland, to Scotland. It's top of the list because of the cold, the currents, and the volume of stinging jellyfish.

Irishman Stephen Redmond was the first to accomplish the incredible Oceans Seven feat in 2012. Freezing in these waters with my wetsuit on, I can only tip my cap to these Vaseline-daubed, knicker-wearing, cold-water machines.

I was back in for the evening tide with a plan to swim for three hours and make the next harbour. After an hour of swimming, Manannán mac Lir, the Celtic sea god whose statue resides in Derry, jabbed his pudgy, saline sausage fingers down my throat. I puked up the tastiest lunch of the tour sponsored by Donaghadee's Pier 36. Skinner whizzed the boat alongside me. Gavin gripped my wetsuit by the shoulders to hoist my mouth above the splashing waves as I spewed, hanging me from the side of the RIB like a jumper pegged to a clothesline. Although the swim ended abruptly, we still managed twelve kilometres.

On day thirteen, a cloud of impenetrable fog smothered Donaghadee and the seas around it, preventing any swimming. Once we could see our noses again, we continued the swim past Ballywalter and Portavogie towards Strangford Lough.

I was getting more comfortable with the separation between the boat and me. Although the crew spotted lots of seals, I hadn't seen any wildlife other than the bubbles that had scared the bejaysus out of me on day one. They did still catch me out from time to time.

The new crew tested my limits, hovering the boat around 400 metres ahead of me for the day.

I reached my right hand forwards to glide and touched something solid and heavy. I jerked up and saw a fin. I jumped out of my skin, and kicked and punched the creature with all four limbs at once, pulling a face that had just encountered the boogie man.

It's only a container from a trawler! I was having palpitations. *It's only a chunk of plastic. Chill the beans, ya eejit.*

Gavin and Skinner pulled up in hysterics laughing.

'With all the sea to swim in, how'd you manage to swim into that yoke, hey?'

'Why didn't you tell me! I nearly died of fright!'

'We didn't think you'd hit, and when we realised you would, shur, it was too late. Pretty funny, though. What are the chances of hitting that, heh?'

'I need you to stay a bit closer to me. I'm bricking it here. Ugh, me heart.'

From Belfast onwards, locals warned us of the dangers around Strangford Lough. Its name originates from the Vikings and translates to 'fjord of the strong currents', with rapid tides reaching 7.5 knots (fourteen kilometres per hour). It's the largest lough in the British Isles and has a narrow mouth. People told us that, whether the vast lough is filling or emptying, its mouth sucks you in, chews you up over vicious overfalls, or spits you miles out to sea, never to be seen again.

'You've got some company in the water today,' Skinner said.

'What? More seals?'

'Yeah.'

'Tell them to feck off.' I gave the stalkers two fingers.

'I'll look after you, pet,' Skinner said, inhaling his cigarette.

I was already on edge with the warnings. I waited for something to happen. I did my best to power past the hazard, hoping the river rescue man would pull me out if things went awry.

I was nearing three hours and thirty minutes, and tiring.

'Are we ever going to get across this feckin' lough or what?'

'Look behind you.' Gavin pointed.

I turned around, on the defensive, half expecting a killer whale.

'You were suckin' diesel, kid. That's it there away off in the distance,' Skinner said. 'Going at slack tide and giving it a wide berth did the trick, so it did.'

I covered sixty-six kilometres during week two, making it to Portaferry Marina before Gavin and Skinner returned to their day jobs.

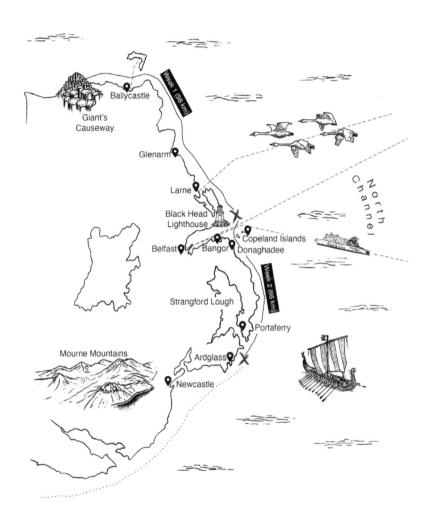

SEVEN
Murphy's Law
336 Kilometres Remaining

Hanging from the Harbour

Despite Emagine's slick promo clip, radio and newspaper interviews, and social media cries for volunteers, I was all out of boat operators.

My childhood running friend, Billy Ryan, flew from London to Dublin to provide land support, but I couldn't swim anywhere without someone to safely handle the support boat.

I got a last-minute offer from a stranger called Mike, who was willing to drive six hours cross-country from West Cork to operate the RIB for three days. I was still stuck, though, uncomfortable with the idea of only having one person on the support boat. I'd known Billy to struggle with motion sickness on bus journeys. I wasn't going to ask him to thrash among the waves for hours on end.

'I'm going to be a little late. I kinda crashed the car rental coming out of the parking space at the airport,' Billy said on the phone. 'They won't give me another one, so I'll ask my sister for a lift up.'

I sat on a bench on Portaferry's waterfront, awaiting the team's arrival, watching the ferry battle the tide over and back to Strangford on the opposite side of the channel. I got a phone call from Mike.

'Here, listen, got some bad news. Two hours into my drive and I got tyre problems. I'm not going to make it up, sorry. Best of luck, though.'

When Billy arrived, we spammed social media, called radio stations, and searched for locals who might help. I met Mark Stevenson working in the town's RNLI station. He was game to support the following day, day nineteen, with one of his friends, Stuart Macrory. I was hoping to progress from Portaferry and reach Ardglass Marina.

Billy and I skipped out the door in the morning and made our way to meet Mark and his pal, Stuart, at the RIB. When I saw the boat, my jaw hit the floor.

'Has this been a problem?' Mark said.

'No, we had leaks and engine trouble alright, but fixed those over the last two weeks. It's been sitting there the last three days without a bother on it. Feckin' typical.'

The inflated tube that supported the right half of the boat was flat as a board. We puffed up the lungs with the pump and checked for punctures. It seemed fine, so we ventured out of the lough, and my swim began off Gunn's Island.

I stopped fearing the cold. I had habituated to it over the nineteen days of the challenge. It was now the last day of May, and I was much further south than when I'd started, so the sea had warmed up a degree or two. I'm sure the slightly thicker wetsuit since Belfast helped matters, along with the extra pounds of lard gained while sitting around eating and waiting for green lights to swim.

Winds howled. The seething waves bashed me around. Some struck my head with the force of a punch. I felt zen. The challenge seemed doomed with no crew in the pipeline, so the opportunity to advance became a dwindling gift to savour. The shift from infinite to finite altered my attitude. *You won't get to do this much longer, so enjoy it*, I thought. An hour and a half in, I stopped to refuel.

'Eh, we've tried pumping the tube up twice, but it's nearly flat again,' Mark said. 'The waves are fairly big. Without the air holding, we're sitting lower in the water. If one comes over the top, we could be in trouble.'

'Do you want to call it a day?'

'I want to help you progress. How much longer do you want to go for?'

'I'm happy to go as long as you feel it's safe. I'm grand down here, but I'm worried about you in the boat if you say it's not holding air. No pushback from me.'

'Yeah, I think we should head into port.'

'Grand job, let's get out of here.'

With another six kilometres covered, we'd progressed enough to justify moving our base camp from Portaferry to Ardglass Marina, where I hired another handyman to attend to the boat.

After another day off the water, Jonny O'Hare, a nearby army medic with RIB experience, volunteered to save the day. Billy was up for joining him on board.

'Are you sure? Don't you get motion sickness?'

'*Al*, those bus trips were like *ten* years ago. I'll be grand,' Billy said.

'Okay then, your call. Sound out for helping me.'

The sun glistened off the water. The marina's flag flopped. The repaired tubes puffed their chest up, and we loaded the gear for a day at sea. The medic turned the ignition key. Battery dead.

'Jesus Christ, give us a break.'

We loaded the spare battery. Nada. We phoned the marina's handyman, who came down to give us a jumpstart. Never a dull moment.

On day twenty-one, the waves were smaller than the previous swim but were closer together. They hit from an awkward angle, splashing over my face and mouth when I tried to breathe. I exaggerated my roll to get some air.

I stopped for my first refuel after thirty minutes. Billy was on his hands and knees, puking over the edge.

'I'm fine; keep swimming!'

I stopped for my second feed after another thirty minutes.

Billy was puking over the edge again.

'He's great company,' Jonny said with a nod.

'It's just when we stop – *blarg* – and float. Can we do faster – *blech* – feeds, ugh, so we can keep the boat moving?'

'Don't kill yourself. If you're too unwell, call it a day any time, yeah?'

'Keep going, Al. I want to get you to that next port,' Billy said.

Having trained as 400-metre sprinters together, I knew he had no quit, but it was impressive.

My stomach wasn't handling the concoction of carbohydrate drinks and gels by the time the fifth feed rolled around. I rushed aboard, stripped down my wetsuit, and hung my bare back over the sea. With the boat stopped and bobbing, Billy keeled over the side to start his bi-hourly spew. A local fishing boat drove past, its skipper staring perplexed at the half-naked man relieving himself, the kneeling man puking overboard, and the driver at the helm laughing.

I waved with a nod. 'Howya?'

'Wait 'til I tell my wife about the day I had with two strange Waterford men,' Jonny said before bursting with laughter.

I wanted to go to bed for a lie-down. I wanted to progress to the next harbour more. With our stomachs emptied, it was back to work as I returned to swimming.

Billy endured the hardship – an impressive nine pukes over the thirteen-kilometre swim: some man, Bill. I felt terrible for being the cause of his bleak day, but it was a little bit funny having a partner join the misery-fest. Swimming in the sea didn't seem so bad after all.

Once the tide slowed and the swim ended, we drove across Dundrum Bay towards Newcastle, County Down, a little town on a long sandy beach. The forests of Slieve Donard, the highest peak in Northern Ireland, dominated the skyline. We reached the harbour, where small fishing boats lined the protective walls, with a scattering of motorboats anchored in the middle. Jonny found space against the pier, looped our docking rope in a figure of eight around the harbour's metal cleat, and headed home. Billy and I checked into our accommodation and got showered and fed. After a few hours, we returned to the harbour to check up on the boat before bedtime.

'Ah, for feck's sake. Give me a break.'

It turns out Newcastle Harbour is tidal. The receding tide had tightened the rope's tension and hoisted my boat's nose at a forty-five-degree angle into the air. We walked ten metres to the pub and ordered two pints of the black stuff.

'Look behind you, Al.'

I read the sign hanging on the wall over my head: *'Murphy's Law – Anything that can go wrong will go wrong.'*

'Cheers to Murphy's Law and my last night.'

'Sláinte, Billy, and thanks for helping me out this week.'

After our first pint, the barman helped us lower the boat down to the water and safely retied it with enough slack to account for the rise and fall of the tide.

'That's tomorrow's headache. Let's get another round.'

Seamus

Jack Molloy and I grew up across the road from each other. Arriving on Saturday morning to replace Billy, Jack drew the short straw by volunteering to help on week four.

'What's the plan today so? Have we got a driver for the boat?'

'Eh, no, no driver until Monday. We got bigger problems. The batteries are dead, so we need to charge them first. We have to check if there's much damage from last night. The boat might be wrecked after the incident.'

'Incident?'

'I'll show you.'

I peered down from the wall. The boat was gone. 'What now? Someone's hardly nicked it?'

'Is that it over there?'

Someone had moved the boat to the other side of the harbour, taking it away from the access ladder. We had no way to retrieve the flat batteries or check for damage. I told the barman about our predicament, and within no time, ten of the town's RNLI and Coastguard members arrived in full battle garb – hard hats, lifejackets, team overalls, high-vis, VHFs, and steel-toe boots.

The Coastguard manned the land as the RNLI retrieved my boat.

'There are a few holes, and it's taking on water. Yeah, you're not going anywhere in this thing. We'll have to take it out, so it doesn't sink.'

They towed my wounded banger out of the harbour and beached it on the sand. The boat's seating bracket had lost the tug of war with the harbour's metal cleat. A water fountain sprouted from the holes where the seat bolts used to be, and plastic items floated in half a foot of water. The local sea dippers saw the commotion and helped us tug the boat by hand up the slipway to the edge of the car park. The Coastguard wrapped their tape around the disfigured machine like a crime scene to discourage kids from climbing aboard.

'Sorry to see it end like this, Al,' Jack said.

'A sorry sight that, but swimming here from the Giant's

Causeway, Jesus, that's no mean feat, eh?' said the RNLI man.

'Here, I can fix that,' a stranger said. 'No problem. Good as new for tomorrow.'

'Huh?'

'Ah, 'tis only a surface wound. I'll patch her up for you at no charge, and you'll be on your way swimming again in no time. It'll be grand. I'd hate to see you stuck after getting this far.'

Seamus McConkey, who had been tending to his fishing boat *Mary Lou*, saw my difficulty, and thought he could help. With nothing to lose, I was happy to roll the dice and see if the nice man knew what he was talking about.

The following day, Seamus had bolted the seat back in place, and the holes were no longer. *Legend!* Nothing like the goodwill of a stranger to lift spirits.

I needed more help since I didn't have a car with a hitch and a boat trailer. I felt like a right nuisance phoning the local water safety volunteers to see if they might help me re-launch the boat into the sea on a Sunday to test Seamus' handiwork. They were down in numbers to heave the RIB back down the slip. I couldn't get over the generosity of strangers giving up their time like that to help someone succeed.

We watched for two hours as the boat floated. It was watertight.

'We're back in business to swim tomorrow.'

My mobile rang.

'Sorry for the late notice, but something's come up. I can't drive your boat tomorrow,' said the volunteer scheduled to get me on the water.

Save Our Souls

I awoke frustrated on Monday morning. With all the drama of the boat resolved, the volunteer bailing was a blow. But my sourpuss was short-lived as I found out the fundraising tally had increased to €9,000. It seemed like the public enjoyed the unravelling chaos.

Jonny felt awful about his error tying up the boat and saw my crewing issues through social media. He connected me with a local, Michelle Chambers, who knew first aid and could drive a

RIB. She was willing to stand in to rescue the day's swim at the last minute. On, off, on, off, and on. I was exhausted, but I'd swim if I had support.

Arriving at the harbour after lunch, Michelle, Jack, and I were pleased to see the boat was in one piece and hadn't taken on water overnight.

'Back out swimming, you are?' two men at the harbour wall said, as we loaded our gear aboard the RIB.

'Yeah, we're over to St John's Point Lighthouse to try to get across the bay.'

'Will it take you long?'

'Ah, about four hours of swimming. I should be done maybe by eight-ish, I'd say. We're heading out early before the tide goes out and traps us in the muck.'

With the batteries recharged, the engine started without skipping a beat. We left the harbour, heading north for the lighthouse. With two hours to kill until the now feeble tide turned, we admired the black and custard bands of paint wrapped around the towering beacon rising from the rocky peninsula.

Michelle said, 'Forty metres, that. Tallest onshore lighthouse on the island of Ireland.'

I plunged into the water, but jerked my head straight out.

'You alright, Al?' Jack said.

'No, there's about a million jellyfish beneath me. I haven't seen any until now. Ugh! I don't like this.'

It felt unnatural to swim with so much activity below. *What are you doing? Get out, ya dope,* was my brain's intuitive response. If I were going for a dip and saw a fraction of the number of jellyfish in the water, I wouldn't get in. This wasn't a dip. It was a length-of-Ireland charity swim, so I'd have to fight the natural urge to flee and get used to my new polka-dot view.

At least five translucent brains larger than dinner plates glided inches below me with each stroke, forcing my face out of the sea. *Pull yourself together, man! Just swim.*

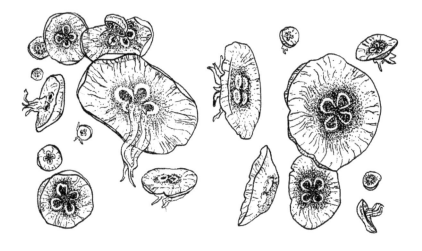

I surprised myself at how quickly I became accustomed to the wildlife display. I even grew to admire the four purple balls on the jelly domes, their tentacles flowing like a frilly skirt in the wind, and pulsing strokes propelling them through the tide with grace. It was beautiful to watch, a distraction, but I'd jolt to a stop when I touched one. Still a scaredy-cat, but improving.

Other than the hundreds of threatening jellyfish, another predator seal, and a wedgie causing all sorts of male discomfort, the swim felt the best yet. The feeds were as snappy as a Formula One pitstop. I even perfected the front crawl pee – a more challenging skill than it may sound – gaining at least five minutes of additional swim time by removing the breaks.

I climbed aboard at eight o'clock in the evening after four hours of swimming and just over sixteen kilometres covered. Jack unzipped my wetsuit. I dried my head and torso, stuck on dry, warm layers, and we were good to go. The sky was grey as an ashtray. Sharp spears of rain punctured the water like bullets. Michelle turned the ignition key, and the engine purred. The whirling propellers spun beneath the surface, accelerating with the wind at our back towards Newcastle Harbour.

A minute later, the engine spluttered and died without warning. We couldn't revive it, floating at the mercy of the wind and waves. Jack hadn't brought waterproof clothing. His knees began to jump as the rain seeped. We tried the spare engine and couldn't get it to start.

'It worked grand the last seven hours,' Michelle said. 'Not a bother on the engine.'

'Yeah, but Murphy's Law,' I said. 'At least the tubes are full of air, and we're not taking on any water.'

Daylight was falling as the RIB wallowed in the swell. We had an hour before dark. After several failed attempts at starting the engines, Michelle phoned her friend, who owned a vessel in the harbour.

'He's on the way there now to tow us in, so he is. Not to worry, we're grand.'

Given my journey to Dundrum Bay, it felt like any other day waiting for the next bus to town.

Mother nature rolled a thin blanket of fog over the bay to reduce visibility. Jack was quieter than usual, tense, tired, staring towards the harbour, blood draining from his face. Never mind fire, his first day on boat support was unravelling into a baptism of ice water for someone not used to being on the sea, especially not on a faltering boat in rain and fog at dusk.

'Do you think he'll be much longer? I'm getting pretty cold now,' Jack said, shivering.

Michelle rang her friend again. I was getting concerned for Jack, but I'd only brought enough clothes to keep me warm and dry after the swim.

'Bob asked if we'd called the RNLI,' Michelle said. 'When he pulled into the harbour, he said the crew were already launching the big boat out of the station. Since the RNLI are on the water, he's leaving 'em to it.'

'Ah, Christ. That thing's big enough to rescue a small army. We only phoned your friend. How'd the RNLI know? Mam's going to have a conniption when she hears about this.'

As we drifted, we saw the million-pound rescue vessel speed from the harbour with a milk-white wake foaming behind.

'Where the feck are they off to?' I waved my bright orange rescue flag overhead to increase our visibility. 'We're over here! Seems like they're heading north to the lighthouse where we started.'

We jiggled the high-vis flag and waved our hands, but they didn't adjust their course.

'It's probably too dark for them to see us now,' Jack said.

'Should we light up the flare?' I asked.

Michelle said, 'It's as good a time as any, I suppose.'

I pulled a flare from the box and checked it wasn't a rocket. Things were already embarrassing enough without exploding a red star into the sky and dousing the town in a red hue.

The lifeboat's searching headlights turned to us once the hand-held flare's searing red flame sizzled, and smoke plumed into the blackness.

'Good evening, Alan. Everyone okay?'

'Howya, Ronan. Yeah, all good. Sorry to bother you again.'

'Sure you know yourself, that's what we're here for.'

We climbed up, and the crew members guided us into the cabin's comfort.

'You don't look well,' a volunteer told Jack. 'You're as white as a ghost. Here, eat this,' he said, handing him a chocolate bar.

'Ah, nice one, thanks; I haven't eaten since we left.'

'Feckin' hell, Jack, that's about eight hours ago. No wonder you're shook. Jesus.'

Once the sugar hit, Jack's colour returned with a relieved smile.

'How'd you know our engine failed?' I said.

'People were expecting you ashore at eight, and when you didn't show, they alerted us to a missing swimmer, saying you were headed for the lighthouse.'

'G'way. I only told those lads I'd be done around eight in passing. I'd just climbed out of the water by then, and we were motoring in grand by five past eight.'

'All's well that ends well.'

'Thanks for getting us, and sorry again for the hassle.'

We pulled ashore to a nuisance's welcome, blue emergency

lights twirling, lighting the harbour and the twenty volunteers on standby. The RNLI handed it over to the Coastguard, who tied the RIB to the pier wall.

The RNLI invited us into their lifeboat station for chocolate bars and fizzy drinks. It was a trap. We stood in the principal's office like naughty children getting told off for our poor behaviour.

'I think enough's enough with that boat. Time to call it a day on the swim,' the lady behind the desk said.

I phoned my mother to let her know we were safe and sound and I was going to bed.

'That's enough, Al. It's too dangerous,' she said. 'Come home, please. Please.'

Orange Submarine

Jack's time in support was over the morning after the rescue. He drove home to Waterford with some stories to tell, and I was back on my own. I booked a repair man to come the following day to inspect the boat and revive it to total health. My brother rang.

'You have to come home. Enough's enough. Mam's calling me every day in a panic. She's in tears after last night.'

'I can't live my life based on Mam's tolerance to risk, Ev. I'm doing my best here. I hired several mechanics to service the engine, and it worked fine until it didn't. They never flagged any fatal issues when they fixed it. It was just bad luck and we got home safe. I have a mechanic repairing it again tomorrow.'

'Just stop and come home, will ya.'

The call ended abruptly. *Fuckin' hell.* As if it wasn't bad enough that the original charities bailed or I couldn't convince any major sponsors to support me. The RNLI, Mam, now Ev. They were all pressuring me to quit. I was now standing alone on an island.

What you believe is best for your life won't always align with what others want for you or themselves. It can be hard as hell, especially when loved ones aren't on the same page, but I knew I couldn't please everyone, and it was my responsibility to steer my ship. I couldn't allow the challenging friction to dissuade me. Selfishly to some and sensibly to others, I refused to cave to the outside pressures. I couldn't accept quitting because of a repairable mechanical fault, not after everything. I needed to keep focused on what I could do to progress. With a mechanic booked, I still saw a safe route forward.

The alarm sounded. I ate breakfast and headed off to meet the mechanic. I looked at my phone as I left the accommodation and saw two missed calls from the RNLI. *What's wrong now?* I listened to the voicemail.

'Can you come to the harbour for a chat? I'm here now. Ring me once you get this.'

The harbour was on the other side of town, a thirty-minute walk along the promenade. *May as well enjoy the stroll first before stepping onto today's rake.* I put my phone away and pretended all was right as rain.

The emerald Mourne Mountains loomed above the town, rolling down to the bay where the sun sprinkled glitter on the gentle waves that whooshed over the white sands. In no rush for a telling-off or to hear about a broken something or other, I stopped to grab a takeaway coffee. My phone vibrated. It was a text from Seamus, the local fisherman who had repaired my RIB the other day and got it back on the water for my previous swim.

'*Your boat sank. I'll see you at the harbour, mate.*'

But of course. Nothing could surprise me by day twenty-six. I could only smile at Seamus's straightforward delivery. No amount of haste or panic would unsink the boat, so I sipped my Americano and continued my stroll along the peaceful waterfront.

And now we're back to where my book began, finding good aul' Seamus up to his neck in water, surrounded by jellyfish as he dragged my submarine ashore.

'The sea was rough last night. By the looks of it, one tube went flat. She wouldn't be as buoyant then. If any water leaked in, she wouldn't be as high up as normal, and a wave or two must have dragged her down and finished her off.'

The locals and I pulled the boat up to the car park once more, and I arranged for it to be collected and hauled home to Waterford.

I phoned Thomas Barr, my athletics friend who went halfsies on the boat with me, and broke the terrible news about the overnight incident. I felt terrible. He took a chance on me when nobody else would. Without his encouragement, generosity, and willingness to see me succeed, I couldn't have started, let alone got to Newcastle and raised €9,265 for the Irish Heart Foundation and Solas Cancer Support Centre.

Once everyone left, the disappointment of failure and the trauma of Dad's death crushed me like a ton of bricks. I sat alone on the rocks. My shoulders trembled as I sobbed while trying to process life.

My devastation washed away more and more with each wave that rolled by. I could stand with my chin up, look myself in the mirror with my hand on my heart, and say that I'd done everything in my power to swim the length of Ireland and raise as many charitable donations as possible. I came up short. Despite failing, I wasn't ashamed. I didn't feel like a loser. I thought back to the struggles of the opening pool sessions and looked at the vastness of Dundrum Bay. The giant lighthouse I swam past was now just a tiny pin on the horizon. After a full stop on the project, there was a second to pause and reflect on the journey, the transformation I had achieved, and the hurdles I'd jumped. Although the adventure didn't go swimmingly, it was a whole lot better to create something than do nothing at all. I knew Dad would have been proud of my ambition, drive, and work ethic, not shamefaced because of the defeat. I realised that once you strive to do your best, though it may be a loss on paper and some may see you as a loser, you can be satisfied once you've given your all. I would never be the same whole again without my dad, but as my tears dried in the heat, I felt inner peace from striving.

Mary Lou

Though the challenge was dead in the water, Seamus offered to support me for one more swim. If this was it, I wanted to know that I'd got as far as possible. I grabbed the opportunity. One more swim would mean one more post online that could create the potential for more donations to charity. One more swim would mean ending on a high and crossing Dundrum Bay, not finishing with an RNLI rescue from the middle of the bay and a sinking boat.

Seamus welcomed Michelle and me aboard his small fishing trawler *Mary Lou*. Because of the harbour's tidal nature, I only had a three-hour swim window, so I had to make do.

It was a surreal swim, chasing a fishing vessel on a Friday afternoon with two locals giving up their time to allow a stranger to inch forwards.

With just under eleven kilometres swam, I climbed aboard. Seamus and Michelle looked like giddy school kids.

'What's gotten into you two?' I said.

'We didn't want to tell you when you were in the water, but you had company for the last thirty minutes.'

'Seals again?'

'A massive humpback whale! The size of a bus!' said Michelle.

'I've been on these waters my entire life and never seen anything like it! It was incredible! Incredible,' Seamus said.

'What, like a hundred metres away?'

'More like ten, pal.'

The thought of being swallowed by Moby Dick or a breaching whale landing on me would have been too much to handle. I was glad they had only told me this after the swim, allowing me to maximise progress in blissful ignorance.

This swim route was formidable even with the best support boat and crew. It was impossible with no team on the way, and a destroyed support boat. On day thirty, with only four days of swimming in the previous fourteen, I threw in the towel and had to take the long and lonely bus home to the finish line. For my efforts and the volunteers' efforts, donors enabled my family and me to hand the Irish Heart Foundation and Solas Cancer Support Centre a cheque for €12,655.81.

In my defeat, Jeremy Lyons, an Irish sprint coach, messaged me Theodore Roosevelt's moving 1910 'Citizenship in a Republic' speech:

'It is not the critic who counts; not the man who points out how the strong man stumbles, or where the doer of deeds could have done them better. The credit belongs to the man who is actually in the arena, whose face is marred by dust and sweat and blood; who strives valiantly; who errs, who comes short again and again because there is no effort without error and shortcoming; but who does actually strive to do the deeds; who knows great enthusiasms, the great devotions; who spends himself in a worthy cause; who at the best knows in the end the triumph of high achievement, and who at the worst, if he fails, at least fails while daring greatly, so that his place shall never be with those cold and timid souls who neither know victory nor defeat.'

I welled up reading it. I still do. Roosevelt hit the nail on the head. Don't allow the fear of failure to incapacitate you, because even defeat is better than cowering in bubble wrap your entire life. And if you want to achieve anything substantial, you must be willing to endure criticism, sniggers, failure, and rejection.

END OF ATTEMPT ONE

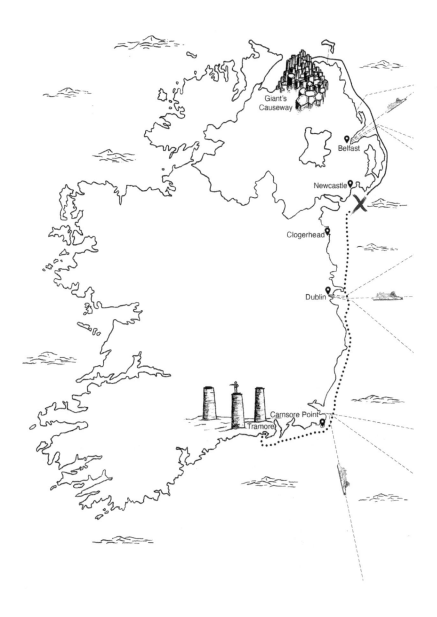

Dad and me at the finish of my thirty-fifth marathon in as many days, 2012. Credit: Noel Browne.

Celebrating my Cardiff University masters graduation with Dad in 2013. Credit: Mam.

Irish Heart Foundation's charity fight night while on the dole, 2013.

Dad, Deirdre, Evan, me, and Mam at Euro 2016, Ireland vs Belgium, Bordeaux, France.

Mam, Evan, and me at the start of my swim from the Giant's Causeway in May 2017.

Leaving Glenarm Marina with Tim Haines and Paul McCarroll. Credit: Darren Doheny.

In Portaferry with Derrick 'Skinner' O'Neill and Gavin Downey.

Seamus McConkey rescuing my sunken support vessel in Newcastle.

Mo and Mam keeping an eye on a seaside training swim. Credit: David Murphy.

Adapting to the perishing Irish waves. Credit: David Murphy.

Kaja on her kayak in Ballycastle, June 2019, on our launch week.

Mam and me at the start of my second attempt, June 2019.

Chris Tweed and me, June 2019, Dundrum Bay, County Down, with the Mourne Mountains in the background.

Tim Atkins, Kaja, Gavin Downey, and me, in Carlingford Marina.

Jonathan Dunne and Ciarán O'Hanlon making our passage plan towards Dublin.

Kaja and me in Wexford after our sixteen-kilometre unsupported leg.

The grind. Credit: JJ Rolfe and EIR.

Cheque presentation: Deirdre, Aoibhe, Me, Jamie, Evan, and Mam. Credit: Garrett FitzGerald Photography.

PART THREE

UNSINKABLE II

EIGHT
Sink to Swim Law

Win or Lose: Learn

I returned to my local authority town planner nine-to-five in London. Confronting the civilised office was strange. You get oddly used to the turmoil and excitement of the sea and the edginess of the cold. The cushioned chair in the air-conditioned open-plan office felt too comfortable. But, like with anything, you settle back in time.

There were no more extreme fifteen or twenty-plus hours of training per week. I hung my wetsuit in the wardrobe and returned to my routine of working, socialising, tipping away in the gym, and Netflix binges with housemates.

A year after the mega sea swim, my local radio station in Waterford, WLR FM, asked me if I'd help them create a radio documentary about open-water swimming. They wanted to interview a speedo-wearing channel swimmer, a 365-day-a-year sea dipper, and me, whatever I was.

I went home to Ireland for a long weekend and popped into the radio studio for my 9 a.m. interview. I only remember the interviewer's final two questions.

'So, what did you learn?'

'Open-water swimming is freezing, and people who do it without a wetsuit are nuts.'

I stand by my statement, though I wish I'd risen earlier, had my Americano, and given a more insightful answer. Truth be told, I hadn't taken the time and energy to reflect on my failure and its lessons in the months prior. I had nothing wiser on the tip of my tongue. I'd lost, chalked it down to a memorable experience, and carried on with life the best I could.

'And would you do it all again?'

'Ah, I suppose I'd go back and do it again, yeah.'

Feck, did I just say that on the radio? The idea of returning to retry the challenge hadn't crossed my mind in the previous twelve months. I was back focused on career progression. Without consideration or hesitation, I'd just blurted out a *yes* as cool as a cucumber.

Those two damn questions lived rent-free in my head, repeatedly playing throughout the following week. They bugged me to the point where, sitting at my kitchen table, I took out the A4 refill pad and biro, and scribbled down what went tits-up with my first attempt. The exercise raised six major flags:

1. The boat sank.
2. I ran out of support crew.
3. I relied too heavily on the volunteers for health and safety.
4. I stressed my mam to high heavens, which distressed my brother and made me doubt my actions.
5. I'm petrified when I'm miles offshore and alone.
6. I'm a wuss when it comes to cold water.

It's not much use pointing out a heap of flaws unless you bring some value to the equation, reflect on the experience, and suggest informed solutions. In winning or losing, reflection is integral to learning and improving, and something I should have done sooner.

Relying on unknown RIB owners via a go-between had left me hanging high and dry. That mistake had forced a brash decision to buy a dud RIB at the last second to salvage the attempt. I reasoned I could overcome this error if I prioritised getting a more substantial support boat early doors without an intermediary. It would be less likely to end on the rocks if I ensured a mechanic fine-tuned it well before the start.

Sean Conway's 2013 Speedo-sponsored length-of-Britain swim had a twenty-seven-foot supporting sailboat, and Maghnus and David's 2015 Costcutter-sponsored around-Ireland swim attempt had a thirty-eight-foot supporting sailboat.

As I considered my options, Ross Edgley had just begun his summer 2018 Red Bull-funded around-Britain swim.

'Look at the size of this monstrous ship, Tommy!' I said to my flatmate.

The goliath sponsor had chartered Ross a fifty-two-foot *mega*-catamaran and professional crew skippered by Matt Knight. The contrast between the jet skis and Red Bull Matadors stunt pilots doing loop-the-loops in the sky over a swimming fitness model was gas compared to my all-expense-spared *Fawlty Towers* show.

I'd have to go big or go home. I'd need to find a sailboat unless I wanted this variable to sink the project again. That would solve the problem of getting to and paying for accommodation and remove the need for a support car.

Hiring a sailboat skipper could cost €200 per day, plus travel and food expenses. That would be more than €12,000 over sixty days. I'd need to find a volunteer skipper and crew, but that was still a significant question mark that I couldn't control too much. My endeavour had more credibility than before, having swum nearly halfway and raised €12,656 for charity. The concept and fundraising tally became tangible. On the face of it, sailing seemed more appealing than asking boating people to sit in an itsy-bitsy open-top inflatable boat that doubled as an ice bath. If I shouted louder and longer and had a proper support vessel in advance, I could increase the odds of enticing more volunteers to join the team effort.

I could attend courses and take more responsibility for the health and safety of the crew and me. It's always beneficial to have more than one person knowing first aid, sea survival skills, and how to use the VHF radio.

Mammy Marie would only be relaxed if I maintained a typical, 'sensible' lifestyle. I could never alleviate all the risks and worry, but with a sturdy vessel, experienced sailors, and safety qualifications to my name, I could reduce her blood pressure by a smidgen.

Though the deep blue often frightened me, I convinced myself to stick it out for over 200 kilometres. The longer the challenge continued, the more comfortable and confident I became offshore. Maybe I could ease the anxiety if I found a support kayaker to paddle alongside me. Fear of open water wasn't a red flag that would stop me from entering the sea again.

On my first attempt, I'd taken about three weeks to acclimatise to the freezing environment. Although stressed to the gills, it had assured me I could power through if needs must. If I were to layer in more specific cold adaption training, refine my gear, and start the next attempt later in the year – when the sea temperature had warmed a degree or two – I could make this variable less traumatic.

I thought my physical readiness was where it needed to be. My body could swim for five hours per day in the sea. Swimming was much kinder to my musculoskeletal system than running con-secutive marathons. I didn't have to bear the brunt of my weight landing on concrete 50,000 times a day. Because of the limiting weather conditions during multi-stage sea swims, there would always be rest days for my body to recoup. I knew the training plan worked – rinse and repeat.

With thoughts written in plain black-and-white, I concluded that my swimming, fears, or sensitivity to the cold wouldn't pre-vent success. With tighter organising, I could resolve the boat and crew issues, and solve the puzzle; and with better readiness, I could give my family more peace of mind. There was only one way to find out: try again.

Shogun of Lorne

This was in June 2018. I decided that I would re-attempt the swim from the Giant's Causeway in June 2019. Instead of only eight months to prepare, like my first attempt, I had the whole year this time.

Finding a suitable support boat was my priority. It turned out that buying a sailboat or renting one for sixty days costs a bomb, roughly €20,000. I didn't train for the first three months. Instead, I focused my lunch, evening, and weekend hours on trying to get corporate sponsors to help with the increased costs. I was somewhat hopeful. I'd accepted not attracting funding when I was a twenty-year-old, non-marathon-running student asking for sponsorship to run a lap of Ireland. I'd been too big of an unknown, and companies hadn't taken me seriously. With that project's success on my CV, I thought I'd have better results for the unprecedented 2017 sea swim, but no joy. Now, with €30,000 raised for charity, the 1,500-kilometre run completed, a decent 210-kilometre first swim attempt, and media exposure to point to, a business might want to join my adventure and back me.

I followed Fiona Quinn on Instagram. She was trying to become the first person to stand up paddleboard (SUP) from Land's End to John O'Groats – the length of Britain. Like the multi-stage sea swimmers, she had a thirty-two-foot sailboat alongside her.

'Do you think you might be selling the boat afterwards?' I asked her.

'I am, actually.'

I ran the boat's specs past Tim Haines from week one of the 2017 swim.

'It looks perfect for what we want, mate. It's got Fiona from Cornwall to Scotland, too, so it's at least tried and tested. Get it surveyed first, though.'

Still, I couldn't afford the price tag of £17,500 (roughly €20,500). My weeks of sponsorship requests were going nowhere. Running a lap of Ireland, swimming from Antrim to Down, and raising tens of thousands of euros were irrelevant to companies that were more interested in the number of social media followers I had – or didn't have, in my case.

Fiona paddled the length of Britain by sea, while Cal Major mostly took inland waterways and narrowly beat her to the title of the first person to SUP the length of Britain.

By August, Fiona's sailboat – *Shogun of Lorne* – was in Portishead Quay Marina, Bristol. I still had no sponsors and needed to make a decision. Given what I was attempting, a boat surveyor offered to waive the £700 inspection fee. Standing in my shirt and tie outside my employer's office, I got a phone call from the surveyor.

'I've had a look at her. She's a lovely vessel. There are no defects of note, and I think the price is fair market value. She's ideal for your swim.'

With no interest from businesses and my mind set on trying again, I took the financially irresponsible decision to take out a bank loan for £13,000 and used savings to make up the difference.

With my poker chips shoved to the centre of the table, I thought I'd better tell my girlfriend, Karolína, affectionately called Kaja [kai-ya]. We'd just become a couple before my first swim attempt, so she had a fair idea of the potential hazards of dating me.

'Eh, remember that NOLS wilderness course you wanted to do but couldn't afford, with the sea kayaking and hiking?'

'Yeah, what about it?'

'Well, I might have an alternative that won't cost you a penny.'

'I'm listening.'

'Well, I've decided to go back and try to swim the length of Ireland next summer, and thought you might be interested in doing some courses with me and maybe being my safety kayaker?'

'Yeah, sure.'

'Huh? Really? I wasn't expecting an answer straight away. Just think it over a bit first, yeah?'

'I want to do it.'

'It's going to be intense, with a lot of training and—'

'Do you want me to come or not?'

'Yeah, that's why I'm asking, but—'

'I'm saying yes. And maybe best not to tell Marie until things are organised, hmm?'

'I'm not taking that as your final answer until you mull it over a week or two, so zero pressure. If you're still keen after that, I'll start booking safety courses for us. Yeah, I was thinking the same about Mam. Give her enough time to digest the news, but not too much time to be overthinking it.'

It was a shot in the dark since Karolína wasn't a kayaker. Kaja's enthusiasm to jump in surprised me. She took no dissuading, and two weeks later, I signed us up for a two-day kayaking course in London. We got the fundamentals down and earned our British Canoeing Two-Star Award. In the meantime, Bantry Bay Canoes agreed to support us by sponsoring her with a kayak and kayaking clothing. The train was out of the station and picking up steam.

Best Laid Plans

By September, I had exchanged contracts with Fiona, and I was the reluctant owner of a thirty-two-foot sailboat that amassed hefty fees to float in Bristol. Wexford County Council in the southeast of Ireland was happy to sponsor a mooring for the year if I could get *Shogun of Lorne* across the Irish Sea. With the mechanic's full-service charge and steep mooring fees, I leapt straight at the council's generosity.

I contacted Fiona's insurance broker to set up boat cover in my name. Straightforward, you would think, since it's the same boat, the same year, and the same set-up with crew popping in to sail.
'It's not good news. I'm afraid the policy we offered Fiona when she had the boat is not being offered again, and they're the only insurance company I work with that provides that kind of cover.'
They suggested another broker, but that broker said no, and referred me to someone else. *Surely to God, someone will insure me if Fiona's annual coverage was about £300.* I followed that lead and tried ten insurance brokers in the UK and Ireland, but none would give me a quote. Some said they didn't have a market for that type of cover. Some had issues with me relying on an alternating team of volunteers to take the helm since I wasn't a sailor. Some had problems with my English address since the boat would be moored in Northern Ireland and the Republic of Ireland as we moved around the coast.
Spending more lunch breaks sitting on hold, just to be repeatedly declined, felt like an utter waste of energy. After the tenth

failed attempt, I concluded I was uninsurable. Sailboats are unlike cars because there's no legal requirement to insure yachts. The rejections weren't fatal, but they meant there would be a significant financial risk. I had to quit on my dream and try to re-sell the sailboat or trust in the volunteer sailors to take care of my property. I was too invested to back out and fail because of bureaucracy, so I chanced my arm.

Tim, who drove the RIB on attempt one, and his sailing friend, Mark Samson, were up for sailing *Shogun* from the UK to Ireland. They had drawn up a passage plan and completed weather checks in advance. We aimed to leave Bristol on Saturday morning, get across St George's Channel overnight to New Ross, County Wexford, and fly back to the UK on Sunday evening to make it to work on Monday.

It was my first ever time on a sailboat. 'Welcome aboard … *my* sailing boat?' I said when Tim and Mark approached with their loaded gear bags on Saturday morning.

'It certainly looks much more promising than the last boat you welcomed me onto,' Tim said. 'You should've seen the RIB, Mark.'

I led them down the timber ladder below deck. At the front of the boat was a two-person cabin; well, more of a poky, V-shaped coffin that made a tent look luxurious. It was wall-to-wall upholstered cushions on top of storage compartments, with just enough headspace to sit upright. When lying down, my head touched one wall while my feet touched the opposite one.

Two blue cushioned benches lined the walls of the middle cabin. These seats doubled as sleeping spaces. A mahogany table ran along the centre, folded down to allow us to shuffle from one end of the boat to the other. In one corner was a gas stove-top with two rings, a fridge that didn't work, and a sink the size of a bucket. The workstation in the corner reminded me of an architect's bench – a sizeable wooden desk to spread maps across and a seat. It wasn't any old chair, but one stuffed with flares, an abandon-ship bag, and boat tools.

We had a toilet the size of a hot press and another claustrophobia-inducing box with two sleeping spaces and a ceiling hovering just inches from the occupant's resting eyes.

We unfurled the docking ropes and departed without delay on our precision-planned operation.

Tim took the tiller. 'Just to warn you, Al, it's going to get bumpy. The forecast has gotten worse over the last two days. If I hadn't seen the misery you endured on the swim, I'd be telling you to sit this one out.'

We meandered around the harbour's motionless water to the lock that released us to the sea. Under the gentle rattle of the engine, I looked out on the Bristol Channel towards Ireland. I slathered on my sunscreen as we relaxed on the deck. *I could get used to this sailing craic. It's pretty nice.*

Once into the Bristol Channel, Tim and Mark killed the engine and hoisted the sails. The boat bolted from its calm horizontal axis, and my insides jumped like speeding over a hump in the road. *We're goners.*

'Is this normal, lads?' I said, flinging my hands out on either side like Stretch Armstrong and grabbing the railing.

'Is what normal?'

'This crazy angle? Jesus. Feels like we're going to tip.'

'This is sailing, mate.' Tim laughed. 'What were you expecting?'

'I dunno, something like the ferry. This feels all kinds of wrong.'

'You'll get used to it. Focus on the horizon if you start feeling seasick.'

The waves increased their might as a black blanket rolled over the late evening sky. Tim and Mark took shifts to sail into the night, slowly zigging and zagging across the channel and past Cardiff. I was the deck boy, ready to come when the skippers needed an extra pair of hands.

I crawled into my tomb at the front of the boat and slid the timber panel shut. I felt seasick for the first time in my life, wrapped in my sleeping bag, driven demented by powerful waves smashing inches from my terrified head. The winds whipped the sails and rattled the rigging. The front of the boat dipped into troughs and ramped up waves before gravity slammed it down with a thunderous thud that shook everything and everybody on board. A hundred litres of water splashed down on my roof. *Christ, please don't sink.*

After a few hours of sweating, tensing, and thinking we would capsize at any moment, I drifted off.

Freezing water drenched me. I shot up and knocked myself down, cracking my head against the ceiling. *We're sinking! Is this a nightmare?* The crashing waves and whipping sails all sounded louder. It was pitch black, and I was disoriented. I tasted the salt water dripping down my terror-stricken face. I tried to sit up again, but a wave rolled me. Another tub of ice water splashed over me. I gasped. My eyes adjusted to the darkness. The force of nature and a dodgy handle had ripped my ceiling hatch open as I slept. I pulled the roof light shut and tried not to puke. *Get me off this yoke.* I was at my wit's end.

With no hope of sleep, I changed into dry waterproofs, clipped my lifejacket on, and inched like a legless drunk towards the deck, grabbing objects in the black as the sea thrashed us about. My stomach turned to mush during the few feet of travel to the exit stairs.

'I know you said it would be bumpy, but are we all good being out here in this?' I asked Mark.

'Yeah, just big seas. It's grimmer than anticipated, but *Shogun* can handle it. Would you mind bringing me up some seasickness pills and keeping me company for a bit? I've crewed loads of yacht races but haven't felt this ill before.'

It was 4 a.m., and raining cats and dogs from the moonless sky. The only colour came from the green and red navigation lights illuminating our position from the top of our mast. I clipped my lifejacket's safety line to the deck to avoid being lost in the stormy abyss and climbed on deck. In the inky darkness, there was no horizon to look at to ease my wishy-washy belly, so I popped some seasick tablets, too.

'That front cabin's taken the brunt of it. Worse than a bloody rollercoaster. I was waiting for a wave to smash through the hull! It's a fair bit better back here.'

There was no response. I turned to Mark, whose head had slumped. He'd dozed off but still had hold of the tiller. An invisible wave struck the boat and frigid spray drenched us like the front row at Sea World. Mark's eyes jumped open.

'Tim! You're up. I'm sleeping at the wheel.'

Tim looked as restless and sick as I felt, appearing from his cabin and poking his head from the entrance hatch.

'Alright, boys. Is anyone else feeling ill? I never feel seasick. This is rough by any standard. How're you coping?'

'I'm bricking it, Tim,' I said. 'That box up the front is pure torture.'

Daylight broke, and we could now at least see the waves gunning for us. We were off the coast of Pembrokeshire, at the end of the Bristol Channel and the start of St George's Channel.

'I think we'll have to call it and abort,' said Tim. 'Some of these waves are fifteen feet. If we go any further, we're committed to the crossing. Given the conditions and forecast and last night's slow progress, it will be miserable, and we might still miss those flights you booked. What do you want to do, Al?'

'If you think it's safe enough and there's a decent shot of making the flights, then I'm happy to plough on,' I told them, 'but if it's sketchy or we won't be back for work on Monday, then just err on the side of caution.'

Mark and Tim consulted the charts, the forecast apps, and their notes. 'Right, best we turn in here to Milford Haven.'

After thirty-six hours of sailing, the second attempt at the swimming project picked up on a similar note to the first attempt.

We diverted in hairy conditions to Wales. We were bruised but lived to fight another day. Part of me was delighted not to spend another night on rough seas. The rest of me stressed the logistics and cost implications – losing three flights, hiring a car rental back to London, Milford mooring fees, and paying a Royal Yacht Association (RYA) certified Yachtmaster to complete the crossing later. An extra thousand euros gone. Poof.

I hired Fiona Quinn's support skipper, John Patrick, to transfer *Shogun* from Wales to Ireland. Once she was docked in New Ross, I recruited a local marine handyman to winterproof and babysit *Shogun* until June. One job done.

Breaking News

After a year out of the water, I returned to pool training in September 2018. Before the mileage and time requirements consumed my mornings and evenings, I pursued several safety qualifications with Kaja.

We passed our November RYA marine radio licence exam and earned the RYA first-aid certificate.

In December, we received our advanced expedition (REC-4) first-aid qualification after a weekend of training in the field and classroom. We obtained our RYA Offshore Safety and Sea Survival credentials after another two days of lectures and training pool exercises.

From radioing the emergency services for assistance to administering defibrillators and CPR, extinguishing fires, and flipping capsized life rafts, Kaja and I learned to be a self-sufficient adventure team. The work gave me peace of mind that we could handle trouble ourselves without overdependence on the volunteer crew for all things health and safety.

In the lead-up to my lap-of-Ireland run, I'd helped establish an annual charity football tournament with my childhood club, Tramore AFC. In 2012, all donations had gone to my chosen charities – my dad and Ophir Zardok's Football Village of Hope, the NRH's stroke unit, and the Irish Heart Foundation's stroke awareness campaign. The local fundraiser continued and grew each year because of the hard work of the dedicated club members, injecting funds into several charities and sporting causes. In 2018, Tramore AFC was once again delighted to host the Christmas tournament in aid of my chosen charities.

With the sailboat docked in New Ross, a mechanic on maintenance duty, five qualifications in my back pocket, and a public fundraiser scheduled, I had to break the bad news to my mam before she heard from someone else.

'You're not serious. I don't believe it. It's all too dangerous.'

'Hear me out. I have a full-on sailboat this time instead of a RIB. Karolína's going to kayak beside me. We're after doing our kayaking qualification, two first-aid courses, offshore safety, and sea survival courses. We got our walkie-talkie licence, too, so we can radio shore and the boat. There's no stone unturned this time around.'

'You're going to get yourself hurt. And now Karolína, too? Don't be putting yourself in harm's way again.'

'Tramore's doing the Christmas football blitz for the charities, so I just wanted you to hear it from me and let you know I'm doing everything in my power to complete it safer and faster than the last time.'

'And what about your job?'

My mother had earned her Biomedical Science degree and had begun her career as a laboratory technician in the health service straight out of university, working in the same haematology lab her entire working life. She valued security and familiarity – nothing wrong with that. Her admirable mission as a mammy was to get her sons educated and into secure jobs so we could fend for ourselves. Deviation from this straight path stresses her out. There's too much risk in leaving public-sector employment.

She wasn't alone. Several friends questioned my career risk when they learned of my swim, concerned about me taking months away from the desk. They were often speechless that I'd hand in my notice to pursue an unpaid – worse yet, costly – passion project.

I didn't have any of that career fear. I'd worked in sports factories, counting jerseys and lifting boxes for minimum wages. I'd scrubbed pots and pans in sweaty kitchens, been on the dole, and worked an unpaid internship. The world didn't end. After those tough jobs, I studied for five years and earned a degree and a master's to have the safety net of better-paid job prospects. What's the point in building a safety net if you don't swing from the trapeze at least once? As Matthew McConaughey eloquently said in *Greenlights*, 'Fuck the box; I'm going for the experience.'

If there was ever a time to strike, I thought that time was now – no kids, no mortgage, full health, and enough work experience to surpass the cesspit of entry-level jobs. I just reasoned I'd get another job, and didn't understand the fuss. Friends looked at me as though I had two heads. I was away with the fairies. It was the same look my mam gave me when I explained my rationale.

'What if jobs dry up or the economy tanks when you're gallivanting, like what happened to Ev?'

Ev had got his college education and had begun his graduate environmental health officer job in the public sector. His college class had kept working, but my brother had decided to travel for a year, seeing Cape Town, South East Asia, Australia, and Las Vegas. Then the 2008 recession hit. When he returned, half of Ireland was unemployed. Ev moved home with Mam and Dad and joined the dole line that snaked around the corner. He eventually found work with the only employer in town, the call centre, listening to complaints until the cows came home.

'Do you regret it? Not staying working and skipping all that dole and call centre shite?' I asked my brother.

'Not at all. I had the time of my life. Ask anyone from my class. They all wished they had travelled in their twenties. Now they're in their thirties and mortgaged to their gills, most with kids, and they can't go backpacking.'

'If the job market sinks,' I said to Mam, 'I'd be fired anyway. In that scenario, I may as well be an unemployed town planner who swam the length of Ireland and raised thousands for charity.'

If I wanted to race up the corporate hierarchy, the swim wasn't the wisest decision, but fast-tracking my way to CEO status wasn't my priority at twenty-eight. I had my whole life to sit at a desk, or I might drop dead tomorrow. I wanted to use my health, freedom, and savings to be more than a job.

'And how are you going to pay for it all?' Mam said, giving up on the safety and career argument, since she knew she was talking to the wall.

It wasn't unusual for my peers to have substantial student loans, mortgages, car loans, and wedding and honeymoon loans. Those debts are kosher. In terms of my cost, my only debt was the sailboat. That put me in the loony bin category, apparently. I planned to get most, if not all, of that money back when I sold the support boat after the challenge. My only significant expense was rent for my room in London, and I'd cover that by subletting it when I was away and hoping the tenant would shag off when I returned.

My mam was looking for any and every reason for me to change my mind. She had valid questions and was worried for me. That's her job as an Irish mammy. You'd be foolish not to consider the risks. There're limits to that, though. There are risks of sitting 'safely' in your job, at the cost of all the other experiences you're missing. I knew that if I got to a ripe old age to sit and reminisce on my deathbed, I'd kick myself for choosing three months of employment over three months of challenging myself to swim around Ireland. Sometimes you have to do what's best for your *soul*, and this sea swim lit mine up like fireworks in the night sky.

'Besides, Mam, didn't I start and finish school early? I was in university at seventeen and never took a gap year. Don't be stressing over a few weeks. I'm a few years ahead of the rat race.'

Mam turned and walked away, shaking her head. 'Oh, look, you have an answer for everything. I don't want to hear anymore.'

I think she regretted taking me to swimming lessons for all those years as a kid. *That went as well as it could have*, I thought, *onwards and upwards*.

Although my dad was my biggest supporter for my marathon running project, I think he would have sided with my mam on this one. He feared and respected the sea, never going beyond his depth. He couldn't swim and joked that he only ever managed to float in the Dead Sea.

When I was around nine, he gave in to my nagging and took Ev and me on a pedal boat rental from Nissi Beach, Ayia Napa, Cyprus.

'Can we go out a bit deeper? We're nearly on the beach.'

'Okay, but stay put, Al.'

I took the opportunity to wind him up a little.

'Sit down, good boy.'

I left my seat, climbed to the back, and stood on the edge to assess the depth.

'Sit back down. We're out too far. Just sit, c'mon, good man.'

I jumped in.

'Alan!'

I splashed about for a few seconds, then stood up, laughing, with the sea around my waist. 'You should have seen your face.'

Ev laughed with me. 'He got you there, Dad.'

'Don't be encouraging him.' Dad smiled. 'I'll kill ya. Give up your blaggarding and come help pedal.'

With the news broken to my family, the local football tournament kicked off with my childhood club raising €2,535 for the Irish

Heart Foundation and Solas Cancer Support Centre.

Cold Tank

At the start of 2019, I scheduled an appointment with one of the UK's leading extreme environments experts. Kaja and I boarded the morning's first train from London to meet with Dr Heather Massey in the University of Portsmouth's laboratory. As well as being a renowned researcher, Dr Massey has swum the English Channel and competed in the World Ice Swimming Championships. If there was anybody I could learn from, it was her.

I hadn't been in cold water for eighteen months. Dr Massey turned the lab's cold-water tank down to a chilly 12°C (54°F) and wanted me to swim for forty-five minutes. By January, I was still six months away from my length-of-Ireland sea swim, and my training volume in the steaming leisure centre was only getting going. Not only did I have to swim in front of an expert, but I'd arranged for videographer Connor Cleary to capture the moment for my *Unsinkable* documentary film. My stomach was a wreck en route to the lab, butterflies whizzing around like before a big exam. I doubted my abilities, and dreaded the cold water tasering me.

When Kaja and I arrived, Dr Massey handed me a wire. At one end was a chunky power connector to attach to a computer and at the other was a rounded piece of plastic no thicker than a mobile phone's charger cable.

'I'll need you to pop this up your backside to monitor your body's core temperature.'

There's nothing like a cable in the arse to add to the morning's discomfort.

'Oh, and Alan, not the thick plug end, the skinny wire end. I didn't think that needed explaining, but I recently had someone come out of the changing room and hand me the wiry end after they'd inserted the plug.'

The six-metre testing pool was above ground, with glass windows for observation. I stepped into the tank, and became a seal in the aquarium. I felt stable, the wetsuit working its insulating magic as the jets at the top of the tank generated a tide to swim against.

'In your own time, Alan. Whenever you're ready.'

I submerged my head and swam. Six strokes in, I stopped in a panic and retreated to the edge of the tank to catch my breath. I bottled it, the natural flight response taking over. *Deep breaths. Relax yourself. You're fine. You've done this before, and you'll do it again. Come on.*

'Do you want to come out?'

'No, no. I just need to relax a tick. I'll be grand in a sec.'

On my next go, I managed to override my body's natural reflex to escape. The sensory attacks still enveloped me, but I focused on a long glide, allowing time to rotate onto my side for deep breaths to fill my lungs. After ten minutes, I was in the groove, and by the end, I wanted to keep going to accumulate more cold-water time.

Delighted with overcoming the morning's fear and adversity, I sat down for a debrief.

'That went well, besides the little wobble at the start. That's to be expected,' Dr Massey said. 'We've studies to show you can actually dull that initial heart rate spike and uncontrolled gasping response by about fifty per cent with just six cold-water training dips. You could use the Serpentine Lake in Hyde Park. Get in gradually, keeping your head above the water, and jump out once your breathing is under control. It will only take one to three minutes to catch your breath. That's enough time to make your body adapt to the cold shock response. The start of your swims will be far less stressful and taxing with some practice.'

'Really? Only six dips to adapt? Could I use a shower instead of trekking to the lake?'

'Cold showers can help, but they're not as effective because they don't cool the skin as much or as quickly as being submerged. And once you've habituated to cold water by repeating immersions, the reduction in the cold shock response remains for quite some time. We've done a study that found cold shock response can still be reduced by twenty-five per cent after fourteen months, even if you haven't been in cold water all that time.'

Under doctor's orders, I dragged myself from beneath my toasty blanket and rode my motorbike to Hyde Park on a nippy Saturday morning before the open-air Serpentine Lido closed to swimmers at 9:30 a.m.

A blanket of withered brown leaves covered the grass. A line of bare London plane, oak, and chestnut trees divided the shark-grey lake and sky. Standing out amidst the drab winter scene were snow-white swans gliding on the water past bobbing seagulls. Dogs barked. Blackbirds crowed. The park was almost void of people, except in the one-hundred-metre swimming cordon where one-piece-wearing women readied themselves on the banks to join the sets of stroking arms front crawling and breaststroking past the ducks. Morning walkers in down jackets, scarfs, hats, and gloves paused with raised eyebrows to observe the spectacle and to ensure they hadn't imagined the lunacy.

Removing four layers and undressing down to my shorts, I regretted asking Dr Massey for her professional opinion.

I scurried over to a dripping swimmer drying off on the lake's edge. 'Do you know the temperature of the lake?'

'Three-point-nine degrees today. The air's about the same, I think. It's up on Twitter every morning. Enjoy.'

The idea of enjoying 3.9°C (39°F) water seemed odd, but the regulars seemed unfazed. They strolled down the ramp without hesitation and began their lengths. Simples.

The water was more than four degrees lower than I'd experienced before. I should have begun in the summertime and allowed my body to adjust to the lowering temperature as the seasons changed. Getting into the lake in the heart of winter was a ruthless assault in broad daylight. The lake knocked the stuffing out of me and transformed me into a huffing and puffing blowfish on speed. The cold seared my skin, and the pain increased as the blood fled from my extremities to protect my vital organs. I lasted the three minutes as prescribed, enduring the inner bedlam until my breathing returned to normal. I dunked my head and didn't dilly-dally a second longer.

Kaja chuckled. 'You look like a lobster.'

Three minutes was enough to burn my skin bright red from the neck down. I dried my water-kissed body and dressed as quick as a wink before heading to the heated pool to clock my day's training mileage which I finished off with a cold shower.

The Déise

From January to March, my training efforts continued to build. The investment in underwater headphones paid off. I listened to an entire Jo Nesbø audiobook as I completed my longest swim – 600 lengths, covering fifteen kilometres in six hours. After several marathon training swims, it was time to tell my town planning manager about my plans to try again.

'Sorry, Steve, but I'm going to give you my notice. I know it's only a week I have to give, but don't worry, I'm not planning on going anywhere for the next three months, so you've plenty of time to find my replacement.'

'Wow.' He smiled, then paused. 'Well, how long do you think it'll take you?'

'Three months, I'd say, allowing some time to get organised beforehand and a little break afterwards.'

'If you could, would you want to come back and still work here?'

'Yeah, a hundred per cent, but I don't want to take the piss.'

'Look, by the time I'd advertise your job, do all the interviews, and help to train them up; it'll take months. I'm happy to hold your position if we can keep you.'

With that great news, I told the public about attempt two and advertised the charity's donation link.

London's Royal Docks opened in April, and Kaja and I tested our kayaking and swimming teamwork in open water. Bar a bump here or there, we worked well together, lapping the 750-metre course and some dead rats. Meanwhile, finding sailing volunteer after sailing volunteer through social media appeals, I steadily filled my spreadsheet with six weeks of support cover.

Before I knew it, it was May. I clocked out of work in London for three months of unpaid leave and returned home to the Déise – Waterford, Ireland.

With experience and more preparation time, 2019 was much more organised than 2017. Instead of allowing myself two weeks of sea preparation before the challenge start date, I took four weeks. I used my time to swim my daily mileage in Dunmore East's crystal-clear sea, and followed each session by removing my ROKA Maverick Pro Thermal wetsuit and acclimatised in my shorts. Feeling toughened by my first attempt, I even squeezed in some night-time training swims in the bay to test myself in darkness. Version 2.0 was willing to do what was necessary to increase the chances of completion, and if that meant swimming day and night, so be it.

I saw Ross Edgley and Red Bull's 2018 bells-and-whistles finish for their round-Britain swim. Red Bull organised hundreds of sea swimmers to join Ross in the sea off Margate and swim in with him. I worked full-time on replicating this concept. It was extra work and stress, but I thought a participation finale had the potential to raise a hell of a lot for the charities and could encourage and inspire others to swim. I met local water safety volunteers and prepared my own detailed thirty-page health and safety report to submit to events insurance companies and Waterford City and County Council. They approved my work. I just needed to pay up €1,500 and declare the start time and date at least one week before the finale. I pitched my final event to EIR, a national telecom provider, and secured their sponsorship for the finale event.

My mam helped me spit-shine the sailboat, and move all the gear, safety equipment, and the kayak on board. Although Mam was opposed to the challenge because she feared for my safety, she still loved and supported me, willing me to succeed since she knew it meant so much to me.

We scraped the name *Shogun of Lorne* from the rear and sides of the boat with a hairdryer and spatula. It was time for a fitting re-naming. Despite the warnings from the superstitious boating community, I slapped on new stickers and christened her *Unsinkable II*, and we were ready to get the show on the road.

John, who had sailed her for Fiona's British paddleboarding extravaganza and transported the boat across the Irish Sea from Wales earlier in the year, was back in action to skipper the vessel. Two strangers, Charlie and Jim, responded to my advert and joined John to sail *Unsinkable II* to Northern Ireland's north coast.

I led them to the boat. 'There's been a slight rebranding, lads.'

'Jeez, "unsinkable", said Jim, 'didn't they say something like that when they launched the *Titanic*?'

I uncoiled the docking line and threw it to Charlie on deck. As John revved the engines to depart, Mam and I waved them off from the marina's pontoon. The boat didn't budge.

'All okay, John? What's up?'

'She's stuck in the muck.'

'Ah for …'

With the tide low, the deep pointing keel fin had stuck in the river's swampy bed. Never a dull moment. John pressed the throttle down as I pushed from the pontoon like a rugby player in a scrum.

'Wahay, and you're off.' I waved. 'Safe trip, men. See you up the north.'

I was relieved to see the back of *Unsinkable II* and have no boat responsibilities for a few days. They sailed her for four days and moored her in Ballycastle on the north coast of Antrim.

Five days before the project start date of 1 June, Kaja and I travelled to Ballycastle to accustom ourselves to our new sleeping quarters. I wanted to be well settled by swim time and avoid the first-night effect of having disrupted sleep in a new environment. *It was just as well,* I thought. Rain pinged the boat like hailstones. Wind howled. *Unsinkable II* sploshed and the protective plastic fenders between the sailboat and pontoon squeaked like a hand against a balloon. The sail rigging jingle-jangled like an uncoordinated triangle player on a loop. The sleeping cabin was a coffin with one person in it. With the two of us in there, we contorted our bodies like an opening circus act, our knees and elbows banging if we moved. I was glad my foresight allowed for a settling-in period, not sleeping much until the third night.

Kaja got into her waterproof kayaking rigout, tied her blonde hair into pigtails and stuck on a woolly hat before pulling a snood over her face and hood over her head. She strapped her high-vis floatation vest around her, put on her neoprene booties and gloves, and mounted her kayak. She paddled out of the marina and headed for Ballycastle Beach. I inflated my tow float, jumped into my wetsuit, and jogged around to meet her on the shore. We tested the northern waters so there'd be no surprises this time on day one when I leapt from the Giant's Causeway. We practised up and down the beach, where we hoped to pass on day two of the challenge. My cold-water dunks and cold showers had paid off, as the first few minutes passed without much of a shock response. Like my first swim attempt, where all my prep was in the pool, Kaja had done all her kayak training on flat city docklands water. The sea was a new frontier for her. Though it was cold and spitting rain, the winds were kind, and the waves were tiny as we prepared without a blip along the shallows.

On my walk from the beach back to the marina, I bumped into Noel Heary, standing next to his spotless Audi A5. He was a successful business owner in his fifties with silver hair and a holiday tan. Noel had owned a thirty-four-foot yacht and described himself as a cautious skipper. He had booked a week out of his busy schedule to use his sailing qualifications and experiences to get me started on my swim. We were joined later that evening by Chris Tweed, a stocky fireman and mixed martial artist in his mid-thirties. He had sailed since he was a boy and lived on his twenty-six-foot sailboat. I felt like I was in very safe hands.

Emagine and Connor Cleary joined us to capture footage of the first two days for the *Unsinkable* documentary film. Noel treated our gang to dinner, and we were all systems go for the launch.

NINE
Attempt Two
June 2019 – 500 Kilometres Remaining

If at First You Don't Succeed …

It was 1 June 2019, and I stood once more on the volcanic rocks of the Giant's Causeway. Evan and Deirdre were on standby expecting their second child, so they couldn't come to Antrim. I had my mam and cousin Pauline at my side. Emotions ran high, looking offshore where my thirty-two-foot sailboat floated and my partner, Kaja, sat on her kayak, awaiting my arrival. It was a much more reassuring sight than the rickety old RIB filled with litres of water, I'll tell you that much. I'd come such a long way in two years, yet I still choked and was in tears when questioned by the documentary crew about Dad and the meaning behind the project. I'd invested so much in achieving this goal and needed to make the finish line this time and do Dad's memory proud.

'I'll see you in a bit, Mam,' I said, as I stepped to the rock's edge.

I took a moment to take in the scenery of grassy cliffs with a stone crown and flat waters sparkling under the sun's glare. *Let's be havin' ya!*, I thought. I pinched my nose and jumped in fins first. I won the first battle – cold shock conquered through weeks and months of preparation. I cruised towards Kaja with a relaxed breathing and stroke pattern.

'Kajo! Ha ha, we're doing it!' I reached up and clasped her hand. 'How're you feeling on the sea?'

'Much better now I'm on the kayak. I nearly vomited on the sail here. Chris and Noel had to take care of me.'

'Yeah, boats suck. Give me a shout if you're feeling dodgy. Look at that view, though.'

We gave Mam and Pauline an energetic wave as they stood among the throngs of tourists speckled on the rocks.

'Ready to make tracks so?'

'Let's go, whoop, whoop!'

Right stroke, left stroke, rotate, and breathe. Kaja was a comforting sight and presence, reducing my anxiety tenfold, compared to 2017 when I was hundreds of metres adrift from the boat.

A rogue critter attacked my outstretched hand. I jumped out of my skin.

Kaja giggled. 'Did the seaweed bite you? Should I radio for help?'

I chucked the slimy seaweed on her lap in retaliation.

'Al!'

'What? Don't be slagging me panic attacks then,' I said with a smile.

After a dreamy first hour, my mind wobbled as my extremities froze and concern kicked in. The sea temperature was much lower than my training ground long swims, and I was two years out of practice with these sensations. It was all about positive self-talk in this moment. *You've been here before, Al, and swam these seas for five hours. Your feet, legs, hands, and arms are grand. They won't fall off. Just keep her lit. Nice and flowy.*

I focused on following Kaja, always to my right, and popped my head forwards every so often to glimpse the sailboat ahead. Chris and Noel circled now and then to ensure Kaja was doing okay on her first offshore jaunt, reassuring her, and giving directional instructions.

On day one of 2017, I'd swum for three hours and nineteen minutes. I was damn determined to better everything about my first attempt and persevered for four hours.

I climbed up the metal ladder to board the back of the sailboat and fist-bumped Chris and Noel.

'Cheers, men. Thanks for that. Four hours. That's a better start than last time. Chuffed with that.' I stopped my GPS watch and saved the swim data. I took my Personal Locator Beacon (PLB) and mobile from my waterproof tow float and switched their tracking off to keep the backup records. Chris and Noel helped Kaja off the kayak and up the ladder before manhandling the craft onto the deck.

'Great stuff,' I said, kissing her.

'Yuck, so slimy and salty,' she said, wiping her mouth in disgust. 'Happy with today?'

'Yeah, four hours! You were brilliant. Thanks for being here and doing all this.'

Kaja and I climbed below the deck.

'What are you so smiley about?' Kaja said.

'I was just thinking about the freezing wind cutting me to shreds when I used to climb onto the RIB to get changed on the last go. This shelter down here is heaven.'

With the three trackers powered off, I loaded www.marathonman.co to see a visual of my progress on the live map and checked the digits on the GPS app. 'Christ, what happened there?'

'What's up?'

'Ugh, fuck's sake. Look.' I showed Kaja my phone. 'Why were we going north for so long? That's no use going in that direction.' The line travelled east on the map, turned north for ages, and then back east again in the desired direction. 'I'm not having a go at you. I just don't know why the lads sent us that way. We're way behind the marker I set on day one in 2017. Four hours of swimming for eight kilometres, with a heap in the wrong direction? Sure, I'd do ten-K in a pool without a tide behind me; these are the biggest tides we'll get on the entire coast.'

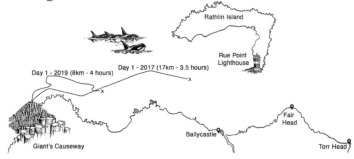

I sulked into the toilet cupboard to wrestle off my wetsuit and text sailor Tim for help.

'Why'd they start you at that time? I'm surprised you didn't go backwards going against that tide,' he replied.

I'd begun swimming at quarter to three in the afternoon on Chris and Noel's instruction. It turned out that I was swimming in slack tide or against the tide until about six.

It was Chris and Noel's first day on the job, and they were volunteering, so I had to be patient, though it was a stark reminder that I could do everything right and still not finish this swim without everyone making the right decisions.

I was tired, irritated, and cold, so I thought it best to enjoy fish and chips in Ballycastle with the team and raise the matter in the morning when we'd be fresh.

I brought take-out coffees and Danishes to Ballycastle's marina for the team, who were just up and moseying around *Unsinkable II*. I hoped the little gesture would start the day on a positive note and make discussing tides and start times easier.

'Here's 2017's swim tracker. That's seventeen-k in three hours and forty minutes. Here's yesterday's tracker with seven-k in four hours; a chunk of that is north, though.'

'Yeah, the tide was being funny. You weren't moving much. We thought you were in an eddy, so we led you into deeper waters, hoping there'd be more of a push east further offshore,' they said. Eddies are anomalies – water currents that flow counter to the prevailing tide because of the lay of the land. 'We'll speak to the local ferryman and sailors around the marina and get it right today. Damn. Sorry about that. That's frustrating now, not getting you off to a better start. We'll fix it.'

'If I'm not moving on future swims, please just give us a shout and let me know,' I said. 'I can't gauge progress down in the water, so I'm relying on you guys to communicate. I'd much rather stop for the day than be stroking away for hours to go nowhere against the tide. Live and learn. We'll dust it off and give it another lash later on.'

Chris and Noel had made an error in their tide checks and swim start time. Everyone makes mistakes; it's human, but what's most important is what you do to fix them. They were visibly annoyed with themselves, clearly wanting to do better. They put themselves about the harbour to get some local information. Their attitude put my mind at ease that I had a team who cared about its performance and would do its best to rectify mistakes.

I'd made the error of delegating tide checks and start times to the sailors, not checking their work, trusting they knew best. From day two onwards, I took more responsibility. I cross-referenced suggested start times against apps and tables, and checked in with Tim to ensure we wouldn't waste more opportunities and energy.

Gale Force & Wild Horses

We left Ballycastle and tumbled around in the waves to the previous day's finish line, confident in the later start time. Chris and Noel navigated the seas from up top while Connor filmed them for the documentary. Kaja and I lay below deck on the benches on either side of the main cabin.

'How are you feeling?'

'Like I'm going to throw up. You?'

'Me too. I'm not sure if we can swim in these … Fuck!' The boat rolled violently to the left. The sea became visible through the rooflight. I shot my arms and legs out wide to prevent myself from ending up in a heap on the floor.

'Are you alright down there? It's going to be a tad bumpy,' Noel said from the helm.

'Define *alright?*'

Sailing was not a hobby Kaja and I were going to pursue. The less time on the boat, the better. It was an odd ratio of ninety per cent slow, boring travel and ten per cent death-defying terror.

'Can you come up on deck when you get a chance, Alan?'

'Coming.'

'What do you think? Have you ever swum in waves like this?' Noel said.

'Nope. The RIB wouldn't have left the marina in these

conditions, and I wouldn't go in waters like this on my own.'

'I don't think we'll get four hours. The wind is due to come up later to a not nice situation. It's a bad idea to put Karolína on the kayak today. Do you want to give it a go, following us on your own?'

'We've come this far; might as well give it a lash if you're certain you can steer a course for me to follow and help me out if needs be.'

Since day one had gone belly-up, I felt I had to push myself on day two. I didn't need to be as cautious as we were in 2017. This time, I had a tow float with my phone, personal locator beacon, live GPS tracker, and snacks. I had Kaja and we'd completed our safety courses. I'd done my cold water prep and bought the best gear to minimise the cold. I went all in on a sturdy boat and found two qualified sailors. The safety net I'd built enabled me to get into more significant swells while feeling relatively safe.

It was too risky to lower the hefty sit-on-top kayak from the deck and get Kaja into it from the rear boat ladder. She sat this one out, nursing a cold. I jumped out of the frying pan and into the fire for a solo battle. Wild white horses whooshed over my head. Boy, did I have a fight on my hands …

There was no capacity to feel the cold or fear the deep, alone, chasing a sailboat towards Rathlin Sound. My brain was as present as possible, homed in on reaching my head above the waves to catch a breath and not lose sight of *Unsinkable II*. It was impossible. The swell hid the boat from my eyes. I only caught glimpses of the top of the mast and my custom Waterford and Ireland ensign flag on every fourth or fifth attempt. Occasionally, *Unsinkable II* would rise to the crest of a wave at the same time as me, and I'd catch the comforting sight of the team on deck.

I swam to the team, noticing we were about three kilometres from Rathlin Island and seven kilometres from the mainland, off our intended course through the centre of the Sound.

'We're too far out! We're getting pushed and pushed and pushed with the tide, wind, and waves,' Chris shouted over the thudding engine. 'Do you want to get a lift back on course? It's up to you now what you want to do, if you want to carry on?'

'Am I getting anywhere today?'

'You're covering lots of miles,' Noel said.

Chris suggested I hop aboard, and we call it a day since we were off-piste with worsening conditions. His option B was for me to climb up, and we'd motor perpendicular to the mainland, and they could dunk me back into the sea in line with where I was but in a more favourable location.

I wanted to continue if they were happy the sea state wasn't too dangerous, and I was progressing well.

There are no rules in these adventures. It's not a competition, and there's no governing body. I wasn't trying to break a Guinness World Record with paid, suited observers noting my every move. It was my challenge with my rules. For me, climbing aboard in the middle of the day's swim to be ferried to a better location wasn't in the spirit of what I wanted to achieve. I told them to do their best to correct the ship's course, and I'd continue swimming after them.

I relished the day's challenge. It was unforgettable to swim on the precipice through testing conditions that few ever have. If it were a channel swim attempt, it wouldn't have begun, swimmers rightly waiting for a weather window that wouldn't scupper their crossing. You'd only be in these ferocious waves if you fell overboard or your ship sank. Because of my swim and logistics preparation, I could continue gaining ground in relative safety, despite the brooding sea around me. The sight of *Unsinkable II* was a much more calming presence than its predecessor.

While I swam, the team listened to the weather forecaster over the marine radio.

'And now the coastal reports at 9 p.m. Malin Head. Gale warning is in effect. South, force six to seven, gale force eight imminent, increasing severe gale force nine soon.'

Chris and Noel monitored the weather throughout the day. They knew we walked a tightrope of safety for the three hours I was in the water, and that the imminent weather front was unsafe for a thirty-two-foot sailboat, never mind the man overboard. The threatening black cauldron of ominous clouds rolled off the mainland towards our position in Rathlin Sound. The dark storm eclipsed the evening sun.

'Alan! We got to call it there! Can you get up as quick as you can? Good lad.'

I climbed up and thanked the team, seeing we'd made it well into the sound with Rathlin Island on one side and Ballycastle on the other.

'Wild swimming,' Chris said. 'It doesn't get much wilder than that.'

'You're some man for going out in that, I'll tell ya. We have gale force eight and above gunning for us. Look at the squally monster sky there. Bit of a change of plan. We can't get back across to Ballycastle, so we need to make a beeline for Rathlin before we get hammered.'

In the three hours, I had covered over eighteen kilometres and was proud of myself and the team for the progress and safety decisions, making up for the previous day's errors.

We just about outran the dangerous weather front and moored in Church Bay under darkness. The storm blew in. Gale-force wind and driving rain engulfed us, rattling Rathlin Island's 150 inhabitants. It was a sleepless night on our rocking boat home, with constant drumming and thrashing like a violent mosh pit at a heavy metal concert.

I was anxious about day three. There was the prospect of whirl-pools, tidal races, eddies, and deadly overfalls of the untamed northeast coast. On my first attempt, the overfalls east of Rathlin Island sloshed me around like I was in a washing machine. Before diving into the middle of the channel at 8 p.m., I warned Kaja to prepare for turbulence.

We dodged the ferry, swimming, kayaking, and sailing past Rathlin Island's Rue Point on our left. A small black-and-white octagonal lighthouse stood alone and stoic at sea level amongst the jagged, wave-sharpened rocks.

We exited the sound as we continued to Fair Head or An Bhinn Mhór (The Great Cliff) on our right, which many have seen in *Game of Thrones*. Fair Head's rugged rocks ramped from the sea before shooting hundreds of metres skywards, a tiara of volcanic rock columns crowning the rounded headland.

I paused to reassure Kaja. 'I think we're in the clear. We're southbound now and past the sketchy spot from last time.'

I was relieved not to face that barrage of turbulent water again. The sun was setting in the west, with a magnificent orange glow radiating over the awe-inspiring cliffs. Conditions were relatively calm with a moderate chop as the racing tide spat us at a rate of knots south to the next target – Torr Head.

Before we reached the headland, a wave broke over my back with a force that knocked my goggles loose and frightened the living daylights out of me. I'd never had a wave strike me like that in deep, offshore water. I bolted upright in a panic to find Kaja. A destructive tornado of jumping water encircled us. Kaja's face looked like she'd seen a ghost as her kayak rose.

'Al!'

A whoosh of salty, white foam bulldozed her ten metres from me. *Shit! No!* She fought the wave and managed not to capsize, but I feared she'd lose that battle if we stayed in the chaos.

'You're okay,' I told her. I waved at *Unsinkable II* up ahead. 'Chris! Noel!'

The waves broke all around us without any pattern as we fought to stay together. *I need to get Kaja aboard the boat and out of danger.* Putting myself in a tricky situation was one thing, but I felt responsible for Kaja's safety since this ordeal had been my bright idea.

We bounced in the overfalls as *Unsinkable II* motored past us and circled back southbound. Noel gripped the helm at the back of the boat in a half squat. Chris stood holding the rigging at the front. *Unsinkable II* ramped up a sharp wave throwing the boat's bow to the heavens. I glimpsed the red fin keel in the middle of the boat's underside. The bow crashed down with the violence of a shotgun blast as the sea sprayed up. Chris was still holding tight, his lifejacket and waterproofs drenched. I realised there was no getting Kaja or me onto the vessel. If the support boat came anywhere near us in this maelstrom, we risked the fatal disaster of the hull striking us.

'Ten minutes south! You need to swim south to escape this! South!' Chris said, swinging his forearm like a darts player and jabbing his pointed hand where he needed us to move.

Kaja bolted like a woman possessed.

'Feckin' wait for me!' I said, trying to put my goggles on and follow her as another wave dragged me under.

Sure enough, after our dash for safety, the overfalls stopped, and the waters calmed down. We paused to relax our overworked hearts and took on some overdue fuel.

'Jesus Christ, that was bonkers! That came from nowhere,' I said.

'I've never been so scared in my life!' Kaja said. 'I don't think my heart can handle more of that. I don't know how I didn't get flipped.'

My 2017 encounter with overfalls resembled a plane hitting turbulence, the 'fasten seatbelt' light pinging on and getting the bejaysus shaken out of me for fifteen minutes – terrifying but knowing we'd survive. This encounter was more like turbulence dropping the plane thirty metres at a time as passengers screamed and prayed for their lives.

We pulled into Glenarm Marina under a star-speckled sky

with the boat and everyone in one piece. Out of harm's way, the team were abuzz with adrenaline.

'A smooth sea never made a skilled sailor,' Chris said. 'Well done on paddling through that one, Karolína. Jeez. I saw you getting clobbered by a few. Fair play.'

I laughed. 'Wasn't much choice. I thought we were goners for a moment, seeing you guys nearly going airborne. Great job handling that shitshow and giving us clear instructions. You were class, lads. Over thirty kilometres, was it? Feck, we were going at a fair lick.'

I competed against the 2017 me, comparing my 2019 progress with the old GPS markers. We fell at the first hurdle – misjudging tides on day one – but because of my investment in the sailboat, we suffered no mechanical faults, and I could swim through seas the RIB couldn't handle. We made ground on day three and surpassed the 2017 GPS marker, unlocking some joy. I didn't invest all importance and value in finishing. I knew more than anyone that the cards were stacked against that outcome. As any seasoned investor will tell you, it's wiser to diversify. Investing all your eggs in a long shot is a recipe for disappointment. I made the journey the centre of focus and invested a little in each step along the path. Surpassing each mini fundraising or swimming target put a pep in my step and spurred me to keep going.

Viking Oarsman

A wet mist engulfed the land for my following swim, removing any reference to progress or orientation. Piercing pellets of rain lashed down, stinging my face as night fell and temperatures dropped. I handed Kaja my mirrored goggles and put on clear ones. Kaja turned on her kayak's green and red navigation light as I clipped a flashing white swim light to the back of my head.

'How're you holding up, Kaja?' I said during my fourth refuelling stop.

'It's hard. I'm soaked. The wind's blowing from behind, so I have to back-paddle to keep your pace. My arms are killing me. I've never paddled backwards in training.'

'Let me know if it gets too much, and we'll call it, yeah?'

'Yeah, yeah. I can't see where we're headed either or if we're moving at all. I'm just following Noel's instructions and aiming for the boat's nav lights. How're you coping down there in the dark?'

'All okay here, I'll survive. Thanks for the grub. See ya in thirty.'

It was a lie. I could hear in Kaja's voice and see in her demeanour that the conditions tested her spirits and grit. I wasn't okay, but I didn't want to burden her further with my struggles. They were for me to overcome.

For the thousandth time, I wanted to quit. Not seeing land demotivated and bugged me. I felt like I was swimming in circles. I couldn't influence the conditions that I allowed to demoralise me. I needed to focus on the things I could control to stop the spiral of doom and gloom. I pulled my horizon as close as possible to trick myself into progressing. I was trying to swim as far as Glenarm. My left stroke became 'Glenarm', and my right hand became 'stroke'. I fought the sea by attrition. My mind roared a mantra on a loop like a clan of feral Vikings rowing a longboat across the high seas: *Glenarm! Stroke! Glenarm! Stroke! You're not beating me tonight!*

Before I knew it, another thirty minutes had passed, and it was time for my next feed, a little chat with Kaja, and a warming wetsuit pee to lift my spirits and temperature momentarily.

Back on oar duty, I adjusted to the bizarre sight that met me with each rotation to my right for a breath. Gone was my girlfriend's lovely face. A hazy red glow in the centre of a black screen replaced her in the night. I clung to that divine port-side kayak light for dear life because I would be a dead man if I lost sight of it. I whimpered forwards, repeating my mantra, inspired by Kaja's mettle to stick with me as we drudged together in a battle of inches.

When the tide dissipated and we climbed back up the support boat's steel ladder, I could see things weren't much brighter for Chris and Noel on deck. They squinted into the wind and downpour, trying to stay warm in gloves, woolly hats, and head-to-toe waterproofs with the hoods gripped tight to their cheeks.

Despite the misery of the Irish weather, they welcomed us back with warm smiles and celebratory backslaps.

'Thanks for putting up with those conditions, lads. Feckin' hard-fought miles tonight.'

'Great job, guys! Brilliant stuff,' said Noel. 'That's Glenarm just in there, so mission accomplished. Go down and get warm. There's hot pasta on the stove. You earned it with that one.'

'Warm food? Ugh, you're stars, lads.'

Kaja and I got dried, fed, and watered. Chris and Noel continued working on deck, navigating in darkness through the elements, dodging the obstacle course of fish farms in Glenarm Bay on the shuttle back to our berth in the marina.

Moored up, exhausted, and asleep by 1:30 a.m., we rose at 7 a.m. to switch from evening to morning tide. With an hour's commute to the start, Kaja and I bonded and moaned about our hatred for sailboats as we rolled up and down and rocked left to right. We sat opposite each other, breathing deeply with our elbows on our knees and our faces in our hands.

'Ugh, I wish I didn't eat the porridge. This is feckin' miserable.'

'I thought you told me we'd get our sea legs,' said Kaja.

'Don't shoot the messenger. That's what all the sailors told me. I'm struggling not to puke here too.'

Chris cut the engine. 'Thirty minutes to go-time, guys.'

We'd always get to the starting coordinates early to allow us time to get into our gear without the excess motion of accelerating through the waves. Even still, moving about the cabin to dress and prepare worsened the seasickness. I filled my bottles with Ribena, water, and maltodextrin carbohydrate powder, and loaded them into Kaja's kayak goodie bag. I took a minute's rest on the bench to cuddle Kaja, the motion of the ocean keeling her over in a depressing ball.

'Ugh, fuckin' boats.'

I stuck a bit of Tina Turner's 'Simply the Best' on the speakers to cheer our dreary mood.

'This one goes out to Kaja, the Czech lady wishing she'd never swiped right for the silly Irishman.'

We gave the karaoke classic some welly as we slimed with disgusted faces into our kayak and swim gear, which were still sopping from the previous expedition a few hours earlier.

'Are you all set to go, guys?'

'Yeah, get us off this shaggin' yoke before we puke on each other.'

Chris and Noel laughed. 'That's the spirit.'

Day five saw us achieve another marathon ten-kilometre-plus swim, traversing Larne's shipping lane without getting squished. The progress justified the commute to the next port of Carrickfergus on the north banks of Belfast Lough.

Headwinds and Quarrels

It was a 5 a.m. start for Chris and Noel on day six as they readied the boat and began our three-and-a-half-hour commute to the previous afternoon's finish point. The two men were doing trojan work, supervising us during the hours of swimming and clocking in first and out last with often tedious shuttles to and from the start and finish points each day. Quickly learning from day one's mistake, we'd all adjusted to our roles nearing the end of week one. As well as crewing the ship, they did all in their power to make the swim and kayak as easy as possible, from prepping food to tip-toeing around as we slept in, squeezing every restorative drop from our uncomfortable shoebox slumber. Their enthusiasm and willingness to pull out all the stops and have some craic along the way lightened the load, making the challenge enjoyable.

Kaja and I hit the water shortly after 9 a.m., heading back towards Belfast Lough under our own steam.

Two days of tailwinds ended in exchange for a bullying wind gusting north and an awkward swell on day six. With us getting on the water as the tide flowed south, the opposing forces of nature churned up the seas.

That meant more exaggerated swim movements to find air when rotating for breaths. Sometimes I'd turn, and the swell would still submerge my head, so I had to hold and try again after another two strokes. The chop could immerse my face yet again on my next attempt. By the sixth stroke, I had to almost roll onto my back or crank my neck to clear my mouth from the suffocating waves.

In the pool, my bent arm would lift from the water, and my fingertips would flow millimetres above the flat surface before gliding in front of my head and initiating the underwater pullback. Facing headwinds in open water is a different sport. My bent arm would rise from the sea, and my pointed elbow would roll forwards, but my hand or forearm mightn't clear the heaving, wind-tossed waves. Forcing my arm against water put a much greater strain on my body than flying it in recovery mode through the air. As well as the physical demands, it was frustrating and taxing on the mind. I wanted to swim, but mother nature was fighting me. I likened it to trying to run a marathon with a gurrier barging a shoulder into you every ten steps. Waves smashed me this way and that, wrapping my arms in sticky treacle, and taunting me: 'Let's see you swim now, boy'.

For Kaja sitting on top of the water, headwinds meant battling waves and fighting the gusts as her body and kayak acted as a sail that propelled her in the wrong direction. She wanted to crawl forwards at my slow swim speed, but needed to multiply her stroke rate to counteract the ripping gusts. The weather put additional strain on her arms, shoulders, and mind, increasing the pain and frustrations.

I stopped at each thirty-minute marker and called Kaja for food and drink. Usually, she'd be beside me or paddle to me, but she'd had enough of competing with the conditions.

'Swim over, Al!' she said.

'Why would I swim to you? That'd mean me swimming thirty metres in the wrong direction.' I wanted my energy used to progress due south, not east, west, or north.

'Well, come over if you want the food and drink.'

Safe to say I was not a happy camper. I swam towards her, but Kaja didn't seem to make any effort to get to me, the wind blowing her further away as she readied the food and drinks.

'You need to paddle, too, Kaja. I can't reach you.'

'Ugh, I'm getting the drinks out of the bag.'

'But I can't swim to you. The wind's pushing you away.'

She handed me my drink and stared forwards, clearly not wanting to be there. I couldn't blame her. I shared the feeling. It was one of those days when the toll from the mileage and cabin fever accumulated and combined with the terrible weather and extreme conditions to test our limitations.

'Stick with me, Kaja,' I said as I drank, watching her not paddle as a gust blew her away.

'I'm tired, Al. I need a break, too.'

'Well, just go back on the boat if you're too tired.'

'No, I'm not quitting.'

'You're making it harder for yourself by getting blown away.'

'Just drink your drink, and let's get back moving.'

I raised my empty protein shaker to show her I'd finished feeding, but the wind had pushed her further away as she rested.

'Swim towards me!'

'Kaja, I'm not swimming feckin' backwards again, and how can I swim holding a bottle!'

It took her a while to grunt through the wind and get back to me. I gave her the bottle and swam away. A few minutes later, she still wasn't by my side. I stopped to look around and found I'd been swimming to shore. My direction was impossible to gauge with limited visibility in the waves, and without my steering companion. The wind had propelled her back when she returned the bottles to the waterproof bag and she couldn't catch up with me despite her effort. I bobbed and waited, all the while getting colder and more frustrated.

Just as Kaja reached me, *Unsinkable II* pulled alongside to give her instruction, a land marker to aim for in the distance.

As I was treading water, still waiting, the wind pushed them further away again. *For fuck's sake,* I thought.

'It's not working today. You're clearly tired and pissed off. Can you just get back on the boat, and I'll try to swim after it for another hour or so?' I said to Kaja when she returned to me.

'No, I'm not getting on the boat if you're still swimming. You need to follow me and not get split up.'

'You're the one allowing the wind to blow you away. I'm not being blown anywhere floating down here in the freezing cold waiting for ya.'

All this bickering and waiting around lowered my body temperature and worsened the situation. The sea is no place to linger and have a lovers' tiff.

I waved for Chris and Noel to come over. 'I think we should call it there. We can't keep together. It's too frustrating with the wind. I'm fit to keep going, but I think it's best to get Karolína and the kayak on board, and I follow the boat instead. But she's having none of it. She's set on kayaking if I'm swimming.'

'Here, we'll stick in closer to you guys, and we can get another thirty minutes together. How does that grab ya?'

'Grand job.'

This was a team effort. *Unsinkable II*, Kaja, and I moved in unison, squeezing more mileage out after reaching our limits. We'd made just over fifteen kilometres to the middle of Belfast Lough.

Once aboard, the mood shifted for the better, and communication breakdowns faded. It helped that we were warm, dry, and satiated with food, three feelings that profoundly affect your mindset. Nature wasn't ripping us apart either. There was no point crying over spilt milk. We were just tired, cold, sore, and hungry, but we were all doing our best. We mopped up the milk, kissed, and moved on.

The sun glared, and the winds huffed – perfect sailing conditions. Chris and Noel killed the noise-polluting motor and hoisted the sails that rustled in the breeze. The four of us sat in the cockpit, full of smiles, as Chris and Noel tried to outdo each other for setting top speed records, crisscrossing our way to Bangor Marina south of Belfast Lough.

Shamu

'*Stena Line, Stena Line, Stena Line*, this is *Unsinkable II, Unsinkable II, Unsinkable II*. We have a sea swimmer here trying to swim across Belfast Lough for charity and wanted to notify you of our intended route as we see you're scheduled to depart soon. Over.'

'*Unsinkable II, Unsinkable II,* this is *Stena Line.* Can you repeat, please? Over.'

'We have a sea swimmer trying to swim across Belfast Lough and wanted to notify you of our intended journey. Over.'

'We heard that bit. We wanted to make sure we heard your vessel's name correctly.' The *Stena Line* passenger ferry captain laughed. 'What happened to *Unsinkable I?* We'll adjust our course to allow you a free run across the lough. Good luck. Over and out.'

At this point in attempt one, I'd switched my short fins for longer fins to jet across the lough and accelerate south before running out of support crew. Having invested much more time in finding support for several weeks, I didn't need to compromise my vision. I continued with my small fins.

We made tracks early when the tide was slack. I shifted gears to pass the shipping lanes, swimming parallel to an anchored one-hundred-metre-long cargo ship. I whizzed into the warmer shallows of Donaghadee Sound, where the tide fired me like a cannonball through the narrow channel between Copeland Island and mainland County Down, thankfully avoiding the overfalls which occur here.

The previous week I'd felt as though I was fighting to remain afloat, biting down on my gumshield and swinging for the fences – surviving. On day seven, I moved with the grace and poise of a synchronised swimmer expressing their art form through the water. Everything clicked into place to make it an idyllic four-hour swim that gained another sixteen kilometres. It had taken me an extra five days to reach this point in 2017.

Mooring up against the harbour wall in Donaghadee, I couldn't get too carried away with our progress or start counting my chickens, because the third sailor in as many weeks had changed their mind about joining the team. I was down one sailor for weeks three, four, and five. One volunteer had health issues, the second had got a new job, and the third sailor didn't say why. I dreaded the thought that the project could be derailed due to a lack of support and hated the lack of control.

I could swim daily with the larger sailboat in support, but the physical toll accumulated without forced rest days. There was no hanging about due to inclement weather or mechanical failure. My body ached during breakfast, knackered from enjoying the unhindered swim streak. I made too much hay in the sunshine.

Day eight was Chris and Noel's final day, and I wanted their leg to end on a high. I put my body's soreness to the back of my mind. With all the hours of training, I knew my body. I knew what discomfort I could safely manage and what pain level raised the alarm bells for me to stop.

I put my head in the sea for another four hours. My efforts were rewarded, making enough progress to warrant moving our floating base from Donaghadee pier wall to Portavogie's port.

'Best we lower the tricolour pulling in here.'

'I grew up on the south coast. You know best. Work away.'

'Just in case it might rub up the locals the wrong way, ya know.'

We lowered the Waterford and Irish flag, and inched towards the port entrance, a bit uncertain of ourselves.

Portavogie is a small village with about 2,000 inhabitants and a fleet of about fifty fishing vessels in its port.

Unsinkable II crept like a snail around the chicane of concrete walls as seagulls heckled us for the day's catch. The pungent waft of prawns and herring violated our noses. Rusty empty trawlers in blues, reds, greens, and yellows lined the walls two or three deep on both sides of us. It was eerily quiet this Saturday evening. We were a lone sailboat, pulling in along the metal dock.

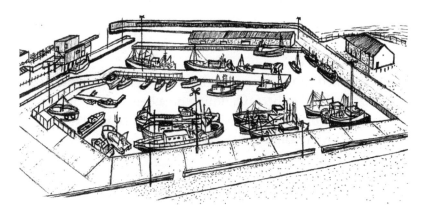

A seal popped its fat head to the surface.

'Jeepers, is that a whale? Look at the size of that fella.'

'They keep him well fed anyway.'

Shamu looked us in the eyes one by one, floated his round body to the surface, farted, and dove.

'Do you think we'll be okay here, or will they tell us to piss off?'

'We don't exactly look like the fleet, but hopefully, you'll be grand here for a wee while until you make the next marina.'

'Can we help you, boys?' two men said, walking towards us along the gangway. They wore jeans, hoodies, and stern faces.

'This man here is swimming the length of Ireland for charity. We're hoping to stay a night or two before he can move on to Ardglass, if that's alright?'

'God love you, you mustn't be right in the head, so you mustn't,' one of the men said, beaming. Their wariness flipped to open arms. 'C'mon down here, and we get a photo with you. Nutter. Yeah, no problem staying here for a wee while.'

Kaja and I waved goodbye to Chris and Noel. We were sad to see them go and would miss their upbeat vibes. Eight days, twenty-six hours of sea swimming and 136 kilometres travelled. They'd helped get me off to a belter.

Happy to have some quality time with just the two of us, we strolled out of the port's gates to explore the village. I noticed the footpaths had curbs painted in the Union Jack's red, white, and blue. Then we passed a black-and-white Ulster Freedom Fighter's emblem emblazoned on a bungalow's gable wall.

'What's that about?' Kaja said.

'That's why Chris lowered our Irish colours. Let's keep moving. I'll tell you on the way.'

We turned to the coastal path lined by canary yellow plants and buzzing worker bees. Cuddling on a bench, we watched the soft sands and open sea as groups of teens and dog walkers passed by. The sun lowered and transformed the sky from blue to magical peach.

'Let's get back to the boat before it's too dark.'

TEN
Lion's Mane
364 Kilometres Remaining

New Crew

Kaja and I were due to welcome two new sailors, Charlie and Jim, on board in the morning to swim the first tide. They were both sailboat owners and familiar with my boat, having spent four days helping John transfer *Unsinkable II* from the south coast to the north before the swim began.

I expected my school friend, Enda Loughman, to arrive that evening. He didn't have any boating experience, but I invited him along for company.

Charlie arrived late.

'Good morning. Welcome back aboard,' I said. 'Ready to hit the road soon? Hopefully, Jim will arrive in the meantime.'

'Jim told me he wouldn't be able to make it this morning. He'll be along later,' Charlie said.

'Eh, right. Good to know.'

I was annoyed Jim was a no-show for the first tide of the new team. Even more so for not getting a text or a call. It's not unusual for sailors to sail on their own. I knew Charlie had recently earned his Royal Yacht Association's Day Skipper qualification, and he volunteered, taking children boating. Still, I felt uneasy about having just one person on the deck while Kaja and I were overboard in the water. Having two sailors at all times provided a margin for error if one wasn't comfortable navigating, needed a second sailing opinion, fell in the sea, or had a health emergency. Having two people was much safer for all involved.

'The wind's looking a bit stronger today. Will you be able to handle the boat on your own?'

'Aye, I should be okay.'

'If you're confident, let's head to the starting point and see what the sea's doing. We can make a call then.'

'Okay.'

Once out of the sheltered port, the bashing began, rocking and rolling us. Charlie operated the helm on deck. Kaja and I took our usual commute positions, lying on the benches below deck in the main cabin.

Paper charts and route plotting apparatus slid off the table and onto the wet floor.

'Why did he leave them out in these conditions? They were never going to stay put,' I whispered in annoyance to Kaja. It was my first lesson on the maiden voyage from Bristol with Tim and Mark – secure everything before setting out to avoid carnage or getting struck by a wayward object in the waves.

I picked up the soggy maps, shook the salt water off, and stored them away.

'Alan, would you mind coming up here for a tick?' Charlie called.

'Coming.'

'Can you steer? I need to go below and get into my waterproofs.'

There wasn't much choice, but I wish he'd had them on before we left port.

'Eh, I've steered a boat twice for about five seconds. I'm useless,' I said.

'I'll be quick; just keep her steady.'

Charlie climbed down to his cabin. I felt worse than a teenager on their first driving lesson, tense, sweaty, and out of my depth. Now I had passengers and no driving instructor next to me to override my mistakes. The car traffic saw the big 'L' plates and adjusted their behaviour, giving me a wide berth when learning to drive. The sea didn't give a flying fiddle that I hadn't a clue what I was doing. I gripped the wooden tiller hard, desperate to keep a straight course.

A wave hit the stern of the boat, my hand moved an inch to counter the force, and *Unsinkable II* sling-shotted ninety degrees to the right.

'Charlie! Can you take back control, *please?*'

He climbed into the cockpit dressed for a storm, took the tiller back, and quickly corrected my blunder.

'I think it's safest if you stick to the sailing bits and just let me know if I can bring you anything. We're usually at the starting waypoint thirty minutes before go time. Could you give us a shout once we're there, please? It takes us a while to get our gear on after you cut the engine.'

'Okay.'

I retreated to my bench and Kaja.

'The stress of that. I can't steer to save my life.'

'Yeah, let's not give you the wheel again.'

'I think we're about thirty minutes out if you want to get into your gear,' Charlie called.

Checking my watch and the boat's GPS, I realised we wouldn't have the usual thirty minutes of pre-swim bobbing at the start point to get dressed if I wanted to maximise the tide. Running behind, Kaja and I struggled to get ready as the boat continued to steam through arching waves, knocking us over and making us feel seasick.

Thirty minutes passed. We were worse for wear but were snug as two bugs in a rug and dressed for action. Another ten minutes passed, but the engine still rattled us forwards. We started to overheat in our gear.

'Do you think we're far off, Charlie?'

'Maybe ten minutes or so.'

Ten minutes passed.

'How are we looking, Charlie?'

'It'll be another wee while.'

I couldn't take the heat anymore, stripped off the top part of my wetsuit, and lay down. It was part of the challenge. New people were coming in, and it took time to hit the ground. I expected that. It was Charlie's first day. We were short a pair of hands; and the moody seas, wind, and bucketing rain threw a lot his way.

'Okay, we're here, I think.'

I climbed up to assess the risks.

'What do you think, Charlie?'

'I'm not sure. What do you think?'

I had no doubts about fireman Chris' physical ability to lug the hefty kayak from the sea and onto the boat during week one. He had Noel there to lend another pair of hands. Charlie was an older man, recently retired, and was sailing solo.

'I think it's too risky getting the kayak on and off the boat and putting Karolína on it,' I said. 'The way the waves are hitting, and we're rocking, there's a fair chance she could fall in before we even start. You could fall in the sink while unloading, too, and then we'd be in right trouble.'

'Okay.'

While it was an easy call about Kaja and Charlie's safety, I took a bit longer to ponder *my* risk tolerance.

'Do you think you could manage to motor a relatively straight line for me to follow?'

'It'd be tricky.'

He was a man of few words and hard to read. He seemed unsure.

'Let's leave it off today and fight tomorrow. It's too risky. We'll have Enda along tonight and hopefully Jim, too.'

'Alright.'

The conditions were borderline, similar to conditions I'd swum through before, but my gut told me it was better to err on the side of caution and be patient given the circumstance. As annoying as it was, it was the right call and allowed my body its first day's rest in nine days.

Jim and Enda joined us that afternoon. We made a plan of action and the five of us got an early night in Portavogie Harbour.

Perils

In the morning, the harbour was teeming with fishermen. Before long, we were the only vessel left. I slathered on my factor-fifty anti-jellyfish sunscreen to fend off the blistering UV rays. A slight breeze blew at our back, ironing the sea flat, and pushing us south with the tide.

Kaja and I stroked for four hours to reach in line with Quintin Bay, north of Strangford Lough's treacherous mouth. Our progress put us in perfect striking distance to cross the following day at calm, slack tide.

I'd swum far enough to justify a commute to Ardglass Marina. After nights tied to a pier wall in an industrial fishing port, we were excited about the simple pleasures of a shower and electricity.

After an overdue scrub in the marina's shower, I returned to *Unsinkable II* to find Jim was gone.

'Jim's away home. He'll be back tomorrow,' Charlie said.

The following morning, we waited as long as we could, later than our discussed departure time, but Jim was nowhere to be seen.

'I don't want to miss our window to get across Strangford. Right, are we ready to crack on?'

'Okay then,' Charlie said.

Forty minutes into our commute, I heard Jim's voice shouting. He'd got a local man he knew to catch him up with us on his powerboat. It was quite the entrance. Jim climbed aboard and joined Charlie and Enda in the cockpit.

'The lads say we're thirty minutes out, if you want to start getting ready,' Enda said from above.

Fifty minutes passed. Kaja and I were sweating in our gear as the engines continued to hum north.

We were late and overheated. I worried about the increased chances of the incoming tide pushing us into Strangford Lough and harm's way.

I stood on deck, waiting for Kaja to board her craft. Up to this point, we'd managed this by one person steadying the front of the kayak and one person steadying the back as she descended the boat's ladder to her seat.

Splash!

'Kaja, you okay? Is she okay?' I said, unable to see her as

Charlie, Jim, and Enda stood in a line across the back of the boat.

For fuck's sake, I thought. I knew she'd fallen in, and worried about the boat bobbing and hitting her on the head.

'I'm okay!'

'She's okay. She's back on the ladder.'

She'll be too cold. I'll have to swim on my own. Why couldn't they be more careful? They were there and doing their best. Nobody wanted her to fall in. Still, it was frustrating when errors accumulated.

Though soaked, Kaja was steely, insisting on supporting me. She gathered herself on deck and descended the ladder again. It was us against the world.

'Right, let's do this, but if you get too cold, tell me and get back on the boat,' I said, as we bobbed in the waves.

'Yeah, I'll be okay. Let's just start moving so I can get warm.'

As I anticipated, she was too stubborn for her own good and kayaked longer than was sensible. I saw her shaking like a leaf after two hours of absorbing the stinging winds. How she endured conditions that long, I wasn't sure.

'You need to stop. You'll get your death.'

She was still reluctant to leave me alone, but accepted my advice and got back on *Unsinkable II.* Just as she left, a ginormous, hideous brown blob skimmed beneath my face, followed by two metres of thick, hair-like tentacles. It was a lion's mane jellyfish, one of the world's largest jellyfish species and one that can pack nasty hospitalising stings, inducing pain, nausea, cramps, and increased blood pressure. It was the first time I saw one in real life.

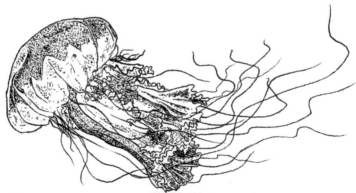

Then came another and another. I didn't want to be alone, but I wanted to get past Strangford Lough more. I popped my face up time and time again, continuing to swim once the threat passed beneath.

We seemed to be getting closer to land, almost swimming west into the lough's mouth instead of south, away from danger.

'What's happening, guys? Are we getting pulled into the lough, or am I good to go?'

'Yeah, best you stop.'

When were they going to tell me? I thought. Two hours and thirty-two minutes, the shortest swim yet.

If we'd left the port on time, started the swim on time, and hadn't dropped Kaja in the sea, we could have swum much further and maintained a straight course south across the lough's entrance. Instead, we had to abort right in the middle of Strangford Lough's mouth and face the hazard again the following day.

When I checked my tracker, I saw that we hadn't stuck to the mission of steering clear of the lough. I'd followed the team straight for Killard Point on the south bank of the lough's entrance for a significant portion of the swim without anyone adjusting our incorrect course.

'Jim, before you leave, can we agree on the logistics for tomorrow, so there's no mix-up with start times?'

We checked the tide times, calculated the commute's duration, and settled on the following day's boat departure and swim start time. I'd be starting at the lough's mouth. Precision timing would be crucial.

Errors

The next day, Jim arrived an hour early and sat in his jeep in the car park. Charlie left the boat to join him.

I walked to the car park as our departure time approached. 'Still on to head off in ten minutes?' I said through his rolled-down window.

'Yeah, all good. We'll come down now in a tick.'

I was delighted to see Charlie and Jim join us on board five minutes before showtime, but they opened the maps and tide books on the chart table and spoke between themselves. Kaja and I exchanged glares across the cabin. Enda was on deck peering into the cabin, glancing from Kaja to me, as if to say, *Why are we feck-arseing around, lads?* Ten minutes passed as they continued to confer, and we were somehow late again.

'Guys, are we okay to go or what's the craic?'

'We think it might be best to wait for tonight's tide in about eight hours instead of going now.'

'We agreed on our plan last night. Why would we change it now?' I said. 'The wind's a bit higher later, and it'll be getting dark if we start at 8 p.m. Let's stick to the plan, no, unless there's a good reason not to?'

'Okay then.'

The sailors continued footering around with maps and apps, murmuring between themselves, as Kaja, Enda, and I sat in awkward silence. Invisible steam blew out my ears, but I had to hold a neutral poker face since they were volunteers.

'Okay, I'll go up and loosen the mooring, and we'll motor on, yeah?' I said, trying to spur on some action.

Twenty minutes late, we headed for Strangford Lough, piling on the pressure to make up time in the water and clear the hazard before the water's flow increased.

Maps and navigation tools were left loose again, falling onto the wet floor once the chop hit.

'Ugh, c'mon, lads,' I said to Kaja under my breath. 'Just put things away, so they don't get destroyed.'

The planned swim start time ticked past as we continued to drive north.

'We're here now if you want to jump in,' the call came from the deck.

Kaja mounted her kayak and awaited my company. I turned on my three GPS trackers in a hurry. Before jumping in, I checked my website to ensure today's marker pinged north of yesterday's finish.

'We're way off, lads. Look,' I said, showing them the live map, where my location pin pinged south of yesterday's finish. It didn't look a million miles off on the digital map, as the boat icon wasn't to scale, but I'd later learn that we were about two kilometres south of the correct starting point.

'Okay, we'll go a little more north, so,' Charlie said.

They motored north, Kaja paddling after the boat.

'That should do it now,' Charlie said.

I zoomed in on the boat's GPS screen mounted to the cockpit where Charlie, Jim, Enda, and I stood.

'The start marker's here,' I said. 'We're still a ways south of it.' There was a silence that suggested I needed to be more explicit. I climbed below deck and grabbed a ruler. I held it straight across the GPS screen. 'See, we need to be north of this line.'

'I think this is as close as we can get,' Charlie said.

I looked around at the 360 degrees of unobstructed waters, confused. There was more silence. We were losing the window for safe crossing. I looked to my friend Enda, the non-sailor, for help, thinking, *Am I missing something here?*

'Why can't we go north, north of the ruler?' Enda asked the two sailors.

'Okay, so,' Charlie replied.

I looked perplexed at Enda again as the boat pointed and moved northeast.

Enda stood up and pointed. 'North. Over that way.'

I didn't have my glasses on. Kaja was becoming a dot in the waves.

'Enda, have you still got eyes on Karolína?'

'Yep, just about.'

I should have called it a day there. It was a botched job. We were way late, and there was too much space between Kaja and the boat. I was disheartened with the week's lack of progress, that we were late again, and all the hullaballoo about driving north of a GPS coordinate. I just wanted to get off the boat and regain control by getting on with the swimming.

'We can't get any further from Karolína.' I pulled my goggles over my eyes. 'Look, here'll do.'

I stepped off the boat and began swimming south. *Unsinkable II* left me and motored towards Kaja's last known location. As the boat became a speck, I worried about how they would find me again if I could barely see a thirty-two-foot sailboat. I was a needle in a haystack, a highlighter-green swim cap and an orange tow float miles offshore in the Irish Sea.

Thirty minutes passed. The boat remained distant, with nobody around to provide water and food at my standard feed time. I had no choice but to keep trying to swim south, but this was slow work with no kayak or boat to steer me. I stopped every minute to gauge my trajectory off the land to my right. With no guarantee of calories or the crew finding me, I contemplated an exit strategy to shore.

I cursed everything as I swam alone at sea. *How could we be late even when they were early? Why did they put Kaja in the water so far from our starting point? Why didn't she have her VHF on her? What if they can't find her? We shouldn't have left Kaja. I'm an idiot for getting in the water. They shouldn't have left me.* It was a dangerous, stupid mess we should have avoided.

While I argued in my head, Kaja was terrified in the waves, alone. She sprinted to chase the boat – stressed, fatigued, pushing beyond her limits, and puking, thinking, *why are they abandoning me?* Once rescued, she was infuriated.

Kaja climbed onto the sailboat. 'Where's Al?'

'He started swimming over that way.'

'You left him in the water! Find him! How long's he been in?'

'Eh, a while.'

After an hour of swimming, the crew relocated me. Kaja got back on her kayak and joined me.

'What happened?' she said.

'They somehow made a bollocks of getting north of the way-point and kept saying we were there or nearly there when we weren't, and then we were miles from you. I should have told them to turn around and get you once I realised we were so off the mark. Sorry. Are you okay?'

'Yeah. You?'

'Fed up.'

'Me too. I want Chris and Noel back. Hopefully, the lads will settle in.'

We continued, but Kaja had a downward thousand-yard stare and a slouched posture. The angst of the worrisome hour of solo swimming had depleted me, too. With only Kaja to look at, it wasn't long until her sombre demeanour fed my deteriorating mood. We kept colliding for the first time, the wind blowing the kayak on top of me and neither of us with the power or concentration to maintain our distance and prevent it.

I grunted and vented underwater as the challenge became wearisome. I gagged on a wave and had to pause.

'My head's fried, and you seem done as well. We keep hitting each other.' Though at my limit, I didn't want to waste the opportunity. I tried to squeeze out the last drops and salvage what we could. 'Let's just do thirty more minutes and call it a day?'

'That's only two hours, though?'

'No point us flogging dead horses. It's not working today. That should get us far enough south to have us out of the lough's pull. That's today's main objective.'

Twelve minutes later, I heard Kaja squeal with excitement. I looked up and saw her smiling like a kid arriving at Disneyland.

'What's happened?' I said.

'Dolphins!'

Kaja's screech pierced my earplugs. Her sudden cheeriness and giddy celebration about large, wild animals zooming around me in the water grated and stressed me. 'Where? How many?'

'Maybe four, right beside you. Can't you see them? Wow, they're right there.'

'Here, call the boat, please. Get me out. I'm done.'

My brain melted after eight kilometres of swimming. Exhausted, I couldn't cope.

We beat yesterday's record for the shortest swim, setting a new low of an hour and forty-two minutes. Reaching Waterford felt like a pipedream.

Gun

Charlie and Jim thought the boat's engine sounded off. More water came up from the floorboards and sloshed about the cabin, seeping into the carpet in the sleeping quarters. It's normal for sailboats to have some water, but not this amount. I booked a mechanic for the morning, and Jim was to come with his dive gear to inspect the propeller.

The mechanic repaired the starter cable and replaced some bolts and the propeller seal. I was hoping to be on the water for an evening swim.

'Running late this morning. I'll be there at lunchtime,' Jim texted.

Jim came down the gangway at 5 p.m. carrying his scuba gear. There was nothing to report after his underwater propeller inspection, but we were too late to catch the evening tide. No swim.

We motored out of Ardglass Marina on Friday, uncertain if conditions would allow a swim. It was one thing to read the weather apps, but given week two's tedious slowness, I wanted the peace of mind of seeing the swell for myself and making a decision on-site.

With diminished confidence in the team and waves lapping the boat, I made the easy call not to take a chance.

Getting past 2017's end point was turning out to be a lot harder and more frustrating than I'd bargained for. I got several texts asking if everything was okay and why had we all but stopped. With Chris and Noel, I'd swum twenty-six hours and covered 136 kilometres in the first eight days. Between the jigs and the reels, I only swam for eight hours and covered twenty-seven kilometres during the six days with Charlie and Jim.

The sailors seemed lovely, well-intentioned, and had volunteered their time to help me, but it was a much different dynamic than week one. They kept themselves to themselves and didn't click into the team like Chris and Noel. Objectively, they weren't punctual, I couldn't swim much, and more things were going wrong.

I zipped it. I couldn't risk upsetting and losing volunteers. Without deep pockets to hire a skipper and crew, I needed them much more than they needed me. I just had to wait for flat-calm weather and hope they showed up.

On Saturday, 15 June, day fifteen, I was down to one sailor for the weekend, Charlie. The winds whipped up, more substantial than the previous day. Being more risk-averse with only one sailor, we stayed put in the marina, not wasting diesel checking the sea state at the starting waypoint.

'The weather's staying like this for the weekend, so I'm going to pop home for a wee while. I'll see you on Monday,' Charlie said.

I was saving a pint to celebrate the occasion when I would beat my 2017 effort, but after the week we'd had, and the winterish weather swamping us, Kaja, Enda, and I found a pub with an open fire to decompress.

'Remember when Jim was late and flew out to us on the speedboat?' Enda said.

'Yeah. What about it?'

'He had a gun.'

'You're only coddin' me; he didn't … did he?'

'Swear to God. Not messing. He had it in a locked box and showed it to me. He was dropping it somewhere but was running late and couldn't leave it in his car, so he took it on the boat for safekeeping.'

'Jaypers. Who takes a gun to a charity swim?'

'Jim,' Enda said with a laugh and a sip of his pint. 'Aw, man. When you were swimming, he joked they might be the first people to get fired from volunteering – for being late, for Karolína tipping over, and for making a hames of crossing Strangford Lough. Charlie goes, the second day went great, though, and Jim tells him that's the only flat, sunny day we had, and a smooth sea never made a skilled sailor.' Enda laughed again. 'Nice fellas, though, to be fair to them.'

'I dunno about you, but I need another pint. Another round?' I said.

The strain and stalling of the week chipped away at my optimistic spirits. It was a crushing reminder that so much was out of my control. I'd done all the courses and training, and had put myself in financial debt. Still, the intangibles could scupper it all. I knew I could swim the distance, and Kaja had my back to the end. I knew I could maintain *Unsinkable II* to finish the journey. I developed severe doubts about having a long enough weather window, and enough enthusiastic and capable sailors slotted into the spreadsheet, to make it home.

As a beggar, I didn't have the privilege of being a chooser. You made the team if you had yachting qualifications and were generous enough to offer your time. I had to take what people gave me and be grateful for it, no matter the result. It wasn't easy to absorb when things weren't working as well as planned.

On the plus side, I was delighted I'd invited Enda, and that he'd come along. He soaked up our woes, shared our struggles, and lightened the load with some laughs. Enda wasn't a sailor, but he kept us afloat. Though it's often undervalued and ignored as a Key Performance Indicator, being able to cheer people up and sustain morale is an invaluable contribution to any team.

Unsupported

With no swim on the cards for Saturday or Sunday, we hugged goodbye to Enda. I booked Kaja and me into a B&B to get a break from the stench of the rocking boat, and we grabbed some takeaway fish and chips.

On Sunday, Mam visited, treated us to lunch, and helped me refuel the boat and spare canisters with diesel.

'I know you're frustrated, but I'm just glad you're both safe and not taking silly risks. You can't be going out with only one sailor.'

'I know, Mam. I know. Thanks for worrying about us.'

We welcomed Kaja's best friend from Prague on Monday, Adriana Van Leeuwen. She wasn't a sailor. She came to fill Enda's shoes as a morale booster. Charlie was back, volunteering for the entirety of week three. Though Jim had only offered to volunteer for week two, he said he didn't want to see us stuck in week three, and offered to help out for one tide on Monday and another on Tuesday.

Jim hoisted the Czech Republic's flag up the mast. The little effort I'd made to order their nation's flag for the Czech takeover did the trick and gave us all a smile to start the new week on a good foot.

'*We're back in action,*' I posted to social media with excitement as we sailed from the marina. The closer we got to the start point, the more the waves chopped up. Winds gusted. It was wilder than the forecast had suggested. I chomped at the bit to progress, but had to weigh that up against my faith in the team when it wasn't fair-weather sailing conditions. Being patient and safe was difficult, but with Mam's voice in my head, I decided not to take the risk when the sailors seemed hesitant. '*Aaaand we're cancelled,*' I posted to social media.

'We're heading home. We'll see you tomorrow,' Jim said when we returned to safe harbour.

It was Tuesday morning, 18 June. I got a text from Charlie telling me he didn't think the weather would suit swimming that day or the next two days.

'*I'll be down for Friday morning,*' he texted.

The waters looked perfect from the shoreline. I checked several sailing apps and weather forecast sites. They all displayed white, light blue, and green shades, not amber, red, pink, or purple – sunny and a gentle breeze from four to fourteen knots on Tuesday, Wednesday, and Thursday. I felt let down and frustrated.

'If he couldn't or didn't want to help, why did he put his name down for week three? You could have found someone more willing and able if you knew this would happen,' Kaja said.

'Yeah, it's a pain in the arse, but it is what it is,' I said. 'There's always that risk with people. Maybe he's got something else going on that he's not telling us.'

Charlie was out, but there was still Jim. It was meant to be his last shift in support, but he wasn't at the marina either. Jim didn't respond to my texts. We sat on the boat, assuming he'd arrive late again.

I looked at my phone and back up at Kaja and Adriana. 'We're too late now. I guess we're not swimming today, so.'

Week three was playing out worse than week two, with circumstances knocking the wind out of my sails. A vengeful *I'll show them* attitude crept in. If I could do anything to improve matters, I would. I couldn't sit there and take the bad hand. Having lost Monday, I didn't want to lose Tuesday, Wednesday, and Thursday. To salvage something from the day, I created handmade signs seeking volunteer sailors to help us south in the favourable weather and stuck them to the marina door.

I updated Chris and Noel about the circumstance.

'Some good news for a change,' I said to Kaja and Adriana. 'Chris and Noel are coming back to get us moving again on Thursday, Friday, and Saturday.'

The inability to move without sailors irritated me, and I was going stir-crazy. There's only so much documentary filming and boat chores to do.

'I'm sick of fannying around here,' I said to Kaja and Adriana. 'I checked the maps and weather forecast. I think we can go unsupported if you're up for it?'

'Okay, I trust you. This evening? Tomorrow?' Kaja said.

'We have a beach to exit. I can see that on Google Streetview, but I'm not sure about having a safe entry point. It looks a bit rocky on aerials. Are you guys up for taking a stroll to see if it's accessible today, and then I'll jump in tomorrow if it's safe?'

'Sure. It beats sunning ourselves in the marina.'

We walked for over an hour, Kaja and Adriana stopping to pet and talk with every good doggy we passed. We reached an overgrown trail headed towards the sea. The nettles stung and thorns scratched. The track opened out to a rocky shoreline and still waters.

'I can get out there, no problem.'

I levitated back to the marina, feeling empowered by problem-solving, and the possibility and hope of progression.

I must have done the calculations at least five times, working out the strength of the tide and factoring in the forecast wind and my projected hourly swim distance. The start point was to the north of our base. Ardglass Marina offered an early exit point in the middle if needed. All things going well, I'd be able to exit the sea from Coney Island beach to the south of the marina.

I loved doing something to better our situation rather than being a hapless damsel in distress waiting for assistance. But with action came pressure. The decisions were on me, not a team of certified sailors. I had to be sure I wouldn't put Kaja or myself in danger.

Adriana helped me carry my gear to the entry point early the following morning. Like clockwork, Kaja pulled into view on her kayak bang on schedule, floating on the lake-like sea in the sunshine.

Adriana and I cheered from shore with big overhead waves. 'Kajo! Woohoo. Over here.'

I waded in and swam out to Kaja. Her face glowed.

'That was so nice paddling along the coast on my own. The cutest seal followed me for ages.'

'Lovely jubbly. This is our adventure today. Let's make it a good'n.'

Within my first few strokes, I saw my first barrel jellyfish – a thick, white mushroom dome the size of my torso with a bunch of leg-like tentacles doubling its size.

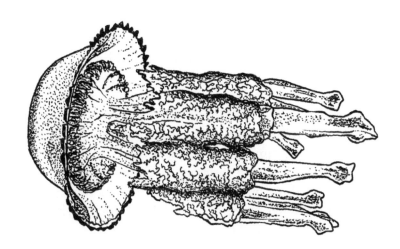

We were two happy campers, having fun and comforted by the shoreline's proximity and the sea's tranquillity.

I heard Kaja's squeak, a noise that meant only one thing.

'What's in the water now?'

She grinned with pure joy. 'Another seal.'

I turned around, and there was the curious cratur stopped ten metres behind me with her puppy eyes poking above the water. The atmosphere was the polar opposite of the previous few days. We were buzzing to be moving again. With a serene seascape, headspace, and the land only a stone's throw, I didn't so much as flinch at the humongous jellyfish or seals. I shared in Kaja's wildlife excitement for a change and was delighted to see her so upbeat after some testing days.

'Nice to see you smiling at the animals instead of crying,' she said with a teasing smile.

I gave her a playful splash. 'Cheek.'

We continued with Sally the seal in tow the rest of the way. A few of her buddies popped up to check out the swim-kayak duo as Kaja celebrated the sight of each one.

After covering seven kilometres in two hours, I decided not to continue to Coney Island beach, an hour's swim due west – wasted energy adding nothing to my progress south. With Kaja needing to paddle back to the marina solo, I didn't want to push our luck and risk landing her into an opposing tide or changing conditions.

'I'll just climb out here instead,' I said, pointing to the rocks that sloped into the sea. 'Good luck. Be safe. I'll see you back on the boat.'

I scurried to shore, scrambled across the sharp rocks like a crocodile, and waved bye to Kaja as she retraced her strokes.

A slight problem with the duathlon approach was the trek back to camp. I clambered across a hape of rocks and through knee-high grassland and shrubberies. Changing the plan on the hop had landed me on a fancy golf course. For twenty minutes, I endured the stares of the dapper club members as, head to toe in neoprene, I hugged the perimeter and tried not to get myself killed by a stray golf ball. Now that would be an embarrassing way to go after swimming all that way.

I nodded and waved to the silent stares. 'Hi there, a great evening for it.'

We regrouped back at the marina and celebrated a triumphant day nineteen. We'd shaken off the glum cobwebs of days nine to eighteen and finally pushed the GPS tracker south of Ardglass Marina.

ELEVEN
Slack Tides
330 Kilometres Remaining

Personal Record

I blasted 'The Boys Are Back in Town' to welcome Chris and Noel's unexpected return on Thursday – day twenty.

I took out my camera to film the good times. 'Welcome back. Good to have ya back on board.'

'We're not meant to be here,' Noel said, laughing over Thin Lizzy's tune.

Another day of headwinds meant for most of the breaths I attempted, I found my face either still underwater or getting slapped by a wave – leading to an overdose of salt water in my mouth. I spluttered often, and then I retched. Once I stopped heaving, I floated to compose myself with some deep breaths before continuing onwards.

'Kaja, there's something in the water,' I said.

'A seal or a dolphin or something?'

'No, smaller but quick as lightning.'

I racked my brain to identify the divil, but I couldn't place it for the life of me. Bullets shot past with white streams in their wake. One nearly hit me.

'It's a feckin' bird,' I said, laughing. 'Birds, I can handle.'

I swam for four hours and reached St John's Point Lighthouse at the tip of Dundrum Bay, the locality of attempt one's demise.

It was Friday, 21 June. St John's Point Lighthouse marked the beginning of phase two of three. In tide books, this part of the Irish Sea is 'SLACK'. The southbound tide from the north counteracts the northbound tide from the south to create an area without tidal flow between County Down and County Louth.

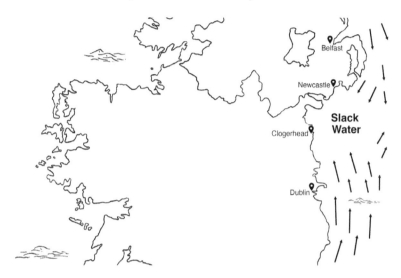

I made it four more hours south. Though Newcastle was the nearest port, I'd already learned my lesson the hard way that it was tidal. We took the long commute back north to Ardglass Marina.

During the drive, I checked the data.

I smiled as I melted into the bench. 'We did it. Thank feck for that anyway.' I'd made it past the point of failure in 2017 and set a hard-fought personal record. Although behind schedule with the lack of swimming on days nine to eighteen, I still beat 2017's marker by seven days. I was elated.

The team cheered. 'Wahey!'

'Some more good news,' Kaja told me. 'I got my results. I'm officially a neuroscientist.'

'And Karolína's just aced her degree!' I shouted up to the deck. 'We got a brain box onboard.'

'Good on you, guys. Wow, great work. We're celebrating tonight, then.'

On shore, we were straight to the fish and chips takeaway, followed by the off-licence for cheap Prosecco to spray about the marina. The evening's red sky blazed as the team nattered on deck. We sipped from boozy mugs and savoured the great times, happy faces, and cheery company.

Saturday arrived. It was Chris and Noel's final day, having gone above and beyond after returning to help us out of a rut.

Charity fundraising reached €4,775. I'd passed 2017's endpoint, but I had a lot of swimming and promoting left to exceed 2017's €12,656 fundraising tally.

Lion's mane breezed below me every thirty minutes, putting me on edge and forcing me to doggy paddle. I tried the neoprene balaclava to protect my face and neck, but it did more harm than good by restricting my vision and breathing. It made me feel claustrophobic. Instead, I slathered on some Vaseline to put some pudge between the tentacles and my skin.

I put one arm in front of the other at my standard rate (approximately 2.5 kilometres per hour).

'Alan! Karolína!' Chris said after two and a half hours. 'I know it's supposed to be slack, but we don't seem to be moving with the headwind and those waves hitting you from the south. I don't want a repeat of day one. Want to call it a day?'

'I'm feeling strong. Let me try up the pace for thirty minutes and see if I can get anywhere before giving in.'

I clipped along for thirty minutes and checked back in with headquarters.

'You're moving – barely, though. It's not matching the effort you're putting in.'

There was no point continuing for the sake of it. I called it a day there at the three-hour marker, a bit disappointed but more concerned about how we'd figure out the tide since it wasn't supposed to be moving north or south on paper.

'The new crew's not in until Monday evening. How about a Saturday night in the mountains?' Chris said. 'I can take you to a wee cottage up there.'

I looked at Kaja and Adriana to see what they wanted to do. Their eyes were alight.

'You don't need to ask us. If we can get off the boat, let's gooo!'

We chugged across Dundrum Bay towards Ardglass, and enjoyed the best seats in the house for the Newcastle Airshow.

'Now, Alan, would you look at you, eh. You've made it,' Chris said. 'Just like that Red Bull athlete who swam around Britain last year with those fancy stunt pilots doing flips for him.'

Chris turned off the main road, driving up a one-lane track with a grass strip up the middle, lined by thick hedgerows on either side.

'This is as close as we can get by car. The rest'll have to be on foot.'

We unloaded our gear and grocery shopping, and hauled it up the Mourne Mountains. The last thing I needed after a long sea swim was a weighted mountain hike, but it was worth the effort.

We reached a wooden gate hugged by a dry-stone wall, rocks of all sizes balanced in perfect harmony atop one another. I lifted the latch into the front garden and looked up to a mighty ash tree looming over a humble, no-frills cottage. The mountain rose behind the slate roof. I sat on the garden's raised bench and soaked in the view.

The wild beauty of greens and yellows, scrubland and farmland, sheep, trees, hedgerows, and ancient stone walls rolled down the mountainside and into the sea.

'You can't get much better than this.'

After dinner, I explored the landscape with Kaja, and made friends with two roaming white horses straight from a fairy tale.

We relaxed in the heat of the kitchen's open fire before pulling down the ceiling's hatch, unfolding the steep stairs, and climbing to our mattress on the attic floor. I was lax about refuelling. I got caught up in the excitement of going somewhere new and knowing there was no swim the following day. I became lethargic and passed out seconds after hitting the pillow.

I woke in the middle of the night to use the bathroom. Half asleep, and still exhausted, I felt around for the ceiling hatch. The narrow steps were almost vertical, like on the sailboat. I let go of the handrails and reached my foot for the floor, but it wasn't there. The stairs were much longer than my sleeping muscles remembered from *Unsinkable II*. I fell a metre, trying to grab the stairs in the darkness, and splattered like a dropped egg on the kitchen's rustic red-sand tiles.

'Is everything okay out there?' Chris said from his bedroom.

I tensed my core and fists to bottle my yell of agony, blood swelling to my pressurised head.

'Al, are you okay?' Kaja said from the attic, realising I wasn't beside her.

'Yeah. All good. Sorry. Just tripped,' I said, holding my breath and tensing between each statement. Tears dripped down my cheeks. The pain was as intense as all the injuries of the thirty-five marathons, localised on my shin and condensed into minutes, not weeks. It was 3 a.m., and it was a twenty-minute hike down the mountain. Even then, we were still in the sticks, miles up a back lane, and nowhere near a hospital. There was no point making a song and a dance, getting everyone flustered.

I tried to stand but couldn't bear any weight on my right leg. *Fuck*. It was too dark to see any damage. I rubbed my shin and felt a golf ball. I hopped to the toilet and pulled the light cord. My left-hand fingers were sliced open and bleeding at the creases, inflicting the pain of several wayward cuts on a chopping board. My shin was in bits, cut, bleeding, and swollen. I tried to walk again but couldn't. The agony swirled the contents of my stomach, and I felt like puking. I stood on one leg, leaning my forehead against my forearm in the doorframe. I closed my eyes and focused on deep breathing, trying to calm the roaring sensations rattling my nervous system.

I shimmied one-handed and one-legged back up to the mattress in the attic.

'What happened?' Kaja said. 'Are you okay?'

'Just slipped on the stairs. I'll be grand. Go back to sleep.'

The cuts on my fingers felt like surface wounds, but I wondered if I'd fractured my shin when it collided with the jagged edge of the step. I tried to remain quiet in my suffering, but I feared this could end my second attempt. Thoughts swirled. *Can I swim with a cast on my leg? I'll only go in circles kicking with my right leg. Christy*

Brown figured out a way to paint with his left foot. I'll manage.

We got up on Sunday morning. Despite the gross swelling and blue discolouration, I could bear weight and muster a limp down the mountainside. The pain decreased from a ten to a six out of ten. I ruled out a fracture. I had the lesser problem of maintaining open wounds beneath a clammy and often urine-warmed neoprene layer – not an ideal healing ground.

Kaja and I hugged Adriana and Chris goodbye, and waited for the next team to arrive.

The Republic

Gavin Downey and Tim Atkins injected fresh blood for week four, arriving on Monday evening. Both men were in their late twenties and were excited to crack on. Gavin had my back in 2012 on the lap-of-Ireland run and in 2017 on my first swim attempt. You'd think he'd have more sense than to join forces again, but having him back on board was invaluable. Tim was a stranger, a mature medical student with a rugby build and long hair. He responded to my social media plea for volunteers and travelled across the pond from England to use his extensive sailing background to help me progress.

We were straight to business on Monday night, stretching the charts and tide books out on the table to make our passage plans for Tuesday. Though I was progressing down the coast, it hadn't felt like it for weeks two and three. We had arrived in Ardglass on day ten. It was now day twenty-four, so the goal was clear – get the feck out of here and onto the next marina for the sake of my head.

We weren't sure what was going on with the tide during the last swim since the charts declared it was 'slack' (no tidal movement north or south), but progress had slowed to a snail's pace in the third hour – nothing some trial and error couldn't solve.

I plopped into the sea on Tuesday, 25 June, unsure how the tide would treat us. Tim and Gav monitored the tide's behaviour on the boat's navigation equipment as we swam and kayaked.

'Karolína! Alan!' Tim said from the deck. 'We've slowed right down. Climb back up, and we'll keep monitoring and tell you when to go again.'

After two hours of working, we clambered aboard for a break. I couldn't face getting out of, and back into, the wetsuit. Instead, I turned my fleece-lined changing robe inside out, zipped it, and stuck the hood up.

Kaja laughed, nearly spitting out her tea. 'You look like a sunburned baby chicken.'

Much to her delight, I flapped my little wings towards the Nutella and ate calorie-dense spoonfuls from the jar like an animal.

'The tide seems to be back moving again. Let's give it another go,' Tim said two hours later.

We climbed back into the water. A gigantic lion's mane jellyfish came alongside me to show me he was longer than my six-foot-two frame. Not good for my ticker. I incorporated some double-arm backcrawl. This technique allowed me the freedom to swear at the bastard and escape simultaneously.

The change in routine did the trick, with no treadmill swimming like day twenty-two in Dundrum Bay.

It was a long auld introduction for Tim and Gav, manning the boat for twelve hours between the commutes and supervising my swim.

With four hours of swimming and outsmarting the tidal anomalies with the mid-swim break, we accomplished our day's goal of progressing enough to justify commuting to the next port of Carlingford Marina in the Republic of Ireland. We moored up in the flat waters, shielded by concrete slabs. Though now in the Republic of Ireland, I still had a lot of work to achieve this milestone under my own propulsion. Still, it was a marker worth celebrating.

'No pasta and sauce tonight, lads. Dinner's on me. To the Republic, yup ya boyo!' I said and climbed on deck. 'Oh, wow, that's an epic change of scenery.'

We bobbed at the valley's base in a marina packed with sailboats. The Cooley Mountains rose south of the fjord. Legend has it that the rolling hills formed over the body of the sleeping giant Fionn mac Cumhaill, the same giant that forged the Giant's Causeway. The Mourne Mountains climbed north on the other side of the narrow inlet. Grazed farmlands and territorial hedgerows covered the lowlands, rising to unspoiled forests and uncultivated heaths of ferns, heathers, and gorse up high.

The ancient stones of Carlingford Castle dominated the shoreline. We meandered medieval lanes past hen parties with inflated willies and stag parties in rural uniform – checked shirts, denim jeans, and brown leather shoes – before settling into PJ O'Hare's pub for dinner and a well-earned pint of Guinness.

A violent commotion woke me during the night. I leapt and nearly knocked myself out when my head hit the coffin's ceiling.

'What's happening?' Kaja said in a panic.

'Not a notion.'

It was pitch dark. It felt like a magnitude-seven earthquake. I groped for the light switch but couldn't place it during the jolting tremors. The only explanation my sleeping mind had was that the boat must have come loose, and we'd drifted into the lough during a storm. I hurried out of our front cabin to muster the crew and get us back to safety. A wave knocked me over onto the bench. Tim rushed from his rear cabin, and we met in the middle.

'Everyone okay?' I said. 'What's going on?'

Gav was out of his sleeping bag in the main cabin. His headlight shone from me to Tim like a lighthouse, then back to his phone screen.

'We're grand; it's a ferry heading to England,' he said. 'It's the wake. She's a big girl, and she's moving.' All the displaced water funnelled through the marina's entrance, hitting us with its full force. 'Not the smartest parking spot. We'll have to move out of the marina's mouth for tomorrow night. Well, back to sleep, I suppose.'

Tim and Gav were as good as gold and took to their roles like ducks to water. We gelled, and they restored team spirits. Their personalities and nautical diligence allowed Kaja and me to relax and focus on our swimming, kayaking, and documenting roles.

Though fatigued from the 3 a.m. heart palpitations, I clocked four hours of swimming on the following afternoon – day twenty-six.

I completed four more hours on day twenty-seven. I took my goggles off in the water to look to land and see if I'd done enough to swim south of the lough and into the Republic.

'Ah, feck's sake. Still north of the yoke,' I said to Kaja as I rolled onto my back in frustration.

'You've done great. All these four-hour swims, we'll be south in no time.'

Feeling defeated, I heaved myself up the boat's ladder as the water slapped up. I fist-bumped the men.

'Thanks for another big day.'

Tim and Gav helped Kaja onboard. I switched off the GPS trackers and checked the live website map.

'Wahay! Get in, you beaut! Lads, we did it. We *are* south. We're in Ireland. It just doesn't look it from here, is all. Unreal!'

I blared 'Fisherman's Blues' on the speakers and listened to The Waterboys' anthem with a broad smile on deck, allowing a flood of joy to wash over me.

As I said, diversifying your investment with mini-goals is essential. It allowed me to accomplish things along the journey and motivated me to reach the next target. Completing Northern Ireland and making it to the Republic had eluded me by a few kilometres in 2017. Reaching the milestone was a monumental victory worth cheering about and definitely justified another round of butter chickens and Cokes from the marina's Indian takeout.

My diary entry from day twenty-seven read:

I'm overwhelmed by Kaja's support, taking up kayaking in September, doing all the safety courses with me during the year, training her arse off and sticking out the last twenty-seven days even when the going got tough; what a partner in crime to share this journey.

The bad thing about all this consistent swimming is swimming consistently. I'm tired and sore, but that's far outweighed by seeing that tracker move each day, little by little but getting there. These are the donkey miles with no tide, but I'm keeping my head down, and although not covering massive ground, I know it's my own steam which is satisfying in and of itself.

The Republic is one massive target reached. The next target is in the scope – Clogherhead. It mightn't be well-known and seems a strange goal compared to 'make Belfast in a week' or 'swim the length of Northern Ireland', but Clogherhead is a pivotal point on my route as it marks the beginning of the third and final phase of the swim. Phase three is where the tide picks up again, and progress should accelerate once my team, mother nature, and Unsinkable II *enable me to get in the water.*

Rip

The sun blazed in a cloudless sky. Temperatures reached the mid-twenties, but the wind raged. The forecast looked border-line for safe sea swimming on day twenty-eight. We were keen to keep the ball rolling with a competent crew and twelve hours of swimming over the last three days. We motored from Carlingford Marina into the lough, hoisting the sails with the sheets rippling in the wind. Sailboats and jet skis frolicked on the sheltered waters as we journeyed east towards the start coordinates. The village of row upon row of magnolia caravans emptied on the north shore as families jammed the golden sands of Greencastle Beach, kids with buckets and spades splashing in the shoreline's shallows.

We edged out of the lough and left the motherly protection of the roaming shamrock mountains to face the dangers of the open sea.

As the amusement ride began, Kaja and I retreated below deck. We lay as usual in the main cabin, where seasickness had reduced powers on our innards. Surviving storms had assured us we wouldn't flip over and sink, and we'd become accustomed to that sinking feeling in our stomachs like being on a rollercoaster, but our hands still had the innate reflex to grab the nearest fixed object to brace ourselves for the crash after ramping a wave.

Unsinkable II launched off a crest. One second passed, but the hull didn't collide with the sea like usual. Two seconds passed, and we remained suspended in space. On the third second, Kaja and I frowned across the cabin at each other.

'Shite.'

Wallop, like a whiplashing car crash. The boat returned to its resting position in the water.

'Sorry, guys,' Tim said from the cockpit. 'I should have seen that one coming.'

That was a decent indication that a swim wouldn't be on the cards.

Once at the waypoint, we met on deck for a risk assessment. A monster wave broke off the side of the boat, taking us all by surprise and drenching Gav like the ice bucket challenge.

'Ah, fresh and warm that,' Gav said.

Tim caught some sea spray on his face, too. 'Bloody hell, what do you consider cold then?'

'What height are they? Two, three metres? It's not a day for kayaking,' I said.

'Yeah, it'd be risky leaning over and trying to lift the kayak off and on,' Gavin said.

'Would you be able to steer a course for me to follow in this?' I asked Tim.

'Realistically, it won't be near an efficient line with the winds and waves. It's fun sailing conditions, but idling under motor near you will be pretty nasty on the boat. I think we're best leaving this one off.'

'Looking at the height and frequency, you'd probably only have eyes on me in the water, what, ten or twenty per cent of the time. Yeah, look, it's not worth the risk.'

As we retreated to the protection of the lough and marina, there was a hullaballoo on the marine radio. We heard there was a missing swimmer. The Irish Coastguard launched their Rescue 116 helicopter from Dublin, and rescue boats deployed from Skerries and Clogherhead.

'That's worrying,' I said to the others. 'I hope they're okay.'

The following day, Saturday, 29 June, we learned that a fourteen-year-old girl had been caught in a rip current while swimming at the beach. The teenager died. The accident consumed my thoughts for the day's four hours of swimming, covering twelve kilometres.

Rip currents drag bathers directly away from shore, sometimes at speeds that even Olympians can't counter. When they realise their predicament, instinct makes them naturally make a beeline for the beach. It's easy for panic to ensue when they notice they're not progressing or the sea is dragging them further offshore. People stroke and kick harder, sprinting to reach safety but often get exhausted.

These powerful currents are in channels generally no wider than twenty-five metres, the length of a typical swimming pool. With even the strongest swimmers unable to beat the outbound rip, counterintuitively, you must swim parallel to the beach to escape the suction of the dangerous narrow channel. Once freed from the rip by swimming to the left or the right, you can begin swimming to shore.

Irish beaches are a fantastic asset, and swimming is a great activity, but things can go wrong quickly at sea, even if you're careful. As an island nation, we need to know about rip currents and the dangers of cold water. Water safety and first aid should be in every school's curriculum to equip people with the knowledge to avoid trouble, save themselves, and be able to help others.

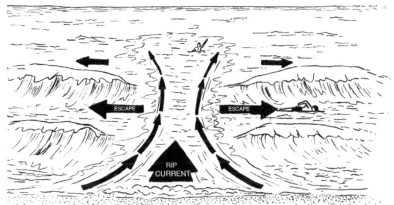

A full moon illuminated the glassy water of the silent lough as we shut the hatch to snuggle in for the night. A menacing howl woke us. Five seconds later, an avalanche of destructive wind accelerated down the Cooley Mountains and engulfed the marina. Wind and waves shook us left, right, up, and down, causing a racket of clinking metals. Eerie calmness followed.

'That was mental.'

'Go back to sleep.'

Just as I was about to drift off again, a whistle built to a roar. We tensed up as the gale-force gust rocked us once more.

The alarm sounded at 6:30 a.m. on Sunday, and I climbed on deck to inspect the weather.

'Seems alright.'

A gust sucker-punched me, nearly knocking me overboard.

'Maybe not.'

We inspected the weather apps – Magic Seaweed, Windy, Windguru – and concluded it wasn't a day to swim a mile offshore.

'Thanks for everything, lads,' I said to Tim and Gav as they packed the car to leave. 'Sixteen hours of swimming this week, out of Ardglass, out of the North, and nearly out of slack waters. Couldn't be happier with you. Smashed it!'

We were one month in, with over sixty hours swum, and around 230 kilometres covered. My day's diary entry read:

I'm not as far as I planned to have been by day thirty, but it's a marathon and not a sprint. There are a lot of variables out of my control. I must do my best to be patient, roll with the punches, and swim my heart out when possible. On day thirty in 2017, I made a lonely solo bus journey from Newcastle back to Waterford after my support boat sank and killed my first attempt. If I still fail, I'm delighted to have improved upon my last effort and bettered myself. I'm hopeful of reaching Tramore Beach by the end of July, and if I don't, it won't be for lack of trying.

The Summit

The gusts dissipated by Monday night. Jonathan Dunne and

Ciarán O'Hanlon joined Kaja and me in Carlingford Lough on Tuesday, 2 July. Both men were in their mid-twenties, down-to-earth, and raring to go. We set sail for day thirty-two.

Kaja's wildlife reflex disrupted my meditative swim rhythm. Even though she knows I hate being in the water with anything not human, she can't contain her excitement. The alarm meant something more significant than a jellyfish in the water. Her excited squeal was sharper and more prolonged than in previous incidences, making me uneasy.

'Christ, what is it now? More dolphins?'

'Something *really* big, but I don't know what.'

'What do you mean, *something really big?*' I said, pivoting left and right, expecting to see a great white.

A lone dorsal fin slowly breached through the satin surface.

'It's about five metres long!'

'It's not an orca or a shark, thank fuck. Probably a whale. Minke, maybe.'

As I flicked my eyes up on each breath, I caught Kaja dancing about the kayak and celebrating each whale breach with cheers as I focused on the more immediate creatures – the swarms of jellyfish and lion's mane, which I could see, and feel, all too often.

With another four-hour swim banked, we reached Clogherhead, but fishing boats lined every inch of the pier wall, two and three deep. The team moored *Unsinkable II* alongside a trawler parked against another fishing ship. Fat seals honked in the water, begging for the day's fishing haul. Sparks flew on a trawler's deck as an angle grinder machine-gunned our eardrums.

'I miss the marina already,' I said as I climbed across the ships' decks, tripping over fishing nets to reach the comforting solid ground beneath my feet. Though lacking creature comforts, I was chuffed to bits to reach my mountain's summit. This point of my journey marked the end of stage two, with the coldest, deepest, most volatile, fastest, and slowest seas behind us. I was proud, but I knew the summit was only half the work. Descents can often be at least as treacherous.

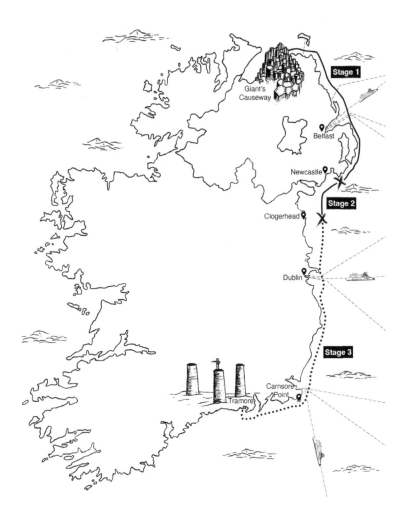

Having reached this significant milestone, I announced the swim's finale plans with no date yet set in stone. I invited participants to register for the 600-metre open-water event, with all profits going to the Heart Foundation and Solas Centre.

Four-hour swims were now the norm, and I had secured an entire crew for weeks five, six, seven, and eight. Importantly, we had tidal assistance from Clogherhead all the way home to Waterford. Although I was a long way from home, reaching the finish line seemed realistic.

Morale was sky-high. Jonathan and Ciarán injected another shot of youthful enthusiasm and craic into the mission. Fair-weather sailing conditions helped the atmosphere, the sea a sun-drenched soup. Though the weather was favourable, it wasn't easy. I kept swimming into the kayak with the gentle wind and waves not aligning with our desired direction. I became pessimistic about everything. That doesn't do anyone any good, but I recognised it. I stopped two or three extra times in the third hour, chatting with Kaja or taking a floating breather or unscheduled feed. It took a bit longer than forcing progress in a sulk, but it worked, and I finished the fourth hour in a good place and still with my partner beside me on day thirty-three.

The project was flowing once more. Ticking Antrim, Down, and now Louth off the to-do list, we were just south of Drogheda, into County Meath waters.

Conditions had spoiled us earlier in the week, but we were back to slogging it on day thirty-four. Headwinds made life unpleasant for Kaja and me for the first two hours on the water. Her paddling was hard and constant, doubling the previous day's stroke rate to fight the relentless wind shoving her north.

'Are you alright?' I said. 'That wind sucks. You're doing great.'

'Yeah, I'm good. Keep it up.'

I could tell she wasn't. Rogue waves splashed and soaked her with added layers of misery.

Things weren't much better in the water. I turned to breathe every second stroke, but my head was still in a wave, or I'd squeeze a half breath before a wave slapped me on the chin. The swell and chop often restricted my breathing to every fourth or sixth stroke. Despite all my training and getting this far down the coast, I hadn't taken the time to learn bilateral breathing to the right *and* left. With limited prep time, I couldn't do it all. I could only breathe to the right side. Taking a breath to the left was akin to writing with my bad hand. It was ugly. It felt wrong and uncontrolled, upsetting my body's position in the water, slowing my pace and ruining my rhythm. Breathing to the left might have come in handy on this day of limited oxygen supply, but it was too late to learn. I held the air until my face turned blue and flipped onto my back if that was the only way for my mouth to clear the surface. In the pool, I trained my shoulders and elbows to recover while flying through the air's freeness before they glided into the water, caught it, and scooped it backwards to propel myself forwards. Now, surrounded by high waves, I could rarely free my hand from the thick molasses. When I did find a pocket of air to swing my arm through, a wave usually forced my hand and forearm back like an aggressive police officer restraining an assailant. The sea deprived me of any recovery during the strokes.

It's easy to stay motivated when things are going well. What would get me to the finish line in Tramore was not spiralling downwards in challenging conditions like these. *I can't swim like this. Sod the sodding waves ruining my progress. I might call it a day and come back tomorrow when it's fine out.* I'd become adept at catching these internal monologues. I knew conditions out of my control slowed us. My swimming was not pretty. I accepted every day couldn't go my way, and some days I just needed to put in the shift. Hold that thought.

'Lads! We're still moving, we are? We're not stalled or going backwards?'

'Yeah, Rockabill Lighthouse and Skerries are up ahead, and we're gaining.'

'Alright, just checking. Thanks!'

I'd tell myself we're moving forwards, so keep chipping away at it.

I stroked and felt seaweed.

'Kajo! Are ya sure there's nothing I can do to cheer you up, mon?' I said, trying a Jamaican accent, flicking my new hairdo behind my ear and doing my best to make her smile.

Some play released the tension from her furrowed brow. We joked around for a bit before continuing in better spirits, clocking another four hours and completing the Meath coastline.

We pulled into Skerries, North Dublin, that evening. The tide was out, so we dropped anchor offshore and looked to land as we waited for the tide to rise. Sailing and fishing boats rested on the shore's muddy tidal flats, their trousers down and their bare bottoms exposed. Cafés, bars, and restaurants overflowed with sunglass-wearing alfresco drinkers and diners.

'Another hour, and we should have the depth to allow us in,' Jonathan said.

My belly growled. 'I'm tempted to kayak in and get a starter. I'm starving.'

The tide rose. Jonathan and Ciarán tip-toed *Unsinkable II* towards the deepest water at the end of the pier.

'Keep an eye on the depth sensor,' Jonathan said.

'It's dropping,' Ciarán said. The reading let us know how much water we had beneath the boat. 'Twenty foot, nineteen, fifteen ...'

'Almost in.'

'Ten ...'

Beep, beep, beep, came the alarm, warning us we were risking running aground. I sweated.

'Nine, eight, seven ...'

'There!'

We parked with a few inches to spare.

'We should have an hour or two, but let's not arse about. Grab some food, and we'll tie up to a buoy in the bay for the night.'

After dinner, we climbed down the pier's ladder and across two commercial fishing trawlers that stank like guts. Seagulls covered *Unsinkable II* like seaside vinegar on chips. We jumped onto the deck to a scattering of caws and white bombs dropping.

The bay was majestical as we reversed out to anchor down for our first night offshore. The once mud-bound fleet of small fishing boats near the shore now floated on silky blue shallows. The sun was yet to disappear, but a faint silver crescent moon floated above the emerald farmlands that were fading to black. Wispy cloud streaks spanned from the horizon to the heavens like lines on an empty copybook. Where the ocean met the headland, the sky layered upwards from peach, orange, and yellow, to blue.

'Lovely food, great company, and a perfect sunset. Made it to Dublin,' I said with some disbelief to the team while taking in the surroundings on deck. 'We might just pull this feckin' thing off, you know.'

Last Stripe

Day thirty-five's swim began a few kilometres north of The Rock and The Bill islands, known as Rockabill. They sit five kilometres offshore, with Rockabill Lighthouse protruding from the rogue rock like a striped candle on a one-year-old's birthday cake.

The landmark provided Kaja with a helpful bearing as we aimed due south to shoot between the island and Dublin's mainland.

'Al! Karolína!' the call came from the boat. 'We're not going to make it inside the island. There's a current or wind pushing us out, so we're aiming for the outside; otherwise, we're on the rocks.'

We adapted and changed course. I rotated to my side and inhaled. A giant wine-red glob of terror greeted me on my return.

'Ah, the dickhead got me!' I said to Kaja as I lifted my head from the armed lion's mane. I'd swum eighty hours over the previous five weeks and had bashed through thousands of jellyfish. This was the first occasion there was no time to react and jerk my head from the sea. Not a bad statistic in the grand scheme of things, but I got zapped on the nose and cheek and wasn't impressed.

'Do you want to stop and get out?' Kaja said rhetorically. 'Or, I can ask one of the lads to pee on you from the boat?'

'No, but—'

'Well, keep going so.'

'Jesus, no sympathy here, huh?' I laughed. *'Unbelievable.'*

The stings hurt, but Kaja knew it wasn't enough to stop me. There was no point hanging around moaning. Besides, I'd now earned my final stripe and felt like a *real* sea swimmer.

After four more hours of swimming, I climbed back aboard off the coast of Rush and flaunted my battle wound.

'I got stung by a lion's mane in the face.'

'Ouch. Are you alright?'

'Ah, I'll be grand. It wasn't as bad as falling down the bloody stairs. I'd say the scruffy beard and Vaseline minimised the damage.'

With Rockabill dodged the previous day, we worked towards the next, more sizeable island with a history of sinking fifty ships. Lambay Island is a lush square mile where a centuries-old castle sits, and four people, cattle, deer, birds, and *wallabies* roam.

This time we managed to stay on the intended course, tracking an efficient path inside the island and tucking closer to the coast of Donabate and Malahide.

'Ha ha, lads, look! Poolbeg up ahead!' I said.

I paused and removed my goggles to soak up the encouraging sight of south Dublin's famous red-and-white chimney stacks piercing the horizon.

'We're bombing it along this week! Hon, the lads!'

The landmark motivated me through the shoulder pains before finishing the day's four-hour swim at another island.

'What island's that?' I said to Ciarán, the hometown man.

'That's Ireland's Eye. You're probably used to seeing it when you land at Dublin Airport. There's a Martello tower there, too, look.'

A stout round tower stood above the yellow moss-covered rocks.

'There's a few of those around here, built hundreds of years ago to defend the place.'

We were gunning for Howth Marina after two nights off the side of fishing trawlers and two nights anchored at sea. Though we took in the experience with a smile, we looked forward to the electricity, fuel, and much-needed showers awaiting us.

'Ugh,' Jonathan sighed with a smile. 'This is going to be embarrassing.'

'What's that?' I said.

'Howth Marina, Howth Marina, this is *Unsinkable II*, *Unsinkable II* …' he said into the VHF to announce our arrival to the harbourmaster. He laughed and shook his head. 'No sailor in their right mind would name a boat that.'

'There're loopholes for me, though. I'm no sailor, and it's questionable if I'm in my right mind. Made you smile, didn't it?' I grinned. 'That's the main thing.'

It was Jonathan and Ciarán's last night. The young guns had been a massive help in getting us to the most consistent swim stretch – four-hour swims on Tuesday, Wednesday, Thursday, Friday, and Saturday, taking us from Dundalk Bay to Howth in five steps.

TWELVE
Shipping Lanes
215 Kilometres Remaining

Pilot Boat

Brian Hett and Colm Higgins tagged in for Jonathan and Ciarán on day thirty-six. Brian was a business executive and a yacht owner in his fifties with many sailing qualifications. Colm was twenty-four, and although he didn't have many formal certificates, he had lived aboard a small boat that he'd sailed up and down the east coast of Ireland and across to the Isle of Man.

'What's the plan for tomorrow?' Brian asked me.

'We're about two kilometres north of Ireland's Eye. If we can keep up the distances we've been hitting this week, we should get across Dublin Bay. Getting out of the firing line of that shipping lane is the main goal.'

'Right. That's an interesting first day. Have you got permission from the Dublin Port Authority?'

'That, I did not do.'

'I'll give them a call first and make sure we're on their radar, and I can keep in touch over the radio once you're in the water and moving.'

'That sounds like a right plan. Perfect.'

'Are you good to go?' I said to Kaja on the northern edge of Dublin Bay, preparing to up my pace a notch. 'Keep your eyes peeled.'

I entered Ireland's busiest shipping lane with more tension than usual.

'Hold up, Al, there's a ship coming in from your left.'

The white dot looked tiny away in the distance.

'Have Brian or Colm said anything yet?'

'Not yet.'

'Okay, keep an eye on it and flag the guys over if it's looking sketchy.'

I continued.

'Al! Stop there.'

Dublin Port's pilot vessel was alongside *Unsinkable II* when I popped up.

'I hope they're not getting us to abort.'

That teeny-weeny white dot from a few minutes earlier was now a gargantuan passenger ferry ploughing towards our intended path faster than a runaway train.

'We're like sitting ducks here. That's a bit close for my liking. The size and speed of that thing, Christ almighty,' I said to Kaja. 'What else would you be up to on a sunny afternoon?'

'Do you want to hop up to stay warm until it passes?' Brian said from the helm of the support boat. 'The pilot boat tells us to sit tight for ten minutes.'

'I'm good, thanks. I'll be grand down here.'

After repeated cold water immersion, I adapted to the environment. This was helped, of course, by progressing further south and deeper into the summer – into warmer waters.

It was calming to know the new team were looking out for me. The added presence of the Port Authority, now facilitating my crossing, was a welcome blanket of comfort.

We repeated the process three times over the following ninety minutes. I put the pedal to the metal until Kaja told me to stop. A tall ship, cargo ship, or passenger ferry would shoot by, and the unbalanced game of chicken continued.

Working with the Dublin Port Authority, we averted catastrophe and kept trucking. After another consecutive four-hour swim, we moored *Unsinkable II* in Dún Laoghaire, South Dublin, under nightfall.

Safe or Gamble?

For the mass-participation swim off Tramore Beach, County Waterford, I negotiated with the local council and events insurance companies, created a thorough health and safety document, and recruited sea and land support. I convinced EIR to sponsor the finale extravaganza and worked with The Tenth Man creative agency to complete the display. We arranged custom EIR swim caps, a branded inflatable finish banner, and a giant turn buoy that looked like a pink Minion to mark the course. These were custom-made, and brandished with EIR, the Irish Heart Foundation, and Solas Cancer Support Centre logos. I did the heavy lifting and could safely accommodate 300 swimmers.

There was a problem – only eight people registered within the week after I announced the event on my social media pages. I guessed that this was because I couldn't predict the finale's exact date and time with much accuracy. I feared that the event might be a flop.

Worse still, despite my 2017 swim attempt raising shy of €13,000 for charity, my 2019 charity tally sat at just €6,842. I needed the finish to be a success to surpass my previous efforts.

The insurance company required me to pay the cash and confirm (gamble on) the finale's date and time at least one week in advance. I'm sure potential participants wanted similar notice, and it needed to fall on a weekend to ensure the highest participation and the most significant bang for the charity fundraising pot.

I'd reached South Dublin, having swum over 300 kilometres. It was the start of week six, morning thirty-eight, Monday, 8 July 2019.

I thought seriously about when I might reach Waterford and what I could do to make things spicier for the audience online and more challenging for me. I had two options:

1. Keep the pace I'd set the previous two weeks and continue my four hours of daily swimming.

2. Up the ante, put the foot down, and race the clock.

With the first option, while there were no guarantees with weather, boats, and volunteers, continuing on a four-hour-a-day swim programme would *almost* guarantee a 27 July finale, in three weeks, at the end of week eight. There was leeway for delays. But I'd miss Kaja's master's graduation on 25 July. The scheduled skipper for week seven bailed on me, meaning I was short a pair of hands on the sailboat. I'd lose momentum with a thumb-twiddling week off somewhere on the east coast. I felt this would make it less likely to attract charity donations and swimmers to partake in the final swim.

The second option meant creating urgency and extra struggle. I'd have to pull out all the stops for the remainder of week six to land myself in a favourable position on, or close to, the south coast. If I could do that, I could swim beach to beach on sections of the southern shoreline. A big week six could potentially entice volunteer sailors to step in to join Colm on the boat and enable me to finish with a bang in two weeks, at the end of week seven, and make Kaja's graduation. There were a lot of ifs, additional strain, and no guarantees the increased efforts would be worth it.

I took the callipers to the maps and spider-walked it down the coastline. I consulted with Tim Haines from my 2017 swim.

'I don't want to miss Kaja's graduation after all she's done for me, and I don't want to finish in eight weeks if it's possible to sprint and finish in seven.' I believed I could increase my daily efforts. 'Do you think it will be enough?'

'Option one is the sensible choice,' Tim said. 'Option two is possible, but it's a strain.'

It was down to playing it safe with a ninety-five per cent chance of success, accounting for rogue variables, or pushing myself, upping the hours, and striving to achieve something with about a twenty per cent chance of success.

My social media post from this day reads:

This challenge is not about playing it safe and doing what's easy, although four hours of sea swimming a day is certainly not easy. It's about taking measured risks, putting yourself out there for possible failure, and working hard to see what's possible. If my dad taught me anything, it's about giving it a bash and trying, so that's what I'll do. I'm going to push it this week. This coming Sunday, 14 July, I can confirm the finish date, at the end of week seven or eight, knowing I gave it my all.'

Darkness

My shoulders were stiff as pokers, but it didn't compare to the impact road running had on my body. I was grateful to get out and move every day, not having the frustrations of feeling stuck, like in weeks two and three. I had seven four-hour swimming days on the trot.

Four-hour swims were my staple. Why four hours? Because in open-water swimming, the 'marathon' distance is ten kilometres. It took me four hours to swim that distance when doing back-to-back daily marathons. With commuting and work time, four hours allowed enough downtime in the day to recover for the next onslaught.

On evening thirty-eight, though, I added an extra thirty minutes, making it the longest swim of attempt two. I dipped my toes in unnerving darkness, swimming out of Dublin under nightfall. Once Kaja and I climbed aboard, we motored into the next marina – Greystones, County Wicklow. The longer swim went well, and I wanted to ratchet things up again.

Mam visited us in Greystones, and we popped into The Happy Pear café for breakfast. The last time I'd eaten there was in 2012, with Dad, when he insisted we stop in as we drove around the country doing a reconnaissance of my lap-of-Ireland run route. The Happy Pear owners, Steve and Dave, are big into their sea dips, and gave our efforts the nod on social media, with more donations flooding in after their kind endorsement.

Mam sipped her coffee. 'I'm counting down the days until you're home safe and sound so I can sleep again.'

'We're on the home straight now. Be grand, Mam, don't be worrying.'

Swimming from Greystones, the waters felt colder. The sea was at its meanest in weeks, sloshing brine testing my resolve and strained shoulders. Conditions settled a little after the first hour, and I knew I had to make hay – upping it to five hours of swimming.

It was 11 p.m. when we left the pitch black and returned to the boat's warmth. There was no cooking at this hour. I wanted to save time and sleep as soon as possible to be somewhat rested for the morning's tide, sometime between 5 a.m. and 8 a.m., whatever the crew were willing to give me. I boiled the kettle and poured it into my sachet of 600 calories of dried camping food. Yum.

We pulled into a silent Wicklow at 1 a.m. The team was tired after a long day.

'It's going to be too soon to make the next tide,' Brian said. 'I'm concerned about Wicklow Head and don't want to take chances. Let's have a lie-in, which will give us time to take a closer look at the charts and chat with the local RNLI about how's best to approach the next section.'

'Righteo, no worries,' I said. 'Thanks for today. Sleep well.'

'What's the plan today, Al?' Kaja said.

'The guys ruled out swimming the two tides, so I'm planning to try to max the full six hours of the evening tide if you're up for it?'

'Yeah, sure, I'll give it a go. You up for six hours? Aren't your shoulders at you?'

'The most I've done in the sea's five, so I guess I'll find out. The shoulders will be grand, don't mind them.'

I cranked the dimmer switch in my mind and found another strength level. I was fully engaged, amped, the challenge within a challenge hitting like a morning espresso.

I was glad Brian had taken a cautious approach to Wicklow Head and that we consulted the RNLI about start times. Wicklow

Head waters were hard work for the first hour and a half. *Nothing you haven't come through already*, I reminded myself, having spent so long in favourable conditions as of late. The tide flowed south, and the wind blew north, kicking the sea upwards.

I could see Kaja's frustration in her mainly yes or no answers during food-stop chats. She had a constant battle with the head-wind and slopping waves.

'It feels like we're not moving anywhere,' she said.

I'd been there, in the mental rut, when it was just not your day. You're not feeling it.

'It might feel like that with the wind, but we're killing it – look,' I said, showing her the kilometres accumulated on my GPS watch. 'I'm sure it'll calm a bit after the headland. This is where Brian warned it can be volatile.'

My words didn't seem to be of much use. I'd asked a lot of myself, pushing for the finish line. Inadvertently, I'd asked Kaja for the same increased output, but the fatigue of the relentless progress since leaving the Northern Irish border was showing. She'd never been an athlete and had only taken up kayaking this year to help me fulfil a dream. Though she wasn't happy then, seeing her brute strength through the waves at my side was all the inspiration I needed to trudge forwards. I hoped the sight of my progress could lift her spirits even half as much as she did mine.

'Guys! Just to let you know, there's a weather warning with winds picking up later,' the team said.

I wished they hadn't told us. Teetering on the edge of having had enough, speculation about predicted weather only sowed more doubt and offered an out from discomfort.

'Maybe we should stop?' Kaja said to me.

'Well, they said later, not now or in an hour. I'm good to continue on my own if you want to hop on the boat?'

'No. Let's go.'

She was as stubborn as me – two mules – and deserved extra credit for persisting despite the day's difficulty.

Night fell. *Unsinkable II*, Kaja, and I turned on our navigation lights. Whites, greens, and blues shone miles offshore like a '90s Christmas tree.

Not only was this six-hour stint my longest-ever sea swim, but it was also the longest I'd submerged myself in darkness. I splashed forwards, not knowing when or where the next wave would attack. I kept touching things that felt like rubbery blobs. *Feck out of my way, will ya, ya brainless blubber; coming through,* I repeated to myself every time we collided. I smiled. I'd come so far since my initial open-water panic stations.

A noise came from Kaja. I popped up.

'What was that?' she said.

'What was what?'

'A splash! I don't know … There it is again!'

I adjusted my aim for my third attempt.

'Alan! Are you seriously throwing jellyfish at me right now? It's on my lap! Jesus Christ.'

I had to do *something* to create some entertainment in the sensory deprivation tank. I swam over to Kaja and released the chonky goo from the kayak, placing it back into the deep dark sea (*no jellyfish were harmed in the making of this book*).

When the tide stopped pushing south after six hours, a constellation of lights was glowing on the sleeping shore. Tonight's red-eye commute would be into Arklow Town, right there, so only a short trip to moor in the mouth of the Avoca River, thankfully.

Speed Bumps

My body was responding well to the increased toll during week six. Upping my hours with the accelerating tidal flow, we were moving my GPS tracker down the east coast at a rate of knots. We ate up the coast from Howth, North Dublin, along Wicklow to the Wexford border. I was optimistic about my decision to make a sprint finish attempt and complete the task within week seven.

Though recent progress had indicated I might pull off this ambitious aspiration, we were still short of a set of hands on deck for that seventh week. Even if I could get us within striking distance of the finish line and confirm the finale to the insurance company, there were overfalls, shipping lanes, rocky headlands, and a wide river mouth that Kaja and I couldn't safely traverse as a duo. In my mind, though, I convinced myself that the closer to home I could swim in week six, the more likely a sailor would step in and join Colm to finish this project on a high note. Sometimes you must push and hope things will fall in place. I was raring to go.

'I'm guessing you'd like to do another six hours today, but I think three is the best we can muster this evening. I don't want to risk pulling into Courtown's narrow marina in darkness. I'm not familiar with it,' Brian said. 'If we don't pull into Courtown, it will take about three hours to commute back here to Arklow, based on the distance you're covering. Six hours of swimming and a three-hour commute into the night isn't ideal, let's say.'

Brian was one hundred per cent correct to err on the side of caution, skippering someone else's boat with Colm onboard, Kaja in her kayak, and me in the water. Still, the outside factors tested my patience. Anything could put a branch in our spokes, from tide times and strength, wind speed and direction, sea state, visibility, commute durations, navigation into unfamiliar docking locations, or the team's comfort levels and sleep requirements. It was frustrating. I had the ability and desire to push things forwards but felt caged. That was just the nature of the beast. The last thing I wanted was unhappy volunteers. *It is what it is. No point whining to volunteers giving me their time,* I reminded myself. I just had to work my best in the confines they afforded me.

'Righto, if you can give me three hours, I'll push for three hours,' I said with a smile and a thumbs-up. 'Thanks a mil, Brian.'

The good thing for me, but bad for Kaja, was that she was there to listen to me unburden my agitation in private. I felt better having a little moan, and I could keep chipper with Brian and Colm putting in a long shift and doing their utmost to help to get me home safely.

The only thing I could do to influence matters was to find another gear and swim faster in the reduced time window to make Courtown and avoid a miserably long commute back north for us all. I felt determined to work around the obstacle and continue the trajectory of massive headway gains. That was the plan, anyway.

The waves, although humble, were irregular in frequency and

direction. It made it impossible for me to get into a rhythm with breathing, occasionally gagging on mouthfuls of water. My stroke didn't flow either, struggling to clear the waves with my arms, never mind getting my hands free from the syrup. The awkward wind kept blowing Kaja's kayak on top of me. We had never collided so much.

'Just paddle that way.'

'Well, you swim that way.'

The sun lowered to the west over Ireland in the cloudless sky. A clear sunset is usually a thing of beauty to behold. Because I'd only learned to breathe to the right, I cursed it. The glare blinded me and obscured Kaja from my sight, though she paddled feet away. The collisions continued, and we allowed it under our skin, compounding the three-hour deadline, lack of tide, and pressure to reach Courtown.

Finding my all-day pace and then upping it this far into the challenge took my focus and exhaustion to another level. I thought I'd cracked the code but was still finding limitations. These factors made it one of the most challenging swims yet.

I climbed up the ladder at the back of the boat. 'Did I do enough to justify moving on to Courtown?'

'Not quite, no. We're going to trot back to Arklow.'

I checked my GPS tracker map. Seeing the limited progress – roughly a quarter of the previous day – squished my earlier fire like a steamroller. Every day can't be a good one. Day forty-one was a swim to forget. Yet there was a small silver lining. We had completed County Wicklow and entered Wexford waters. That was something.

'What do you want to swim tomorrow?' Brian said.

'I'll take what I'm given. What are you comfortable with?'

'Well, you tell me what you'd like to do.'

'Ideally, I'd be up for trying to swim two full tides.'

'How about we just go for the morning tide and recover a bit in the evening?'

'Grand job so, one tide in the morning it is.'

On the east coast, two six-hour tides flow south roughly every twenty-four hours, moving forwards by approximately one hour each day. If the tide flows south between 5 p.m. and 11 p.m. today, it will begin to flow south at about 5:30 a.m. and again at 6 p.m. tomorrow. As well as shifting tide times, commute durations varied from thirty minutes to over three hours. We needed to eat and sleep too. There was no routine, which was challenging to manage. It was even trickier when we adjusted from swimming the evening tide to the morning one. In this scenario, we might only get about three hours of sleep if we commuted to and from Arklow Town and planned to use the entirety of the morning tide. The only way around that was to sleep offshore, where the swim finished, but the sailors didn't want to do this. Since the sea was too deep, we couldn't drop an anchor to secure us in position. We would be adrift. The two sailors would need to take shifts to watch from the deck through the night. The motion in open seas would deprive us of a more restorative sleep compared to a much calmer marina. Commuting was the least-worst option, given the size of the boat and the small, voluntary, two-person sailing team.

We missed the start of the following tidal flow to allow us all to get some sleep during the early hours of day forty-two. This left only a four-hour and fifteen-minute opportunity to swim.

We began swimming and kayaking five kilometres off Kilmichael Point, County Wexford, hoping we could leapfrog Courtown and reach Cahore Point.

We rebounded from the lull and accomplished the day's mission while returning to swimming in bright daylight rather than twilight and night.

'I'm not certain of the depth here, so I'll bring her in nice and easy,' Brian said.

Cahore Point was no marina but a short boatless pier wall thronged by local dunkers and divers enjoying the sea.

The boat's shallow depth alarm began, a bit like a car parking sensor, but with no change of pattern to gauge the hazard's proximity. We slowed and braced for an impact.

'Ah, we seem to have just about enough under us here,' Colm said.

'Perfect. There looks to be a busy pub up on the hill. Can I treat you to a meal, guys?' I said.

'That'd be lovely.'

After grub, the team returned to the boat while I took in the sights outside the hilltop pub and phoned my mam. Bees buzzed around holidaymakers' pints of cider on packed picnic tables. Friday's work shift was over. The pier was filling up with locals starting their weekend right – chatting, joking, and frolicking in the water.

After reassuring Mam that everything was still okay, I walked back to the pier.

'Where were you?' Kaja said with urgency.

Kids and adults jumped into the waters from up high before rushing back up the ladder to escape the chill. It was a glorious summer scene except for a bang every ten seconds. I climbed down to the boat.

'We need to get out of here,' Brian said.

The fin keel bashed the seabed and jerked us.

'Shite, yeah, let's move. Where to?'

'I asked a local. He said we should be fine for the night tied to that buoy, fifty metres out from the beach. A bit exposed, but best we can do.'

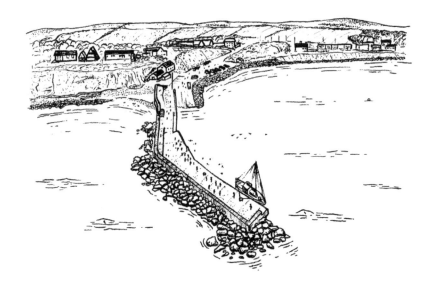

Resolve

It was my worst night's sleep on *Unsinkable II*. The sloshing motions woke me several times, only for the buzzer to sound at 6:30 a.m. for me to prepare to swim. I lacked no motivation to stroke to the next safe port, keen to spare us all from more sleepless nights anchored at Cahore Point.

It was day forty-three, Saturday, 13 July, and skipper Brian's last day in support. Week six was coming to a close. I had to make it count since week seven was still uncertain.

Only Gavin from week four had answered my online pleas for volunteers since the original skipper had cancelled. The gent didn't want me stuck and was returning to dig me out. Gav's a capable problem-solver I'd have on my team any day, but it wasn't ideal since he wasn't a sailor, having a powerboat licence but not much boating experience. He would support Colm, who was interning under Brian's tutelage for the week. Colm was a young sailor and knew his way about the sailboat but wasn't yet at skipper or Yachtmaster level. I hoped he'd picked up enough confidence and experience over his week with Brian, but it was a big ask and a bit of a risk. Still, Gav could only squeeze in tomorrow (Sunday), Wednesday, and Thursday because of his job. The chances of finding enough replacement volunteers to finish in week seven still seemed slim at best. There was little margin for error, with only three crewed days rather than seven. I needed this last swim with Brian to be a big one to keep the dream alive.

The southbound tide was now starting late enough in the day to allow us a more typical night's sleep, though waves ruined the last night. Because of this tide shift, I had nearly double the time to work compared to the previous two swims, which got cut short by late-night commuting demands and the team's early-morning sleep needs. I felt energised about getting to work with the extra hours of tidal assistance, needing every little break I could get at this stage.

I cannonballed off the back of the boat. 'Six hours, let's go,' I said and clapped. 'Thanks, men! Have a good one.'

'Best of luck, guys,' they said to Kaja and me.

I didn't go hell for leather out of the gates. I adjusted my pace for a slower six-hour shift.

After three and a half hours, a call came from the support boat.

'You only have thirty minutes of tide left!'

Wearing earplugs, a neoprene cap, and a silicone cap, I thought I'd misheard. 'What are they shouting, Kaja?'

'They're saying we only have thirty minutes of tide left, and we'll have to call it a day.'

'But we planned it for the full tide, six hours, to get to Rosslare. Agh.' I was agitated, but there was no point in losing more time complaining to Kaja or arguing with the crew. 'Right, let's get cracking. I guess I better try up my speed then.'

I shifted up a gear and worked hard. My watch ticked to four hours, and my surprise thirty-minute deadline expired. I rolled onto my back to float and huffed from the exertion and annoyance of losing swim time.

'What happened to the last two hours of tide?' I asked Kaja.

She signalled the team with a wave to indicate we were ready for extraction. 'No idea, Al.'

Unsinkable II pulled up to us.

'There're thirty minutes of tide left,' the sailors said.

'Another thirty minutes?'

'Yeah, the instruments still say we have tide, so it's up to you if you want to keep going?'

'A hundred per cent,' I said.

Normally, I'd eat every thirty minutes or drink a carbohydrate supplement. Because I thought we'd finished, I didn't bother to refuel while we waited five minutes for the boat to reach us. Since I'd learned there were another few minutes of the tide to work with, I didn't want to waste it refuelling. I put my head down and kept the relatively faster swimming pace up.

We reached the four-and-a-half-hour mark. I pulled out my earplugs, unstrapped the swim cap, and took off my gloves as Kaja signalled the boat for collection.

'That was hard going, thinking it's job done and then having to buckle down and continue,' I said to Kaja as I breathed deep, floating on my back, staring at the passing clouds.

'There's still tide if you want to continue?' the call came from the boat.

'Fuck me,' I said to Kaja.

Kaja paddled closer to me. 'What's going on?'

'Ugh, I don't know. This is a joke,' I said to her.

'Do you want to call it there or keep going?' Brian asked us.

It was the kind of mental warfare that I imagined army drill sergeants inflicted on their fledging troops to break their spirits and test their character.

'Yeah, we'll keep going if the tide isn't against us yet.'

Though fed up with the false alarms and fatigued by the changes in pace, I didn't want to waste any opportunity to progress. I was proud to maintain the right attitude and plough on, dragging my GPS tracker for six hours from Cahore Point to Wexford Town. This slog justified moving our base to Rosslare Harbour.

'Sorry about that,' Brian said. 'The instruments kept suggesting the tide was turning.'

'We got six hours. Don't sweat it. Thanks for the week.'

There was no point reading into it or complaining about how constantly moving the goalposts made it one of my most challenging days in the water. It was Brian's last day, and we had a great week. I chalked it down to a character-building exercise.

'Nice to be getting into a harbour,' I said to Kaja, relieved we weren't returning to Cahore Point's offshore mooring buoy.

'Yeah, I can't wait for a warm shower and some shelter.'

As we pulled in to let Brian go home, we realised it wasn't one of those harbours. Massive *Stena Line* and *Britanny Ferries* ships were docked on one side, preparing to take passengers to Britain, France, and Spain. On the vacant side read a sign, '*DANGER. Do not berth alongside if logs are stacked on quay*'.

I strained my neck upwards at the towering pile of felled trees. 'I guess we're not sleeping here then?'

'No. Let's make this quick. The harbour's only for commercial ships,' Colm said. 'We'll have to drop an anchor offshore around the corner for the night.'

'I was hoping you wouldn't say that.'

We gave Brian a parting hug and pushed off the harbour's wall to find a safe location to sleep.

'Eh … now,' the newly promoted Colm said from the helm.

I dropped the anchor off the boat's bow, feeding the heavy, rusty chain into the sea. We struck sand and ground to a halt.

'I'm not sure we're secure here. Eh, sorry, could you pull it back up, and I'll try another spot?' Colm asked.

Heaving the weighted anchor from the sea was a challenge fit for the Crossfit Games and not the best recovery protocol after a six-hour sea swim, but it was better than running *Unsinkable II* aground as we slept.

Colm's cautiousness reassured me that he was safe. His hesitance about where to anchor made me a little concerned too.

'Get ready. Hold. Hold. Now!'

I dropped anchor again. The captain was satisfied we wouldn't drift.

'I'll set my alarm to check on it throughout the night. I'm a bit uneasy mooring off an anchor close to land,' Colm said, embracing the responsibility of his new role.

I sat on the deck, swallowed a seasickness tablet for the night ahead, and became hypnotised by the world reflecting off the sleeping sea. The screen split in two, the sun and moon co-existing in the same sky. The fireball was lowering over Rosslare Beach to our right, dipping to kiss the rural hills as we swayed lazily to the boat's seesawing squeaks. A full moon crept up to our left, shining a snaking torch on the faint ripples.

Though the sun had vanished before us, its parting glows smothered Mount Leinster and the horizon with soft sheets of pink, peach, and yellow hues. I felt lucky to be alive and out in nature to experience the sight.

THIRTEEN
Not Home or Dry
110 Kilometres Remaining

Flat 7UP or Exploding Prosecco

It was Sunday, the last day of week six – day forty-four. I sipped my black coffee in the cockpit, looking for Gavin to appear in the dawn's glow.

'That's him there, is it?' Kaja said.

Since we'd anchored offshore, Gav had parked at a tiny, tidal harbour next to Rosslare Europort and kayaked out to us.

'A fine aul' morning for a paddle,' Gav said.

'Well, what's the craic, Gav? Great to have you back, my man,' I said.

Colm turned the ignition, the motors came to life, and we chugged to the previous day's finish point, seven kilometres off-shore of Wexford Town.

Without Gavin and a complete support team for the next two days – Monday and Tuesday – I needed to progress past the daunting shipping lanes on this Sunday swim. Succeed, and I'd unlock the opportunity to navigate from beach to beach with Kaja on her kayak to start week seven. Fail, and we'd have to sit tight for two days until Gav returned. If I failed this mission, the finale would be like flat 7UP in two weeks on 27 July, not exploding Prosecco in one week on 21 July. The challenge was that the shipping lane was sixteen kilometres south of my start point.

I created extra pressure by wanting to finish as soon as I could. It made it exciting and engaging to push for the line instead of coasting within my new comfort zone.

As I swam, I regretted the coffee.

'Kaja, if it comes to it, I'm sorry, but I'm not stopping for the jacks. We're beating these ferries.'

'Christ, just get back on the boat if you need to go.'

'We don't have time. Do you want me at your graduation or not?'

She laughed. 'I'm not sure I do if you crap your wetsuit.'

Luckily, desperate times didn't call for desperate measures, and I retained my invitation to Kaja's big day.

Gavin and Colm monitored the shipping traffic and ferry timetables. Thankfully, there were no close calls or forced stops as we had in Dublin Bay. After four hours and forty-five minutes of swimming, I crossed the danger zone and lined up perfectly with Carne Beach, County Wexford, near the southeast tip of Ireland.

'Whoop. Job done. We can start from the beach tomorrow.'

We halted the swim early, without maximising the full tide, as Colm needed to tackle the nautical challenges of our three-hour transfer to Kilmore Quay Marina on the south coast during calmer tide times. We rounded Carnsore Point at Ireland's southeast corner and approached the Saltee Islands, both areas known for their ship-sinking histories and known by some as 'The Cemetery of a Thousand Ships'.

The Saltee Islands consist of Little Saltee Island, off Kilmore Quay, and Great Saltee Island beyond. The inviting direct route to the marina between the mainland and Little Saltee Island would likely wreck us on a reef. The fairway between the islands looked welcoming to the naked eye, too, but the shallow sound hid menacing shoals and rocks. Colm had done his diligent homework. The digital and paper charts were a minefield of cloaked obstacles – circles, crosses, waves, and contour lines marking the umpteen death traps that encircled the islands. The crew remained silent as Colm focused on following his passage plan through the sound, walking the tightrope between underwater obstructions.

We orbited around the south of Little Saltee, hoisted on the racing swell that propelled us forwards. The islands' beauty matched their danger. High cliffs framed the unspoiled apple-green isles. The skies bustled with birds – gannets, guillemots, and gulls. With over 200 species recorded around the protected wild-life sanctuary, birdwatchers flock here from around the world. A family of resting puffins had painted the local peak white. Shallow, isolated sandy bays punctuated the rugged rockface with resting seals guarding the shore, but we were all a little too on edge to enjoy the sightseeing.

We relaxed as we finally approached Kilmore Quay Marina, seemingly out of harm's way. Then *Unsinkable II* missed the last-second turn into the marina. We were on a short collision course with the beach.

'Colm! Shit, reverse, reverse!'

'Sorry!' he said, backing her into reverse gear. 'Close one. I wouldn't live that down after making it through the islands.'

My heart! We moored up safe and sound and congratulated our new skipper. 'Great first day in charge, Colm.'

'Well, that was scary and stressful.'

'We're all in one piece and made it further than we hoped. Good man. Thanks a mil for that,' I said to him.

'If you can swim past the marina with Karolína over the next two days, that would help, so I don't have to deal with navigating the Saltee Islands again on Wednesday.'

'I'll do my best, Colm. Right, I need to find someplace to stay within kayak-carrying distance of Carne Beach. Could you hang on for a bit and help us transfer the kayak, Gav?'

'I'll ask Rachael. She's picking me up. Should be grand since she's dropping me to the car in Rosslare Harbour anyway.'

There was no rest or time to celebrate. Colm held down the fort in Kilmore Quay while Kaja and I made our way to an Airbnb a mile from the next day's beach start point.

'It's going to be a miserable time trying to carry the kayak to the beach in the morning, but it's the closest place available.'

As Gavin's girlfriend, Rachael, drove us to the Airbnb, I announced on social media:

'The swim finale will take place at 6 p.m. next Sunday, 21 July, on Tramore Beach. I'm insured to have 300 participants, so please do spread the word. Currently, I only have thirty-two hardy souls signed up.'

'No going back now with insurance locked in,' Gav said.

I checked week six's stats on my phone. 'Thirty-four hours of swimming and one hundred kilometres done this week.'

'You guys crushed it. You covered nearly half the east coast. Now you *only* have about one hundred kilometres to make Tramore for next Sunday, and you're home dry.'

'No bother, yeah. Ugh, Jaysus.'

We arrived at our Airbnb. The couple who owned the home greeted us and showed us to their spare room.

'What are you two up to, if you don't mind me asking?' said the man.

It seemed a bit of an intrusive question before I realised the cut of me. I'd forgotten about my appearance the previous month, never looking too out of sorts in marinas and hanging off harbour walls and trawlers. We must have looked like the right pair pulling up with a banana-yellow kayak, a black sack of swim equipment, and a bulging waterproof gear bag. Then there were my grubby shorts, flip-flops, black woollen hat, and fawn oversized knitted fisherman's jumper. It was a far cry from the shirt and trousers of office employment.

'We're swimming and kayaking the length of Ireland from the Giant's Causeway for charity.'

'Janey Mackers.'

When he picked his jaw up from the driveway, we chatted about the adventure, and he offered to drive us and the kayak to the beach in the morning to save us from a Navy Seals boat carry exercise.

Proud

It was just the two of us on morning forty-five. Kaja and I sat on Carne Beach for a moment before the launch.

'I loved that last day we had in Ardglass together. It's nice when it's just the two of us, isn't it?' Kaja said.

'Fuckin' lovely,' I said, quoting my dad, and grinned back.

'Are you ready to swim the length of Ireland?'

'Are you ready to kayak the length of Ireland? First Czech person to do it.'

'Am I?'

'No idea, but what would any Czech person be up to kayaking the length of Ireland before now?'

Swimming south and breathing to my right, I caught sight of the rotating turbines of the wind farm marking Carnsore Point at the southeast tip of Ireland, where I'd complete the length of Ireland's east coast and begin my swim west towards home. I'd worked so damn hard for this. We turned the corner. I stopped. My throat tightened, my eyes welled up, and I exhaled with puffed cheeks.

'We did it!' I squeezed Kaja's neoprene hand in mine and kissed it. 'Couldn't have done it without you. You're some woman for one woman.'

'Good job. You made it.' Kaja smiled. 'I'm so proud of you.'

The stars aligned for this one. A solitary moment for the two of us to relish. I floated on my back, smiling, crying, and overcome with emotion. *I did it, Dad,* I thought. We stayed there, floating, steeping in the moment of victory.

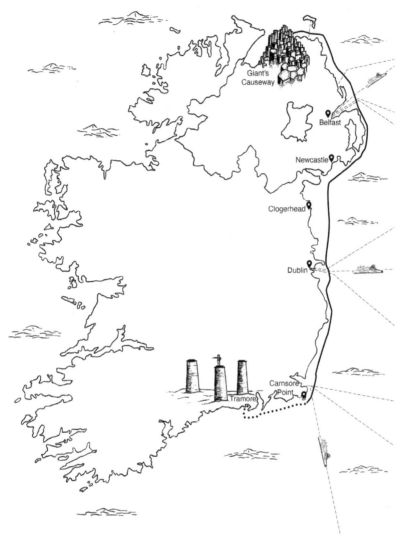

I faced west.

'Right, let's get me home to Waterford. Just one hundred K that way is all.'

I returned to the task, cognisant of the tide times and my responsibility to get us safely away from Carnsore Point and ashore. We were a kilometre or two out from the beach. At the four-hour mark, I angled thirty degrees towards the shore, not wanting to lose too much progress to swimming north and inland when our final target was west. After fifteen minutes, I reassessed, swimming at forty-five degrees to shore since we were still a long way out. With four hours and thirty covered, I popped up.

'Aren't we supposed to be in by now,' Kaja said. My mam had offered to collect us between Kilmore Quay and Carnsore Point when our day's work ended since we were laden with an awkward thirty-kilogram kayak and our gear bag of civvy clothes. I calculated we'd be done swimming by 2:30 p.m.

'Yeah, you're right – sod progress west. We need to get in. Aim straight for the beach, and I'll follow.'

Fifteen minutes later than planned, my feet touched the comforting shore of Rostoonstown Beach.

We were a little late, but it didn't matter. Knowing my mam's worry thresholds, I added an hour to our estimated arrival time. The last thing I wanted was the mammy tearing her hair out on the beach and phoning the Coastguard about a late swimmer and kayaker.

I texted Mam the details of the nearest extraction point. The golden sands stretched nearly thirty kilometres with only a few entry points. Thankfully, we only had a two-kilometre trek to the nearest car park. I removed my neoprene socks and felt the sand warm my toes as Kaja paddled her vessel beside me in the shallows.

Some holidaymakers were on the beach as we neared the public access point. 'Alan!' a man said as he approached me. 'We've been following your live tracker. Well done. You must be thrilled to bits. Do you want a hand with the kayak?'

The man, his wife, and two kids hoisted the kayak from the beach to the car park – a lovely random act of kindness to add icing to the day's celebration.

'I did it, Mam. I just swam the length of Ireland,' I said with open arms as Mam stepped out of her car.

'Well done, Al.' She gave me a big hug. 'I'm delighted for you. I'm just glad you're both safe. You're brilliant, Karolína. Well done.'

Saint Patrick's Bridge

My big brother, Ev, took the morning off work to drive the kayak, Kaja, and me from Kilmore Quay Marina to Rostoonstown Beach.

It was a team and family effort to navigate the logistics of shore-to-shore swimming.

'That's not a promising sign,' Ev said, nodding at the warning post – a red circle with a red diagonal line across a swimmer in waves – as we carried the kayak over the dune of marram grass and down the shimmering shore.

'Yeah, it's a sharp drop down at the shoreline, and the waves can dump you and drag you out. Once you're out a few metres, 'tis grand.'

This inadvisable beach entry made it tricky to launch Kaja off the shore.

'Go! No! Wait, stop … Okay, and, now, jump! Go, go, go!'

I was apprehensive in these waters without the support boat as the tides were contrary, working off their own clock. While the sea flows west in our desired direction along the south coast of Ireland, it doesn't flow that way for six hours around the Saltee Islands or closer inshore at Kilmore Quay. This place was the exception rather than the rule, with notorious local counter-currents firing at peculiar times at rapid speeds.

We could monitor the tides before getting in when we had *Unsinkable II* and a team. The crew could continually check progress onscreen and pull me out when I stopped moving forwards. Without the boat, there was much more risk. If I wasn't moving forwards because of the currents, it was near impossible to gauge it in the water. Even if I was sure the treadmill had begun, we couldn't step out; we had to swim and kayak to safety.

The tide was due to be in our favour at 11:30 a.m., but since we weren't exactly sure when it would turn against us, I decided to start early, at 11 a.m., during slack waters. We spent the first hour aiming outwards to get into deep waters and more helpful tidal flows. We straightened our course towards Kilmore Quay and Little Saltee for the next two hours. That got us to 2 p.m. The three-hour mid-tide mark was when sailors advised us to be more vigilant of our movement.

As I swam, I observed floating buoys and their anchor ropes, checking which way they swayed. The ropes moved like flowing hair in the wind.

I told Kaja, 'The tide's still with us.'

The longer we moved, the more they straightened upright.

Though we were a long way offshore, the water became shallow. Rather than deep blue, I grazed the top of a seaweed forest.

'There's loads of seals whizzing around, Al. Just to warn you, in case one zips out and scares you.'

Seals were the least of my worries in these waters. Swimming over aquatic ferns gave me peace of mind, a constant tool to monitor the tidal direction and strength.

'The seaweed's starting to sway against us. What are we, four hours in, and it's turning. I need to up it to reach the marina before things get rapid.'

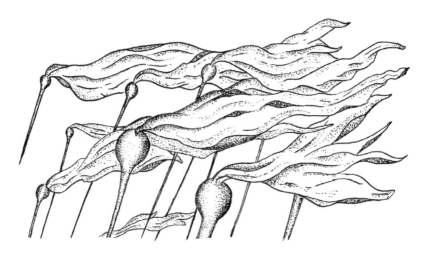

I found myself swimming in five feet of water, then four, three, two, and one. I was a kilometre offshore, but it was too shallow and rocky to swim. I stood up like a neoprene-wearing Jesus and began walking on water.

Kaja laughed while recording my magic shuffle on camera. 'Woohoo, go, Al, *swimming* the length of Ireland, yeah!'

I later learned that this oddity was Saint Patrick's Bridge, a submerged causeway linking the mainland to Little Saltee Island, three kilometres out to sea.

Though it's said that a glacier dragged these foreign rocks here many millennia ago, I prefer the old wives' tale. The story goes that the devil got into it with Saint Patrick at the Galtee Mountains in County Tipperary. Saint Patrick took a run at the divil and sent him on his bike but not before the fuming dark lord bit off a chunk of the nearby hill, now aptly named the Devil's Bit Mountain. Ireland's patron saint chased the bugger from Tipperary, over one hundred kilometres to Kilmore Quay. He thought he had cornered him. The devil scurried into the sea, and our nation's saint began pelting him with rocks from his reinforced bottomless tote bag, leaving a causeway in the bombardment's wake – Saint Patrick's Bridge. Saint Patrick had one Hail Mary throw left. He catapulted a boulder at the devil. It came up short, splashed with a monstrous ripple, and lodged in the seabed. It still stands alone when the tide's out, protruding like a lost iceberg. They named it Saint Patrick's Rock. The dropping bomb was enough to make the devil deep-dive in fear, but not before he spat out the stolen bite from the Tipperary hillside. With that, Little Saltee Island appeared. There you have it, some Irish folklore for you.

After some clambering over the underwater ridge like a gorilla on skates, the causeway ended. I returned to swimming hard to beat the temperamental tide and reach the marina before the sea rammed us backwards.

We just about made it in by the skin of our teeth, exhausted from my sprint to the marina's breakwater boulders. I knew we were cutting it fine since, beneath the surface, the currents tugged the seaweed against us. I climbed up the rocks, slipping and bashing my shin again. It seemed dry land was causing me more difficulty and injuries than the sea.

Overboard!

The finale was building. Sixty people had registered to join in, but the charity donation pot was still relatively low compared to my 2012 haul of €15,000 and 2017's haul of €13,000. On day forty-seven, with over ninety per cent of the distance swum, donations reached €7,476.

Gavin returned to join Colm on deck, and we were back to progress with a safety net of *Unsinkable II* ready to scoop us out if things went awry.

It was Wednesday, 17 July. I needed big swims and favourable weather to make Sunday's looming deadline. There was still the tall order of eighty kilometres to cover from Kilmore Quay, County Wexford, to Tramore, County Waterford.

The marina flags rippled in the wind.

'Do you think we're safe to go?' I asked Colm.

'I think "safe" has a different definition for this challenge,' he replied. 'The wind's close to our upper limits.'

We set out from Kilmore Quay to our drop point between the marina and Little Saltee.

'We can't linger here with the wind, waves, currents, rocks, and ridges,' Colm said.

'Okay, we'll jump in and go. Pushing for six hours today. Let's give it socks. Thanks, guys.'

'Best of luck.'

I turned my GPS trackers live and jumped from the windswept cockpit into the lumpy waves. I looked westward with the boat bobbing and drifting away behind me. *Make this one count, Al.*

'Ah!' Kaja said.

I turned around. A wave had capsized Kaja into the sea, the hefty kayak striking her head in the process.

'Shit.'

'The kayak!' Gavin said as the €1,000 piece of equipment whooshed eastward on the crest of a wave.

'Fuck the kayak! Get Kaja onboard!' I sprinted to her. 'You're okay. I'm here. We'll get you out.'

Kaja gasped for air, suffering cold shock. Her floatation vest did its job and kept her head above water as we waited for Colm to manoeuvre *Unsinkable II* within swimming distance for Kaja. As he reversed the boat's ladder to us, the boat shot up and slapped down. Ten metres away, he cut the engine. The last thing we wanted was to be minced by a propeller.

'Go, Kaja, kick!' I said.

She kicked her legs and swung her arms, but the sea kept shifting the goalposts, drifting the support boat away faster than she could swim.

'Why'd I wear this stupid hoody,' she said as she gave up the chase, panting.

For the first time, she'd added an extra civvy layer beneath her kayak-specific gear. The hoody was drenched and doubled in weight, restricting movement and making swimming even harder.

'Okay, we'll go again, guys!' I said. 'A little closer this time if you can, Colm.' I locked eyes with Kaja. 'Just try to get your breath back. I'll give you a little push this time to get you going. We'll get there.'

The situation was dire. We had two people overboard in testing seas, close to hazards that could endanger the ship, and Gav and Colm on board. The only saving grace was that we were just two kilometres south of the marina, and Kilmore Quay had an RNLI Lifeboat Station, given the dangers of the village waters.

'Get ready!' Gav said.

The second the engine cut, I shoved Kaja towards the boat, and she sprinted. She got within two arms' length. The ship blew away.

'Just there, keep pushing, Kaja.'

She gave it her all and clawed the distance back, but the swell yanked the boat out of reach again. Exhausted, she stopped.

'I think we need to call for help,' Colm said.

'One more try like this. We'll try to do it together.' I thought back to primary school swim lifesaving classes. 'I'll tow her,' I told the boat crew. 'I'll hold you, Kaja. When they shout, *go*, you kick with me, okay?'

'Okay, I'll try,' she said, visibly tired from the weighted swim sprints.

'We'll get out of this, okay? I'm staying with you.'

As the minutes passed, the life-threatening reality of the situation intensified, but we had to focus.

'Three, two, one, *go*!' Gav said.

Kaja was floating on her back, kicking her legs up and down. My arm hooked over her shoulder, around her chest, and gripped her armpit. On my side, I grabbed the water with my left hand and ripped it back, fluttering my legs as hard as possible.

I reached for the ladder and missed. I went for the ladder

again and missed. No matter how hard I tried, I could only get within arm's length before the swell taunted us and tugged the boat away. We were ten minutes into the failed rescue attempt. Hypothermia was becoming a greater risk for Kaja.

'I think we need to make a distress call,' Colm repeated.

'Wait, I have an idea,' Gav said. He had better recall of his lifesaving swim classes than I did. He began coiling a rope around his hand and elbow.

'We're good, Kaja. This'll work,' I said, trying to reassure her as the moment spiralled and cold dug its claws in.

Colm motored around and switched the engine off. Gav threw his lasso. It came up short, so I swam for it. Again, the sea wouldn't play ball. We were getting dragged closer and closer to danger.

'Again, Gav! I'll get the next one.'

Please work, I thought. Gav coiled the rope quicker this time and put more elbow grease into the throw. I swam at full tilt.

'Got it! Thank fuck!' I swam the rope to Kaja. 'Hold tight.'

Gav pulled Kaja in, and she clambered on board. Colm surveyed the scene, glancing from me to Kaja, to the mainland, and then to the islands. The sea hammered the jagged rocks. I swam for the boat and had the same difficulty as Kaja. Gav threw me a line and got me aboard. Kaja gripped the metal hand railing as she keeled over the side of the boat. A concoction of cold shock, fear, adrenaline, seawater, and relief puked out of her. I felt several shades whiter than usual, breathing deeply to calm myself.

We caught up with the runaway kayak and tied a safety line around me. I jumped in and retrieved it, Gav and Colm dragging the craft aboard.

'Right, let's get the feck out of here, lads, and back into the marina.'

Kaja and I climbed below deck and sat in silence for a moment. I rested my frazzled head back against the wall. 'Jesus, that got sketchy quickly. You alright?'

Kaja sat with her elbows on her knees and her head in her hands. 'Yeah. I'm okay. I just got a fright, and then the cold water and this stupid wet hoody weighing me down.'

'What happened? How'd you end up falling in?'

'I climbed down the ladder fine and sat on the kayak. I just reached to take the feed bag from Gavin, and a wave hit me side-on and flipped me.' Kaja sat up. 'I'll be okay. When are we going back out? I can do it.'

'You just need to rest up and grab a warm shower once we're back in. Don't worry about doing anything else today. We're not going offshore again.'

'I know you needed a big day. Sorry, I should have been more careful.'

'I'm just glad we're alright. That's the main thing. You handled it so well.'

Though there was some annoyance about losing a six-hour swim window and now likely missing the finale, it felt trivial in the context. Relief was my main feeling. So much could have gone drastically worse, but thankfully it didn't.

Colm manoeuvred the boat towards our marina berth. Gavin and I coiled the mooring lines in our hands, stood ready at either end of *Unsinkable II*, and awaited Colm's signal.

'Now,' Colm said to us.

We hurried off the deck, onto the dock, and wrapped the lines around the steal docking cleats.

'Quick thinking with tossing us the rope, Gav. Lifesaver. Nice work getting the boat close enough to us, Colm. I think we handled that pretty well, all things considered.'

'I'm just glad to be back in,' Colm said.

'So, what are you thinking now?' Gav asked me. 'I'm up for supporting you on the kayak along the beach if you want to give it a shot? We can still make the finale.'

The westbound tide wasn't waiting for us to recover from the ordeal. We had to move fast if we didn't want to miss the opportunity.

'Yeah, fuck it, let's go, Gav. We need to salvage something from today if we're going to make it to Tramore for Sunday. Getting more west of the islands will make things simpler for Colm on the next one, too.'

Noel appeared at the boat with a set of binoculars in his hand. He was the sailor who'd supported me during week one and had come in on short notice to help rescue week three with Chris.

'Noel, great to see you. What are you doing here?'

'Just thought I'd call over and see how you're progressing. Looks a bit rough out there. Are you finished up for the day?'

'No. We had a bit of a shitshow. We're going along the beach now instead. I'll let Colm and Kaja fill you in.'

'Right. Go on. Best of luck, men.'

Gav put on his wetsuit and floatation vest and paddled to the marina's mouth. I jogged around and climbed down the marina's ladder to join him. In the rush of the moment, we never discussed how long we planned to swim; we just got going, knowing we had the tide at our backs.

It was time to feed after thirty minutes.

I gulped my calories. 'We had the tide until about three yesterday. So we have until about four until it turns against us, which can help carry you back to the marina.'

'I'll keep an eye on the sea. It's lumpy, alright.'

Progress waned by 4:30 p.m. I stopped fighting the sea's pull to shore and let the rising waves wash me in. I crashed belly-first on the hard sand and commando-crawled as the sea tugged my legs back.

It was like winter on the beach – desolate – and I had a ten-kilometre beach walk back to base. I shouted over the cutting wind and exploding waves to record a piece for the documentary film.

'This is turning into proper fuckin' torture,' I said, trudging in thick wet sand. My legs became heavier and heavier. I was out of food and could feel my energy stores nearing empty. There was no car park near, so I *had to* walk out. I tried to keep my eyes on Gavin, who paddled at a similar pace, fighting through gusts.

Then I lost sight of him. I paused, squinted, and scanned. 'Balls, where's he gone?' Eventually, he rose from the gully onto the swell's crest. It was more stressful from land, unable to communicate with him as he bobbed in and out of sight among the waves. Now I had a taste of what the boat team felt like watching me – from watching paint dry to panicking in a flash.

I ran out of sinking sand, the tide forcing my feet onto the crunch of punishing pebbles. The long walk wore through the soles of my neoprene socks, my bare heels and the balls of my feet flinching on the shingle.

Eventually, we made it back to the marina. The day had well and truly flattened me. Worse, I didn't know if it was enough progress to make the finale, with a planned six-hour offshore swim shortened to a three-hour, five-minute coastline swim.

'At least we don't need to go near the Saltees ever again,' Colm said.

The ordeal earlier that day reminded me how quickly things could go wrong at sea and how important it was to have at least two capable people on the deck. Shit happens, but I couldn't have been happier with everyone's response to the emergency.

'The Wall'

The hope of making the announced finale in time dwindled after the near-catastrophic day off Little Saltee. Every hour and second counted this week, and we had lost valuable time, but it ain't over until the fat lady sings. The odds-makers had written us off, but there was still some time on the clock, with Thursday, Friday, Saturday, and Sunday to make Tramore. Each tide was crucial.

Skinner, who'd skippered week two on attempt one, joined Gav and Colm for the day. The sea state was more forgiving than yesterday's start, but it was still testing. Kaja's launch went smoothly, and we got out of the blocks. The swell increased as the tide and opposing winds picked up speed. Blustery winds pushed Kaja back. She dipped her head and powered through, needing to maintain a high stroke rate to progress. On occasion, she had overcome these conditions down the east coast, but those days were four hours long, not six, which we needed to complete today. Around the four-and-a-half-hour mark, her strokes looked a bit lethargic. I'd hit 'the wall' twice, crashing with no energy in a glycogen-depleted state. I had a hunch she was on this trajectory as I monitored her body language with each breath I took.

'Kaja, you okay?'

'Yeah, fine.'

'You can tell me, you know? We've Skinner today, too, so Gav can kayak. You can swap with him if it's too much. Don't overdo it.'

She mulled it over.

'Okay. I'll do fifteen more minutes.'

I signalled the boat over.

'Kaja's wrecked. Can you get ready to kayak, Gav? She wants to do another fifteen minutes.'

'I'll get into my wetsuit now then, yeah.'

Five minutes later, my partner in crime had fallen behind. I stopped and waited for her to catch up. Her head and shoulders flopped, and her arms barely turned over as though paddling through wet cement.

'Let's get you out of here.'

I waved and called for the boat as I floated beside her. I was concerned for my girlfriend but annoyed she'd pushed herself to this vulnerable state. Ten kilometres offshore in high winds is not the time or place for that discussion. The only objective was to stop the swim and get her on the boat as soon as possible.

'I'm exhausted, Al.'

'You're okay. You're just out of fuel. Drink some of my drink and eat some of my food. You need to stay with me and be ready to get aboard.'

Though I'd stopped swimming and moving, the wind and waves colluded to drag her away from me. The conditions had a much more significant impact on the kayak above the water. I swam back towards her.

'You need to stay with me, Kaja. We can't risk separating.'

Gav wasn't expecting the call so soon and wasn't ready to tag in.

'Just get Karolína on board. That's priority. Worry about the changeover after,' I shouted to Gav, Colm, and Skinner.

She still struggled to stay with me and *Unsinkable II* wasn't coming much closer.

I gestured at the boat. 'Lads, we need to get her out of here. Quick.'

The boat came within thirty metres of us, but not as close as we needed. Karolína had a rush of blood to the head and made a beeline for it.

'Kaja! Stay with me until they reach us.'

Jesus Christ, I thought as she continued her slow paddle over the lumps and bumps. We were back in the realms of yesterday's dangers with another potential mayday on our hands. *We're five hours in, and Kaja's shattered.* I floated and watched as she emptied her depleted tank, paddling away from me, trying to make the boat. My concern turned to worry; my annoyance turned to anger. *What if she flips like yesterday but in that zombie state? I can't reach her from here. What if the boat engine fails, and everyone's drifting on their own? Why is this happening? Argh!*

We'd drifted a few hundred metres apart. I couldn't see what was going on or if Kaja had made it. I was isolated, floating on my own as the team was hopefully rescuing her. They were moving further and further away from me. I thought about pinging off my SOS device and looked to shore with notions of swimming in. I could make land four kilometres to the north, near Cullenstown Strand, or about five kilometres to the west, near Fethard. I felt abandoned and in danger. *Why didn't she stay with me? How are they going to find me?*

The whipping winds spread us at least a kilometre apart. I was losing them, seeing them on the crest of a distant wave or glimpsing the top of the mast when they dipped into a valley. As I was treading water, assessing my options, things didn't look good. I jiggled my bright orange tow float overhead to increase my visibility.

After what felt like a lifetime, the boat became larger. I saw yellow paddles flying through the air – left, right, left, right. I sighed in relief.

'I didn't think you'd find me. Is Kaja alright?'

'She's knackered but grand,' Gav said. 'She's below deck, having some food and a lie-down. Listen, the weather for tomorrow's gone cat. We need to swim this tide out if we're to make Tramore for Sunday.'

After the chaotic thirty-minute pause that pushed us backwards, we were once again in forward motion through the high seas to round off the six hours in the water.

Disaster, thankfully, had been averted again. Though frustrated to lose yet more progress, I was glad to live with that outcome in the grand scheme of things.

By the end of the day, I felt stretched to breaking. The others looked how I felt. Rather than debrief when nobody was in the mood, I thanked everyone, flopped into bed beside Kaja, and fell into a ten-hour coma.

FOURTEEN
Red Flag and Bubbles
33 Kilometres Remaining

Debrief

It was day forty-nine, Friday, 19 July. The closer we got to the finish deadline, the more we needed things to go right, and the more they went wrong. Yet the upshot was that the more things went wrong, the more people liked and shared social media posts, and donated. It didn't offset the years the last two days had taken off my life, but I was encouraged by seeing the charity fundraising total increase to €8,981.

Poor Skinner puked through the night. A boat cabin is not where you want to be when unwell. It's difficult enough at the best of times. I felt terrible but grateful that Skinner hung in to get me closer to that finish line. It was a colossal team effort that was dependent on volunteers.

The excellent news for Skinner – but terrible news for the project – was that the wind gauge turned red. We weren't getting any breaks. The gusts surpassed thirty knots and tried to rip flags off their poles. The water was too rough to swim in. We hunkered down in Kilmore Quay Marina for our first day's rest in nearly three weeks.

I contacted the insurance company to ask if we could defer the event if we didn't make it in time.

'We won't accept a deferment or cancellation unless it's twenty-four hours before the scheduled event. We're closed for the weekend. We'll need to know today if you're cancelling it.'

With Friday out of the picture, that left Saturday and Sunday to cover fifty kilometres. The dream finish didn't seem realistic, with just two tides left in my favour with boat support. The distance was too great. But I felt I was too close to defer the public finale by an entire week. I crafted a post for social media:

'The team are giving it our all to make Tramore for the 6 p.m. finale on Sunday, but sometimes your best isn't good enough. Despite the setbacks this week, there's still some fight left. We hope to see you all there in the waters with the event's pink swim caps on.'

My phone pinged. It was a text from Noel.
'I can help you guys through the night on Saturday.'
Impossible moved to maybe possible with the opportunity to swim an additional tide. It was well worth a shot. I updated social media:

'Weather permitting, I plan to swim at 2:30 p.m. tomorrow, Saturday, for five to six hours to get as far as Hook Head, or as close to it as possible, pull into Dunmore East to pick up Noel and turn around for 3 a.m. to swim for five to six hours towards Tramore Beach. If needs be, the tides allow a few more hours of swimming to make the 6 p.m. finale on Sunday evening.

Cutting it very fine, but we've done our best until now and will continue to do so to make Tramore, likely in a delirious state if we pull this off. I hope to see as many of you partaking in the swim as possible.'

During Friday's forced downtime, I spoke with Kaja.
'We can't have a repeat of yesterday. I know you're going above and beyond to help me, but that was crazy dangerous.'
'I know, I know. I was stubborn to go that far and shouldn't have tried to go for the boat. I didn't want to let you down, and then I was too tired and stressed to think straight.'
'C'mere, you eejit,' I said, hugging her. 'You've nothing to prove. You're not going to let me down by getting out when you're feeling shattered, for feck's sake. Look how far you bloody got us. Come on.'

'I know, but after falling in the day before, I was trying to make it up so we can make Sunday.'

'If we don't make Sunday, we don't make Sunday. I want to push it and be there, but there are more important things like keeping everyone in one piece, yeah?'

'Yeah, I should have handled it better.'

'I've made the same mistake twice now. Five or six hours of moving in these conditions is a massive ask for your body. Make sure you're staying on top of regular fueling. Live and learn. And just tell me if you're wrecked, and we'll get you out before shit hits the fan, yeah? No biggy.'

Karolína had the best intentions, and I loved her for striving to do her utmost. Doing it to support me was heart-melting, but the risk wasn't worth the reward in that scenario. As determined and supportive as she was, it put us in danger. We needed to remember priorities. It wasn't about finishing at all costs or by an arbitrary date. That was all irrelevant if someone got hurt. Our decisions needed to be measured, even more so when we were close to pulling off the unimaginable.

By Hook or By Crook

Day fifty was Saturday, 20 July. The wind blasted through the teeming Kilmore Quay Marina during the night, the clickety-clank blaring. But my fatigue yelled louder, and I passed out like a drunk log.

Kaja, Colm, Gav, Skinner, and I set out from the marina after lunch. We were on a mission to swim as far as Hook Head, some twelve kilometres west of my last location.

Conditions were … interesting … but swimmable, and just on the threshold for getting Kaja on the water. I felt anxious and sensed Kaja shared the sentiment, knowing we couldn't afford any more feck-ups this week.

We began swimming and kayaking before the tide turned in our favour, hoping the decision to swim in slack waters would buy us more time to progress. We were some fifteen kilometres offshore for this swim, wanting stronger westerly tides. With no visual distraction, I fixed my gaze on Kaja.

Kaja handed me my drink on my feed break. 'Wind in our face again? Seriously!' she said.

'Yeah, gusting twenty knots, according to the app. Them's the breaks.'

The weather created big swells again – intimidating hills washing over me. I hoped the day's rest worked its magic.

I focused on making my technique through the water as efficient as possible with each stroke, continuing through the waves in silent determination. We didn't mess around during the feeds either, making them as snappy as possible, with Kaja making sure to take on fuel too. The crew halted us. It didn't seem like I was swimming for too long. I looked at my watch – five hours and ten minutes.

'That's it there, Al. Hop out. We're starting to get the tidal effects of the estuary.'

We didn't want to hang about with the moon pushing and pulling the waters of the rivers Barrow, Nore, and Suir in and out of the estuary.

For the first time, I checked to get my bearings. It was dusk. I saw the familiar sight of one of the world's oldest operational lighthouses on the headland – Hook Lighthouse, standing to attention in a black-and-white prisoner uniform. Located in Wexford but visible from Waterford, I was never so happy to see this familiar 800-year-old gem flashing at us like police lights. Though I didn't get the entire six hours, we'd reached our intended target for the day, and I was almost home.

When we crossed the estuary by boat and moored under darkness in Dunmore East, County Waterford, I had time for a three-hour catnap before Noel joined us. I set my alarm and conked out before my head hit the pillow.

All Night Long

The alarm sounded at 2 a.m., and it was time for work on day fifty-one. Though I'd conquered my fear of swimming into the abyss, this was the first time I'd start in total darkness. Climbing out of the dark waters along the east coast had felt celebratory. Climbing into blackness felt like a bad idea. *Do you want to finish or not? It's the last push, and you'll get there. Right, let's go,* I told myself.

'Last night of this shitty boat,' I said with a grin.

Kaja smiled back. 'I know, right.'

Hook Lighthouse winked and illuminated the seascape every few seconds. Colm and Noel readied the kayak on the water, its green-and-red navigation lights shining some light on the dark matter below. Kaja turned on her headlamp and boarded her vessel. Colm handed my bag of food and liquids down to her but fumbled it into the water.

'Shit! Shit,' Noel said.

'It's okay. I have it,' Kaja said.

Colm put up his hands. 'Sorry. Sorry.'

'It's grand, Colm,' I said. 'We're all good. Kaja has it.'

Colm had been through enough stress this week to be getting grief about dropping a waterproof bag overboard. It was as well the sea was sleeping, and Kaja caught it, though. Swimming for hours without fuel would have been asking for trouble, and I needed to swim for several hours to ensure I made it to the finale in time.

I turned on the tiny adventure light attached to my goggles, and my head became a beacon. I jumped into the 3 a.m. tide with a little over twenty kilometres to go to Tramore Beach.

'Kaja, look at this. Unreal,' I said.

I was swimming through a scene from *Avatar*, the water glowing blue and purple with bioluminescent plankton.

I felt alive and lucky to be there. I had set out to accomplish something and was doing it. There are few greater feelings in this life.

Time played in fast-forward as I glided on autopilot. Before I knew it, the sun was up, and I was on the Waterford side of the estuary, passing Dunmore East. *I'm going to make it.*

'You're slowing right down, Al. The tide's turned,' Noel said to us from the boat. 'We'll call it a day there.'

I'd been swimming for five hours. By 9 a.m., I'd swum from Hook Head in County Wexford, across Waterford Harbour's mouth to Ballymacaw in County Waterford. It wasn't Tramore, but T-Bay was within striking distance, the Brownstown Head pillars just in front of us. Mathematics still entertained the possibility that if I rested up and started swimming when the tide turned again, I could swim in with the registered participants by 6 p.m.

Mooring back in Dunmore East, we went straight for breakfast with my mam.

'There're 102 people registered, something like €2,000 raised from the finale alone. We're actually going to pull this off,' I said, beaming with a dopey, sleepy head.

'That's great work,' Mam said. 'You've really flown it the last week, and you're all in one piece, more importantly.'

I glanced at Kaja across the table as though to say, *If only she knew the half of it.* Despite all the week's mishaps, we'd still squeezed in twenty-eight and a half hours of swimming.

'Yeah, we put our heads down and got lucky. Glad to be home and ready for a big finish.'

Mam doesn't need to know, I thought. *She can watch it in the film or read it in the book in a few years.*

After breakfast, it was back to *Unsinkable II* for a three-hour power nap before getting up for a sprint finish.

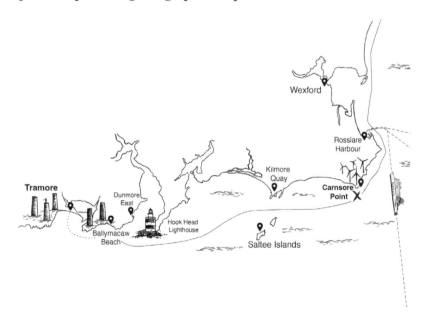

Dead Ends

The wind was moaning when I woke. I turned on my phone and checked the weather.

'Ah, come on. Fuck ye anyway.'

I wanted white, light blues, or green squares on the weather app. The grid lit up yellow, orange, and red, increasing to pink. Winds were up to a constant twenty knots, gusting thirty into Tramore's surfing bay.

Because of the bay's depth, the sailboat could never continue to the beach finish, even during perfect weather. Colm and Noel planned to escort Kaja and me to Brownstown Head at the entrance to Tramore Bay and return to Dunmore East harbour, leaving us to swim and kayak into shore. There was now serious uncertainty about whether Kaja could board her kayak from the boat and remain on her kayak in these windy, wavy conditions. I didn't want a scenario where she couldn't kayak onto the beach with me. We decided Kaja wouldn't join us on *Unsinkable II*. Instead, she'd join the finale's other support kayakers off The Pier, near the beach, where I could meet her on my swim-in. That way, we could still walk up the sand together. As the saying goes, *You can't control the wind, but you can adjust your sails*, so we tacked and made the best of the situation, determined to see the challenge through with everybody in one piece.

It was 1 p.m. We were so close. Once we arrived at the Ballymacaw start line, I would have four hours to swim ten kilometres and reach the EIR buoy in the bay. I could do it.

'Best of luck, and I'll see you in the bay,' Kaja said with a kiss on the gangway before I boarded the sailboat and pulled out of Dunmore East with Colm and Noel.

I sat alone in my cabin, plugged in my headphones and listened to one of Dad's favourite songs – 'Blackbird' by Sharon Shannon. I was ready to finish my mission.

Once we left the seclusion of the harbour and ventured beyond the headland, all of ten minutes out, the sea's blood pressure boiled. The engine hummed as we ramped up and crashed down with jarring thuds through the waves.

I moved to the deck. The RNLI appeared ahead, tugging in a sailboat in distress.

'I don't like the look of this, Alan. That rescue's a sign. I think it's too rough. What do you think?' Noel said.

'It's rough, alright. I don't want to pressure you. I'm not operating the boat, so I'll leave that call to you guys. Whatever you decide, I'm happy to go with.'

'Yeah, look, there's a gale and small craft warning, and it's picking up. I'm going to turn us around. Agh, disappointing.'

'It is what it is,' I said. 'Better safe than sorry, lads.'

Although I was pissed off and dejected, flopping back down to my cabin, there was zero animosity towards Noel's retreat. That was the wise decision. I was just so disappointed, though, having defied the odds and broken our backs to make it the best finish possible, only to be engulfed by gale-force winds.

As we retreated, my friends followed my event plan, setting up the registration desk, giant finish banner, and inflatable turn buoy on Tramore Beach.

We pulled back into Dunmore East harbour with the RNLI rescue tow not far behind. We couldn't progress to the finale with the sailboat. That decision had been made. It was time to spring into action, look ahead, and see what we *could* do. I knew people had travelled from Cork. Anraí Ó Domhnaill, who had ambitions to swim around Ireland, had ventured six hours cross-country from Donegal with his eighty-five-year-old mother to partake in the finish. There was no time to play the victim. It was straight to damage limitations. I met a local Coastguard member.

'I couldn't finish the swim today. The weather's too much.'

'But shur, look it, isn't that it sometimes.'

'If I'm not swimming in myself, can we even carry on with the public event? It's out from the beach, around a floating marker and back for 600 metres.'

'With the weather, I'd be advising you that's off the table. Will safety kayakers go out in that? Doubt it.'

'What *can* we do? The insurance money's locked in for today, and it's Sunday, so I can't get in touch with them. Ugh, some shambles this.'

'Not much you can you do with the Irish weather, lad. Only make the most of a bad lot. I'd say you'd be grand for a splash and dash, like at Christmas. Not a bother. You'd all run in, take a quick dunk rather than a *swim* swim, and then jump out under the finish banner.'

'Ugh. Right. Will have to do, I suppose. Thanks a mil anyway. I'll head out to Tramore so and see what the craic is.'

Without the four-hour swim, I caught up on some sleep before going to check the conditions on-site. I met the support kayak team coordinator at The Pier, a small tidal harbour on the west side of the bay.

'What are you guys thinking? My latest thinking is to swim into the beach from here and have a "fake finale", and tell the participants it's just a splash and dash when I get near the shore instead of a 600-metre swim.'

'We won't be going out in that. Sorry.'

'Yeah, that's fair enough. Thanks for coming down and your help with it.'

'Hard luck. Sorry, Alan.'

'Not at all.'

My health and safety assessment had several support kayakers as part of the package and insurance agreement. It seemed I would be liable if something happened in the water now.

With the wind, waves, and no kayakers, the custom-made turning buoy shipped from England had to remain onshore.

I got a call from Alex at the registration desk on the promenade.

'The crowd's building, but the lifeguards have just raised the red flag. They don't want anyone in the water. What do you want me to do here with registration?'

'Cheers for the heads-up, Alex. Let me call you back in a tick.'

I stood with Gav and Kaja on The Pier overlooking the bay, with sets of surf rolling in. Tramore AFC had their beach football fundraising tournament in full swing on the sands. I got a call from the Coastguard I'd met earlier.

'I'm just down here now on the promenade, and it's rougher than I thought earlier. If I were you, I wouldn't even promote a splash and dash in those waves. The red flag's just gone up.'

'Ah, balls. Thanks for your help.'

'What's he saying?' Kaja said.

'Not to do the splash and dash either. Fuck.'

'If you're going to swim in, I can still kayak with you from here,' Kaja said.

'I think that's a bad idea. Those guys have been kayaking for years and are bailing. I don't want anything happening to you.'

'Can we take a look from a better position? We have time still.'

We drove along the seafront and saw people gathering. Two surf kayakers flipped and rolled about in the waves. Nobody else was in the water.

'You can't go out in that in an open-top kayak. Those guys are strapped in, ready for surfing their kayaks.'

'Yeah, okay. It looks much worse from here. What are you going to do now?'

'I can't cancel at this stage. Everyone's there, in the wind and spittin' rain.'

Surf's Up, Dude

I posted on my social media:

'My hands are tied, so the public swim is officially cancelled due to the red flag on Tramore Beach.

I'm still swimming in from The Pier to the lifeguard hut. ETA as advertised – 6 p.m.

I hope you can all still join me at the shore with your EIR swim caps to show support for the event and its sponsors.'

I donned my wetsuit and gave Gav a hug and Kaja a kiss.

'What time is it?' I said.

'Half five.'

'Tell them if I'm not on the beach in thirty minutes, just wait longer.'

Yes, there was a red flag, and the sea was rough, but the tide was heading into the bay and beach, and the gale and rollers aimed straight for shore too. Even if I just floated, nature would only force me in one direction – towards the sand. I thought I'd earned a place in the 'strong swimmer' category by now as well, and I was confident in my abilities. Though there are always risks with the sea, I made a calculated decision. I didn't feel I was putting myself or anyone else in unacceptable danger.

I swam from the protection of the pier wall. The onslaught of surf began. I missed Kaja guiding me. I needed to breathe left to sight the shore but only knew how to breathe to the right, facing the open Celtic Sea. I craned my neck to sight the lifeguard hut and inflatable finish banner. No matter how hard I strained my eyes, I couldn't see it with the waves, spray, drizzle, and poor eyesight. I paused and took off my goggles for a better look, but it was no use. *Hmm, maybe this wasn't the best idea.* A stud farm of white horses swamped me. *So long as the waves smash you from the right, the beach is parallel to your left. Right, perfect, this way, I suppose, let's go!*

Despite some waves rolling me in the washing machine, I was in my element, calm and happy, doing my best to salvage the day. I'd left my neoprene gloves and socks on the boat in all the commotion, and could feel the cold water with my bare hands and feet for the first time. During the swim from the north coast, I'd envisaged this moment a thousand times over like a bridezilla imagining her big wedding day. My plan to encourage people to swim failed because of the weather. The main pulling force now was walking up the beach with Kaja to the finish banner and embracing my mam and brother. I couldn't have everything, but I still had that vision to fulfil.

Eventually, I caught sight of the lifeguard station's cone roof, and swam until I got perpendicular and turned straight for shore to begin bodysurfing to the beach.

Where are the swimmers? Where's the inflatable finish banner? Aw, lads. My event plan was clear about where the finish should be. It seemed at that moment that the day's salvage job was for nothing, and I'd walk up the beach without my partner, family, or swimmers. My happiness changed to annoyance. *I may as well have driven to the beach and stepped out of the car instead of swimming in on my own like an eejit. What will the finale sponsors make of this after sending a camera crew down from Dublin?* I could only hold up my end of the bargain at that stage and finish where I said I'd finish when I said I'd finish.

But then I saw pink swim caps forming a group, one dot at a time. I wasn't going to finish alone after all. The overpowering emotions hit harder than the waves, with thoughts of celebrating with my family, girlfriend, and friends.

I felt a wave surge at my toes and sprinted to catch the surf. I flew outstretched in Patrick Swayze's *Dirty Dancing* arms, having the time of my life on the wave's crest. The backwash sucked me out, and the subsequent breaking wave barrelled me forwards, ripping the goggles from my head as the raging swell broke on me. My vision blurred with salt water, but the pink pixels lured me in like a kid to a candy store. Without goggles, I had to finish the swim polo-style with my head out of the water.

My feet planted on the Waterford seabed at 6 p.m. A crowd of swimmers in wetsuits and pink caps cheered, clapped, splashed, and hugged me in the waist-deep shallows as the foaming waves washed around us. Friends from my playschool, primary school, and secondary school were there to welcome me. I fought back the tears, an elated grin plastered across my face, but that quickly changed.

'Where's Karolína?'

I was supposed to walk up the beach with her. The swim was a couple's and team effort. She wasn't there, and I couldn't see my mam or brother either. The inflated finish banner was on the other end of the beach, tucked away from the winds behind a grey Portakabin. Onlookers lined the promenade railings and applauded. Swimmers raised my hands triumphantly as I searched for my nearest and dearest.

'Where's my family?'

Gav came running into the sea, dragging the EIR float with him to minimise the sponsor's disappointment and ensure it was in camera shot despite the weather. Kaja waded in behind him.

'Kajo!' I said, before squeezing hold of her.

I held her hand, and we walked from the water together. Jack legged it over to me.

'Your family's at the top of the beach.'

'What are they doing up there?'

'A mix-up with the finish. Smile and wave to the crowd; you did it. C'mon, your mother and brother are waiting for you.'

To be honest, the chaos was a bit of a downer after planning the event to a T, visualising it for so long, and working so damn hard during fifty-one days of swimming to reach it. Then I saw my mam, brother, niece Aoibhe, and nephew Jamie on the slip. The crappy weather and mishaps no longer mattered. Seeing their smiling faces made everything right again. I could feel the euphoria engulf me as I finally embraced my family and the moment's joy.

'Here you go, Al,' Ev said as he handed Kaja and me a bottle of Lidl Prosecco each.

I shook the bottle, bit the cork off, and drenched Kaja as the smiling crowds clapped, cheered, and celebrated our win. Once the bubbles stopped spraying, I opened wide and gave myself a much-needed shower, pouring the dregs over my head in victory.

It wasn't perfect, but that wouldn't spoil the occasion. I gave it my best shot at every turn and couldn't do any more. To have people come out on the worst summer's day to welcome us in and see the emotion on everyone's faces was surprising and powerful.

When you're chugging along the coast with a small team, you don't comprehend the number of well-wishers wanting you to do good. The home crowd support was phenomenal.

The swimmers didn't get to swim, but they didn't care.

'Keep the registration fee, boi. The charities can have it. Good on ya.'

'Glad you're home safe and sound, fella.'

'Failing and coming back like that, your dad would have been proud.'

Emotions hit in waves. I was ecstatic to see so many cheery faces. Then my dad's brother, Liam, hugged me and thumped my back. The family embrace sucked the air from me. It meant so much to finish my memorial tribute to Dad after three hard years.

'You didn't swim to shore in that on your own, did you?' Mam said.

I grinned and hugged her. 'I'm home safe. Ya can stop your worrying.'

'I knew your father,' a stranger said. 'He was a great man. Delighted you managed to finish your tribute to Milo.' It flooded me with grief and sadness not to have Dad there.

The entire journey was relentless and full of ups and downs. That last week and finale were no different, keeping me honest right to the line. Having to overcome so many difficulties and not coasting home made the ending that bit more meaningful – a truer reflection of my dad's legacy and the man he'd raised me to be.

The *Real* Last Swim

After the Sunday evening of free stout and whiskey, I nursed a hard-earned hangover on Monday as the weather front fizzled on.

I had completed the project as far as the public was concerned, but my mission wasn't complete. My GPS spot still floated off Ballymacaw Beach.

The weather broke on Tuesday, 23 July – day fifty-three. My alarm sounded at 5 a.m., and I woke Kaja. Mam made us breakfast, and we hit the road.

We pulled down the rural single-file laneway and into the

narrow cove in Ballymacaw. Getting out of the car, we were greeted
by bird song and a golden retriever.

I did some filming for the project's documentary movie
– *Unsinkable*.

'The last swim. I finally get to Tramore,' I said to the camera.
Mam turned around. 'Sorry?'

'I was saying it's the last swim, the *real* last swim.'

'Will you just get going,' she said as she rolled her eyes.

'Mam wants it over and done with quickly,' I said, laughing
to the camera.

My swim put her through many sleepless nights of worry, but
she was still there, rising before dawn to prepare breakfast and
drive us to an empty cove to finish the job I started. It meant the
world to have her stick with me through thick and thin.

Kaja and I stroked our way out of the sheltered cove, worked
towards Brownstown, and rounded the twin cement pillars that
warned seafarers of the perilous headland.

'I need to pee,' said Kaja.

'Can you hold it? We shouldn't be much longer and don't have
much time until the tide starts pulling out of the bay. Mam will
be stressing on the shore too.'

'No, I *need* to pee.'

'Go for it so.'

'You have to hold the kayak steady for me.'

'Then you'll piss on me!'

'Just hold the kayak, quick.'

There we were, in the middle of the bay, laughing our asses
off as I steadied the kayak in the warming waters.

'Stop looking!'

I chuckled. 'What a way to finish. Covered in your pee.'

As we edged closer to shore, I saw my mam and sister-in-
law, Deirdre, sitting on the empty beach, waiting to cheer us in. I
drained my energy tank and sprinted for home at the four-hour
mark to join up the final dot. I turned to celebrate the end of a
shoeless summer with Kaja, who was a metre from shore. A one-
foot wave flipped her as she tried to step out. I knew I shouldn't
laugh, but I couldn't hold it in.

'Awh, come 'ere, you okay?'

'I had to finish in style, didn't I,' she said, standing up soaking wet. 'Ugh, at least it wasn't in front of the crowd on Sunday.'

The four of us shared hugs for a perfect, low-key, intimate ending. I said I was going to swim the length of Ireland and I swam the length of Ireland. That was pretty damn satisfying.

We sat on the beach with some hot chocolate, cake, and laughs to re-warm after an eventful few weeks of living.

Re-Warming – *0 Kilometres Remaining*

Once I completed my mission, the tally for the Irish Heart Foundation and Solas Cancer Support Centre increased from €8,981 at the end of the last week to €15,996. It worked even better than a woolly hat to defrost my bones. This donation, coupled with my efforts on the first attempt, brought the swim's charity fundraising total to €28,650.

It was with immense pride and joy that I could present this money to the charities with my family and friends in my dad's memory and extend his legacy that little bit longer.

With no time to rest, I drove my motorcycle from Waterford to London for Kaja's graduation ceremony. Afterwards, we took our motorbikes through Britain, France, Switzerland, and Italy for a two-week holiday. Then it was back to reality, as they say, time for me to return to full-time work in London as a town planner to replenish the empty purse.

A year on, Covid exploded. I was so glad I went for the swim in 2019. The pandemic forced me to spend more time in the flat. 'Don't waste a good crisis,' my mam says. With extra time in confinement, I began writing and self-published my award-winning debut memoir, *Marathon Man: My Life, My Father's Stroke, and Running 35 Marathons in 35 Days*.

The Covid pandemic and the writing process were eye-opening, offering a glimpse of a possible future. If I'm fortunate to reach old age, I will likely live under some Covid-like restrictions. At some point, I won't be able to go out to the pub or on holidays with friends and family, or have the good health and ability for a therapeutic hike or sea swim. I'll have time to sit and think about how I lived.

Whilst immobile under strict government instruction, I could tap into life experiences of days once lived to the full. Writing my first book, I laughed, cried, and felt every spectrum of emotion. Recalling my experiences, I was amazed by how visceral it all still felt many years removed. There was a nourishing energy source in reliving old memories. This made me think that I'm taking the right approach to life, for me anyway, pursuing rich experiences in the first part of my life to feed and satisfy me in my later years.

I crowdfunded a small budget to complete the production of the *Unsinkable* documentary film created by Emagine (a creative agency) and me.

With those creative projects nearing completion, I took on a new physical challenge of trying to stand up paddleboard (SUP) around Ireland. One person had covered the distance on and off over three years, but nobody had completed the feat in one go over a summer season. By the summer of 2021, I was game to try. What could possibly go wrong?

EPILOGUE

Back in 2017, I'd attended a town planning conference hosted by the London Irish Town Planners Network. Experts from Ireland had flown to London to discuss Ireland's latest developments. After an entire day of writing technical reports in the office, I could be forgiven for daydreaming when the first slide appeared – an aerial image of Ireland. *I wonder, has anyone paddleboarded around it?*, I thought, as I sipped my caffeine and rubbed my weary eyes, trying to refocus on the besuited speaker.

Pursuing the paddleboarding concept at that point didn't feel right since I had unfinished business. I'd just failed at swimming the length of Ireland the summer beforehand. I put the SUP dream on the back burner until I corrected my blemished record and swam the 500-kilometre distance in 2019. After that, the timing felt right to learn how to paddleboard and see how far I could take it. Besides, with closed gyms and strict social distancing, paddling solo to my heart's content seemed an excellent spin on the sad state of affairs.

Once Covid had struck the world, and my job security was in serious question, I doubled down to get out of debt and paid off the bank loan I owed on *Unsinkable II*. I advertised the boat for sale, wanting to be rid of the financial liability, and wanting money to sponsor myself to do the paddle since companies didn't want in.

I invested thousands, importing the best Black Project paddles from Hawaii and a custom-made ONE board from Australia. I hired Michael Booth, the six-time SUP World Champion, to steer my crash course in the new sport.

At the time, Fiona Quinn was the only person I could find who had accomplished a sea SUP of this magnitude. She'd done it with *Shogun of Lorne* (aka *Unsinkable II*), the thirty-two-foot sailboat at her side. I wanted to go solo and unsupported, removing the cost and risk factors of the boat and volunteer support crews and taking more personal responsibility.

Between my full-time desk job, writing and publishing *Marathon Man*, directing and producing the *Unsinkable* film, and learning to SUP great distances, I didn't have the fuel to devote to pursuing the exact dream I'd visualised. I'd set a personal deadline for the summer of 2021, but hadn't completed enough safety preparation to paddle 1,500 kilometres solo. Persisting would have been foolhardy, yet quitting after building the skills and fitness would be a crying shame. With some encouragement from Kaja to play it safer, I decided to compromise and pivot.

Since I was yet to find a buyer for the sailboat, I thought, why not use it for a bit? I planned for *Unsinkable II* to act as my safety net from Waterford, clockwise up the unfamiliar, unforgiving, Atlantic-exposed Irish west coast, to Donegal. That would provide enough time to get my sea legs, learn on the job, and then I could tackle the familiar east coast solo as *Unsinkable II* would depart for a new home or the sales yard in Dublin. That would then free up cash to get me home to Waterford and fund my emigration to the Canadian Rockies with Kaja. That was the plan anyway.

I'd invited the swim's dream team – Chris Tweed and Noel Heary – back to help me start the SUP journey. They were keen as ever.

The week of my SUP launch, complications with work, Covid, and travel restrictions meant Chris got stuck in the UK and had to defer his plans to join the team. That just left Noel to navigate the support boat.

'We can manage with the two of us,' skipper Noel said. 'But if you know anyone looking for a short adventure, please invite them along.'

'Do you need a body or sailing skills?' I said.

'Just a body if possible.'

Emer, a friend's mother, volunteered at the last minute. Though not a sailor, she'd followed my endurance run and swim and was excited to assist under Noel's qualified watch.

'Things look too good to be true. I don't like it,' I said to Kaja two days before the SUP start.

'What do you mean?'

'Winds typically blow from the southwest to the northeast. All this week, it's nothing but clear skies, perfect low twenty degrees, and the low-to-no wind will blow from east to west, directly behind my back. It never blows that way or that gently. The sea will be a lake. And when I plan to reach the southwest tip of Kerry, it's forecast to change and blow south to north, putting the wind at my back again up the west coast.'

'Enjoy the breaks when you get them, I suppose.'

'I'm not sure ...'

Pain and grief were the accelerants for the lap-of-Ireland run and length-of-Ireland swim. The SUP project was different, a celebration of life rather than therapy to soothe my woes. Life felt on a positive trajectory again in 2021, despite Covid and job insecurity, and I wanted to see if I could accomplish something from a settled mind. Success is often paid for in full and in advance. I demonstrated I could sacrifice and put in the consistent work to prepare without a personal crisis to fuel it and, even better, have a blast doing it.

It had been nearly one year of gruelling expedited training, often training twice a day and over fifteen hours per week. After one million off-balance SUP falls and one torn medial collateral knee ligament, I had taught myself how to paddle for hours on the waves. I had organised my logistics ducks in a row; it was lift-off time.

I hugged my mam for a private, quiet departure from Tramore Beach. I left her behind and paddled from the unusually still Tramore Bay. After seeing me off the beach, my mother drove to the Guillamene, halfway along the headland that grips the bay. As she waved, I became overwhelmed with emotions. It had taken colossal work and personal expense to reach this moment. It was complete, utter joy. I was wholly present, stroking smoothly, smiling, crying, and waving my oar back to Mam on the hillside.

The waters were pristine. No longer *in* the water, I could appreciate the beautiful fishies and jellyfish below, and the curious circling gulls above. I rounded the Metal Man – three 200-year-old white pillars built after 360 people drowned when the *Sea Horse* shipwrecked in Tramore in 1816. A dapper fourteen-foot sailor with white trousers, a red shirt, and a blue jacket stands atop the middle beacon pointing seafarers away from the jagged cliffs.

I took the statue's sage advice to steer clear of rocks and paddled offshore to *Unsinkable II*, where Emer and Noel basked in the sunshine on the deck. 'This is perfect paddling conditions.'

'Just incredible. You're looking smooth, Alan. Much faster than the swimming.'

'Let's make hay when we have conditions this perfect.'

I paddled west, parallel to the cliffs of the Copper Coast.

'Eeep, eeep,' I said to myself when a pod of dolphins jumped past me, arching through the sky like rainbows. I could understand Kaja's uncontrolled awe at wild nature bouncing from the blue now that I was on top of the sea. I loved this vantage point. Birds dropped from the sky, diving for fish. The jagged coastline moved on a conveyer belt as I became absorbed by the seascape and the rhythm of my meditative stroke.

'We were just whale watching,' Noel said. 'Spectacular to watch it breaching the water. What a day.'

It couldn't have gone better, except for the sea breaking into my new dry bag and destroying my phone when I had jumped in to cool down. I covered fifty kilometres during seven and a half hours of flow-state paddling, travelling from Tramore to Ardmore and almost covering County Waterford's entire coastline.

Noel cheered. 'I've booked us for steaks on a mooring at the Cliff House Hotel in Ardmore. My treat. We have to celebrate that massive opening. Great job, you. You'll love their food.'

I was happy with adding hot water to pasta, but I wasn't going to reject Noel's generous offer of a five-star hotel's grub. I climbed below deck, downed my protein shake, and began drafting my day's diary as *Unsinkable II* glided on marble waters in glowing daylight.

BANG!

I shot forwards, the chart table creasing me in two at the abdomen. The floorboards erupted with the explosion of broken planks. The depth alarm blared, and sooty smoke filled the cabin.

'Fuck! Fuck!' Noel said from the helm above.

Coughing, I wafted the smoke from my face and looked out the below-deck window – a wall of rock. *Why, in God's name, are we at a damn cliff?* The water rose from the floor. *Oh shit!*

'I have the life raft ready!' Noel said.

Pure panic and adrenaline coursed through my veins, unlike anything I'd felt before. We'd gone from fair-weather cruising to brunt force emergency in a fraction of a second. It was the last thing I'd expect with a qualified, experienced sailor on flat seas in bright daylight. The impact force, incoming water, alarm, and Noel's life raft call made me fear we'd sink in seconds. The smoke made me feel a fire or explosion would engulf us first.

'Is everyone okay?' I said.

'Yeah, we're fine. Shit! Damn it!'

I hurried to gather the most expensive equipment, like a high-stakes game of *Supermarket Sweep*. If my sailboat went down, I didn't want thousands' worth of gear to sink with it.

'Will I radio a mayday?' I asked Noel.

'Yeah, do, Alan. Fuck, anyway.'

I switched on my EPIRB, an invaluable safety device I'd purchased that notified emergency services of our location and imminent danger with a simple flick of a switch.

I picked up the VHF radio. 'Mayday, mayday, mayday, this is *Unsinkable II, Unsinkable II* …'

The rescue helicopter circled overhead twenty minutes later as two RNLI RIBs speeded to the scene. They attached a line to *Unsinkable II* and dragged her off the rocks before towing the boat and us to Youghal.

'Ah, sorry, mistakes happen,' Noel said. 'You need to be careful with language and words, Alan, naming a boat *Unsinkable*, and someone should have had a flag sticking up there as a warning. And I cannot believe anybody with a boat has no insurance.'

I wasn't convinced the boat's name was responsible for the collision. Although a hero of the swimming adventure, Noel had crashed my SUP dreams. Besides the dangerous blunder of driving a sailboat anywhere near a towering headland, he mustn't have done the essential safety checks of inspecting the digital and physical nautical charts we had on board. If he had checked the navigation tools to see exactly where he was going, he'd have clocked the annotated symbol on the maps that said 'Rocks' and 'Underwater rock … which is considered dangerous to surface navigation.'

Unlike a car, there's no legal requirement to insure a sailboat. The ten brokers I approached all rejected my request for a quote. Still, I took a financial risk pursuing my charity projects that depended on qualified sailors covering the basics and taking adequate care of my boat and the people onboard. Though it could always be worse, it was an expensive risk that came back to bite me in the arse.

My plan to SUP a lap of Ireland, raise a chunk of money for the RNLI and Solas Cancer Support Centre, sell my boat to recover some of my costs, and move to Canada with Kaja was a pipedream, not to be. My endeavour embarrassingly cost the RNLI money on the rescue. You win some; you lose some.

I had bought the boat for €20,500 in 2018 with a sizeable bank loan and expected to sell it for €17,000-plus in 2021. The damage caused during the crash devalued the boat to €5,000, and repairing it without insurance cover wasn't viable. I had to sell for tuppence, losing around €12,000 or more down the swanny. For his part, Noel offset about seventeen per cent of my losses with a €2,000 contribution, insisting accidents just happen and it's my fault for not having insurance.

That's how the cookie crumbled – I was gutted. All I know is that *Unsinkable II* remained afloat like a champion.

I stored my paddleboard and moved with Kaja to Canmore, Alberta, Canada, on a much tighter budget. I wrote this book and returned to my safer hobby of trail running, enjoying roaming the mountainous dirt tracks within a fantastic Rocky Mountains running community. That said, wild bears, wolves, and cougars have reared their terrifying heads. Jellyfish don't seem so bad anymore.

My parting encouragement to anyone reading this is to try not to allow fear to control you, especially fear of failure or what others might think (or deep-sea creatures). Get up, get out into the real world, and pursue the interests that excite *you*.

I've discussed my fears and failures openly, hoping that people can see that it's part of the game, if not integral, provided you're willing to play. You won't always win if you brave the arena. You will slip on seaweed, splash unintentional bellyflops, become overwhelmed, and feel the stings of rejection and criticism. Try not to get too discouraged or be too hard on yourself when you do. You are not alone, and there are often solutions, like taking another run at it.

Heck, this book has had over fifty rejections from the literary gatekeepers. It went much like the start of my town planning career, my lap-of-Ireland run, length-of-Ireland sea swim, lap-of-Ireland SUP attempt, and *Unsinkable* movie. Not one agent or publishing house liked my *Unsinkable* memoir enough to think it was worth making it into a book, so I knuckled down and created it myself. You can't always rely on others to enable your dream. If you do, you're unlikely even to start. Others can often lean towards reasons not to pursue or support an endeavour. Sometimes you need to bet on yourself, get moving, and figure it out on the go. That's been my experience, anyway. I've tried to ask who will stop me rather than who will let me. I guess that's half the fun – being disobedient, persistent, and consistent enough to make things happen regardless of naysayers. You'll just never know what you're capable of accomplishing until you put your money where your mouth is, put in the time and effort, and eat that elephant one damn bite at a time.

We cannot control the sea. The tide will flood and push us forwards. Tides will also ebb, drag us to deep waters, and make life more challenging to soldier through. Joyful and tragic moments are both guaranteed. Savour the current when the tide's at your back, try to remain hopeful and calm in the passing ebb, and give your honest best during both tides.

Being touched by death in my relatively young life, part of what drives me is how I'll feel when the party's nearly over. Never mind judgement from some higher being; I want to pass my own assessment with flying colours. Win, lose, or draw, I'm striving to have a content smile at the end of my story, pushing to create, contribute, and follow my interests with integrity, giving this precarious and precious life a proper whirl. What about you? Go get 'em.

In Loving Memory of my dad,
Milo Corcoran.

Thanks so much for reading my Unsinkable *story.*

I'm an independent self-published author without the power of a literary agent, publicist, or publishing house to market and promote my book. I rely on you to tell your friends, leave a review, or post online.

I'd be extremely grateful if you could please review Unsinkable *on Amazon or Goodreads, as reviews help other readers find my work by telling them what to expect and feeds the algorithms to get* Unsinkable *in the virtual shop window.*

Bonus appreciation for posting a picture of my book on social media.

#Unsinkable

Please check out my Marathon Man *book if you enjoyed this one.*

Instagram: @alan__corcoran
Facebook and Twitter: @35marathonman

Acknowledgements

I want to take the opportunity to thank the staff of Waterford University Hospital for the attention and care they provided my dad, Milo. My exposure to your workplace was eye-opening. Your dedication to showing up day in and day out to help the sick and suffering is extraordinary and greatly appreciated by your patients and their families.

Karolína, I'm eternally grateful for your immeasurable efforts to help me achieve my dream. From learning how to kayak to training in the docklands and taking safety course after safety course, to the slight inconvenience of sharing a dank cabin with me for two months and kayaking for 150 hours on the sea. Your companionship and love were invaluable, and no words can do my appreciation justice.

A special thanks to the mammy, Marie, and big bro, Ev, for all the great memories and your continued love and support.

Thomas Barr, when people were closing doors in my face, left, right, and centre, you opened one without even being asked to and ensured I got to the start line in 2017. I owe attempt one and its many lessons to you for that massive act of kindness and friendship. Your sporting achievements and, more importantly, your character inspire me.

I'm indebted to the 2017 and 2019 volunteers and supporters who gave up their time and made this team effort a success:

2017

Chris Bryan, Tim Haines, Paul McCarroll, Darren Doheny, Gavin Downey, Derrick O'Neill, DJ Magee, Billy Ryan, Jack Molloy, Seamus McConkey, Michelle Chambers, Mark Stevenson, Stuart Macrory, Jonny O' Hare, Thomas Barr, Carrick-on-Suir River Rescue, the community of Newcastle in County Down, Emagine's Peter Grogan, Ted Moran, and Róisín Dunk, Sailfish, Simon Cody, Cully and Sully, ZeroSixZero, Kennedy Movers, and Swim Secure. Aviva Stadium collectors who answered my last-minute plea: Andrew Foley, Adrian Jackman, Thomas Powell, Damien Walsh, Barry Upton, Paul Farrelly, Caroline Farrelly, Tom Raine,

Stephen O'Rourke, Christine Murphy, and those who responded to the Irish Heart Foundation's call.

2019
Tramore AFC, Tim Haines, Mark Sansom, Tommy Keighery, John Patrick, Chris Tweed, Noel Heary, Gavin Downey, Tim Atkins, Charlie, Jim, Brian Hett, Colm Higgins, Jonathan Dunne, Ciarán O'Hanlon, Dublin Port Authority, Owen Marshall, Mark Gaffney, Joe Murphy, Alex Flynn, Jack Molloy, Gavin Downey, Derrick O'Neill, Simon Cody, Enda Loughman, Adriana Van Leeuwen, Gavin and Jim Griffin, Derek Barrett, Connor Cleary, Dr Heather Massey, EIR, The Tenth Man, Emagine's Peter Grogan and Ted Moran, Bantry Bay Canoes, Cully and Sully, David Lloyd's Acton Park, Atlantic Marine Supplies, SPOT, ZeroSixZero, and Swim Secure.

To the RNLI, HM Coastguard, and the Irish Coastguard, thank you for your time, expertise, and service in helping people to stay safe on the water and to get home. The number of lives you save each year is phenomenal – heroes.

Dr Heather Massey and Professor Mike Tipton of the University of Portsmouth's Extreme Environments Research Group for welcoming me into your lab for testing and ensuring my statements about cold water and its physiological impacts were accurate.

Dr Anne Horgan (Consultant Medical Oncologist) and Eoin Tabb (Chief II Pharmacist) of University Hospital Waterford for doing your best with my dad and for reviewing chapter three.

Thank you to everyone who donated to my chosen charities and furthered their missions to help people affected by cancer and stroke.

Thanks to those who left a 'like', a message of encouragement, or shared my online posts. This kindness cost nothing, but didn't go unnoticed, helping lift the team's mood, spread awareness, and ultimately increase charitable donations.

I want to thank all my sporting coaches, training partners, and teammates for creating many fond memories, and instilling good health habits and a love for the freedom to move, play, and be outdoors.

I'd like to thank my bookish team, who helped me refine my memoir. *Unsinkable* is an independent self-published production with no financial support or handholding from literary agents or a big publishing house. I had the pleasure of picking the quality people I wanted to work with. Thanks to my beta readers: Kaja, Catherine Hamilton, Declan O'Reilly (Writerful Books), and David White (The World of Nonfiction Books). A massive thank you to Claire Strömbeck and Ross Jamieson for your thorough copy-editing skills and Jennifer Barclay for your precision proof-reading. To Jack Spowart, whose stunning illustrations completed my vision and elevated my book to the next level.

Last, but by no means least, to my Kickstarter supporters for backing my book: Tom Davies, Joe Murphy, Mary Casey, Richie Casey, Billy Ryan, Niall Moran, Mark Perry, Ian Silk, and Sean Connolly.

Appendix One – Training, Week One, Session One (September 2016)

<u>Pre-Pool</u>
Mobility and shoulder rotations

<u>Warm Up</u>
4 x 50 metres as 25 metres freestyle / 25 metres backstroke
4 x 25 metres kick-only, with fins, on your side
4 x 25 metres fins: 6 kicks and switch sides

<u>Work Set</u>
4 x 50 metres freestyle   30-second rest
8 x 25 metres fins freestyle (focus on rolling) 15-second rest
4 x 50 metres freestyle   30-second rest
8 x 25 metres fins freestyle (focus on rolling) 15-second rest
4 x 50 metres freestyle   30-second rest

<u>Cool Down</u>
100 metres choice easy

Appendix Two – Training, Week Twenty-Three, Session 119, 'Hell Week' (February 2017)

<u>Warm Up</u>
Dryland warm up

<u>Work Set</u>
Choice of gear, no same gear for any two:

4000 metres
3000 metres
2000 metres
1000 metres

<u>Cool Down</u>
100 metres double-arm backcrawl

Appendix Three – Attempt One: Gear

Sailfish 'The One' 1.5–4.5mm wetsuit to Belfast and then Sailfish 1.5–5mm 'Attack' wetsuit to Dundrum Bay
Waterproof H1 10mm High-Visibility Polar Hood
2 x silicone caps
GUL thermal long-sleeved rashguard and leggings
O'Neill 3mm vest
Speedo BioFuse small fins to Belfast and then Mad Wave long fins to Dundrum Bay
O'Neill 5mm gloves
5mm neoprene surfing socks
TYR mask
Speedo silicone earplugs
Vaseline lube
Swim Secure tow float
Nike+ Tom-Tom GPS watch x 2 + cable ties
Dryrobe

Appendix Four – Attempt One: Summary Stats

Day 1 – 3 hours 20 mins – 17km
Day 2 – 5 hours – 36km
Day 3 – 0
Day 4 – 0
Day 5 – 5 hours – 17km
Day 6 – 4 hours 30 mins – 18km
Day 7 – 2 hours 20 mins – 10km
Day 8 – 0
Day 9 – 0
Day 10 – 0
Day 11 – 3 hours 20 mins – 14km
Day 12 – 3 hours 15 mins – 12km
Day 13 – 0
Day 14 – 3 hours 30 mins – 16km
Day 15 – 1 hour 25 mins – 7km
Day 16 – 3 hours 30 mins – 17km
Day 17 – 0
Day 18 – 0
Day 19 – 1 hour 25 mins – 6km
Day 20 – 0
Day 21 – 4 hours – 13km
Day 22 – 0
Day 23 – 0
Day 24 – 4 hours – 16km
Day 25 – 0
Day 26 – 0
Day 27 – 0
Day 28 – 3 hours – 11km
Day 29 – 0
Day 30 – 0

Total completed: 210 kilometres in forty-eight hours over fourteen swim days

Appendix Five – Attempt Two: Gear

ROKA 1.5–5mm Maverick Pro Thermal wetsuit
HUUB 3mm skull cap
2 x silicone caps
Orca longsleeve rashguard
Orca Heatseeker 2mm vest
Speedo BioFuse small fins
HUUB 3mm gloves
HUUB 3mm booties
HUUB Altair goggles
HUUB Aphotic goggles
TYR silicone earplugs
HUUB sports lube
Swim Secure tow donut
SPOT Gen3 satellite GPS tracker + waterproof bag
Whistle
Ocean Signal rescueME Electronic Distress Flare
Smartphone + waterproof bag
Nike+ Tom-Tom GPS watch + cable ties
2 x emergency energy gels
Adventure Lights Guardian Tag-It clip-on light
Dryrobe

Appendix Six – Attempt Two: Summary Stats

Day 1 – 4 hours – 8km
Day 2 – 3 hours – 19km
Day 3 – 3 hours – 33km
Day 4 – 2 hours 45 mins – 18km
Day 5 – 2 hours 20 mins – 12km
Day 6 – 2 hours 45 mins – 16km
Day 7 – 4 hours – 16km
Day 8 – 4 hours – 14km
Day 9 – 0
Day 10 – 4 hours – 8km
Day 11 – 2 hours 30 mins – 11km
Day 12 – 1 hour 40 mins – 8km
Day 13 – 0
Day 14 – 0
Day 15 – 0
Day 16 – 0
Day 17 – 0
Day 18 – 0
Day 19 – 2 hours – 7km
Day 20 – 4 hours – 7km
Day 21 – 4 hours – 8km
Day 22 – 3 hours – 5km
Day 23 – 0
Day 24 – 0
Day 25 (swim one) – 2 hours – 6km
Day 25 (swim two) – 2 hours – 8km
Day 26 – 4 hours – 7km
Day 27 – 4 hours – 7km
Day 28 – 0
Day 29 – 4 hours – 12km
Day 30 – 0
Day 31 – 0
Day 32 – 4 hours – 11km
Day 33 – 4 hours – 11km
Day 34 – 4 hours 10 mins – 12km

Day 35 – 4 hours 15 mins – 15km
Day 36 – 4 hours – 6km
Day 37 – 4 hours – 16km
Day 38 – 4 hours 30 mins – 15km
Day 39 – 5 hours – 21km
Day 40 – 6 hours – 18km
Day 41 – 3 hours 15 mins – 15km
Day 42 – 4 hours 20 mins – 12km
Day 43 – 6 hours – 8km
Day 44 – 4 hours 40 mins – 10km
Day 45 – 4 hours 45 mins – 16km
Day 46 – 4 hours 15 mins – 12km
Day 47 (swim one) – 15 mins – 1km
Day 47 (swim two) – 2 hours 50 mins – 10km
Day 48 – 5 hours 45 mins – 28km
Day 49 – 0
Day 50 – 5 hours 10 mins – 12km
Day 51 – 5 hours – 12km
Day 52 – 0
Day 53 – 4 hours 5 mins – 9km

Total completed: 500 kilometres in 153 hours over thirty-nine swim days